Kiss Me,
Kill Me

Also by Ann Rule
in Large Print:

Green River, Running Red
Without Pity: Ann Rule's Most
    Dangerous Killers
. . . And Never Let Her Go
Bitter Harvest
The Stranger Beside Me
The I-5 Killer
Last Dance, Last Chance and
    Other True Cases
Empty Promises and Other True Cases
A Rage to Kill and Other True Cases
The End of the Dream and
    Other True Cases
In the Name of Love and Other True Cases
Heart Full of Lies: A True Story of
    Desire and Death

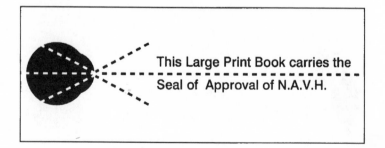

This Large Print Book carries the
Seal of Approval of N.A.V.H.

ANN RULE

Kiss Me, Kill Me

AND OTHER
TRUE CASES
ANN RULE'S
CRIME FILES:
Vol. 9

Thorndike Press • Waterville, Maine

Published in 2005 by arrangement with Pocket Books, an imprint of Simon & Schuster, Inc.

Thorndike Press® Large Print Basic.

The tree indicium is a trademark of Thorndike Press.

The text of this Large Print edition is unabridged.
Other aspects of the book may vary from the original edition.

Set in 16 pt. Plantin by Minnie B. Raven.

Printed in the United States on permanent paper.

Library of Congress Control Number: 2005920430
ISBN 0-7862-7444-1 (lg. print : hc : alk. paper)

Although it is long overdue, this book is dedicated to the memory of Pierce R. Brooks, a cops' cop, a superior detective, an innovator, and a wonderfully kind man. Pierce saved more lives in his long career than any law enforcement officer I ever met.

As the Founder/CEO of NAVH, the only national health agency solely devoted to those who, although not totally blind, have an eye disease which could lead to serious visual impairment, I am pleased to recognize Thorndike Press★ as one of the leading publishers in the large print field.

Founded in 1954 in San Francisco to prepare large print textbooks for partially seeing children, NAVH became the pioneer and standard setting agency in the preparation of large type.

Today, those publishers who meet our standards carry the prestigious "Seal of Approval" indicating high quality large print. We are delighted that Thorndike Press is one of the publishers whose titles meet these standards. We are also pleased to recognize the significant contribution Thorndike Press is making in this important and growing field.

Lorraine H. Marchi, L.H.D.
Founder/CEO
NAVH

★ Thorndike Press encompasses the following imprints: Thorndike, Wheeler, Walker and Large Print Press.

Acknowledgments

Over three decades, any number of detectives have shared their experiences with me, along with their thoughts on the cause and prevention of criminal behavior. Had they not been willing to talk about both their triumphs and their mistakes, and their own emotions as they faced seemingly impenetrable puzzles and tragic loss, I would never have learned what I have about the psychopathology of the criminal mind. And I thank them all.

When I first became the Northwest correspondent for five fact-detective magazines and the New York *Daily News* Justice Stories, I hadn't been out of college very long. The homicide detectives in the Seattle Police Department used to tease me, saying: "Ann, we'll all be retired someday, and you'll probably still be coming down here to get cases to write about. Our grandsons will be the detectives then."

And we laughed. They were older than I was, and that first crew of seventeen detectives are all retired now, and many of my best detective friends are deceased. Then, there was a period when the homicide detectives were the same age I was. And most of *them* are retired. I'm happy to say that, so far, there are no *third* generation detectives! But the world does move on and it would be easy to forget old unsolved cases. That has not happened, and it has been gratifying to see the second platoon of investigators in many Northwest police departments closing cases and catching killers.

I wish to thank scores of detectives who worked on the homicide cases in *Kiss Me, Kill Me* from the following departments: Seattle Police Department; King County Sheriff's Office; University of Washington Police Department; Snohomish County Sheriff's Office; Thurston County Sheriff's Office; Walla Walla County Sheriff's Office; Spokane County Sheriff's Office; Salem, Oregon, Police Department; Marion County, Oregon, Sheriff's Office; Silverton Police Department; Mount Angel Police Department; Oregon State Police; Los Angeles Police Department; Orange County, California, Sheriff's Office; and the Lee County, Florida, Sheriff's Office.

Special thanks to Detectives Greg

Mixsell and Richard Gagnon of the Seattle Police Department's "Cold Case Squad," and Sergeant Dan Brooks, West Covina, California, Police Department, and to Joyce Brooks.

When Pocket Books suggested the concept of a series of books called "Ann Rule's Crime Files" a dozen years ago, none of us knew if there would be more than the first edition. Happily, readers look forward to these original paperbacks. *Kiss Me, Kill Me* is Volume Nine, and there are many more in the works.

I am one of those peculiar authors who never met an editor she didn't like, and I particularly enjoy working with Mitchell Ivers at Pocket Books. He is always encouraging and slow to criticize. His assistant, Josh Martino, is more efficient than it's possible to be, and I appreciate that a great deal.

Once a manuscript leaves my hands, I know that a capable and enthusiastic team at Pocket Books will see that it gets into print in record time. My grateful thanks go to Louise Burke, Donna O'Neill, Stephen Llano, Paolo Pepe, Felice Javit, Linda Dingler, Joy O'Meara, Jaime Putorti, Victor Cataldo, Nancy Inglis, Rodger Weinfeld, and also to copy editor David Chesanow.

As always, I thank my literary agents, who have been in my corner for thirty-five years. I've never had any others because I picked the best the first time out: Joan and Joe Foley of The Foley Agency in New York City. I also appreciate my theatrical agent, Ron Bernstein of International Creative Management in Beverly Hills, California.

And, of course, I thank my readers! Without you, there wouldn't be books at all, and I appreciate you. I hope to meet many of you when I'm signing books this year. My website pages will have my schedule and lots of updates and other information.

Come and visit at www.annrules.com.

Contents

Introduction

While it is true that serial murder cases often tend to draw the biggest headlines — perhaps because that phenomenon was recognized and acknowledged only two decades ago — homicides resulting from interpersonal relationships can be more dramatic and mesmerizing. In this volume of my true crime files series, I have chosen cases from both categories. They all evolved from what began initially out of attraction, but some murders came about through undiluted lust on the part of the killers. Others started with love — or what passed for love.

If I had to sum up the cases I have selected for this book, I would say that the tragic women victims all hoped for something positive from the men they encountered: a conversation with someone who seemed trustworthy, friendship, companionship, a kiss, or a hug — and in many cases, a kiss, romance, and perhaps even a lifetime commitment. Some of the lost women soon had reason to be uncomfortable — even frightened — while others faced death suddenly and with no warning at all. If there are lessons here, I hope that my readers will learn to react to even the first small niggling of doubt and protect themselves from danger before it is too late.

"Kiss Me, Kill Me," the title case in this book, began and ended with pure lust, although there was a strange interlude where a killer and the woman he abducted actually seemed to care for each other. This long section also explores the encouraging phenomenon of "Cold Case Squads," now mobilizing in police departments around the United States, with clever detectives who use the latest technology in forensic science to track down murder suspects who believed they were home free decades ago.

"The Postman Only Killed Once" isn't about "going postal" as it's come to be known after workers for the U.S. Postal Service have faced mass murderers among their fellow employees. This sex-mad killer was ultimately selfish, a glutton who wanted any number of women in his life, and a man who fantasized a crazy plot to free himself of the bonds of marriage while blaming murder on a phantom serial killer. *He just happened to be a mailman.*

14

Neither kisses nor passion last forever; ordinary life settles in and truly good marriages and relationships are based on shared interests, common experiences, trust, and mutual support through both the good and bad times. Of course there will be high points over the years, but no one can live full-time on roller coasters or a diet of ice cream sundaes. And they can't devote every waking thought to someone else's needs and desires.

"What's Love Got to Do with It?" began with an attractive couple who wanted to live a life filled with pleasure, without having to work to pay for it. It would have worked in a movie. It was hard to tell which of them was more attractive, but I suspect *she* was the one who loved the most. The question remains, "Did she love the wrong man too much and pay far too heavy a price for believing in him?" Or was she just as guilty as he was in their plans to have a wonderful life?

That life was Las Vegas, convertibles, drinking and drugging, and cocktail lounges, as empty of substance as a mall theater after the last show. And they were, of course, doomed to fail. Sadly, they took another life in a stupid attempt to fulfill their impossible dreams.

Some of the cruelest murders have been perpetrated by those who promised undying love when what they really meant was that the love object now belonged to them. Ownership of another human being is not love.

Jealousy is not love, either. When men or women fail to trust their partner and allow them to live freely, real love cannot exist. It is inevitable that the object of jealousy will try to break free at some point. Some partners let that happen, and some destroy those they have sworn they will cherish forever. I get letters and emails every day from both men and women who live in fear because an estranged spouse or lover is stalking them and threatening to kill them.

It is important that they realize this is *not* their doing. Those who have not been there can't understand why trapped victims of misplaced "love" couldn't detect the danger behind protestations of affection and caring *before* they exchanged vows or promises with the person they have come to fear so much. And yet it is rarely the fault of the one who is being stalked. Sometimes, yes, there were signs that their lovers were too possessive. More often, the warning signs came when it was too late to run away.

"The Captive Bride" is about the fear that many women — and some men — live with day by day. *I wish that I did have the answers for them, but I don't.* The best I can do is urge them to go online and enter "Domestic Violence" in the slot in search engines.

"Bad Blind Date" is exactly what the title suggests, but, tragically, it takes the concept far beyond an uncomfortable evening with someone who turned out to be a major disappointment. We have all accepted dates with someone we didn't really know. This case illustrates graphically the worst possible result if we allow ourselves to be pushed into spending time alone with a complete stranger.

"The Lonely Hearts Killer" who found his victims in the Personal and "Model Wanted" ads of Los Angeles newspapers was, arguably, the first *serial killer* ever identified by that phrase. His horrifying crimes fit within the parameters of the description of the definition, as chilling today as it was when it happened. His victims were ultimately vulnerable, women seeking love or a way to make a living in Hollywood.

Some of the cases I picked with some hesitation — because they deal with sexual aberration that few of us, thankfully, ever encounter or even read about. "Old Flames Can Burn" and "You Kill Me — Or I'll Kill You" fall within that category. The men who were convicted in these crimes were handsome, much more than presentable socially, and ultimately frightening.

"The Highway Accident" is a case that some of you may have read before. Still, after reading the massive media coverage of both the Lori and Mark Hacking case in Utah and the Laci and Scott Peterson case in California, I felt I had to include it. This case is almost a blueprint for the current cases — particularly the Hacking tragedy — although it goes several steps beyond. It does seem impossible for a wife to be so trusting of her husband, only to find out that she has lived in a lie. But it happens. It happened in "The Highway Accident" in Oregon, and I think you will be as startled as I was to see the similarities with the cases in today's headlines.

"Where Is Julie?" is one of the thousand or more mysteries I have chronicled in the past three decades, and one of perhaps a dozen that I cannot get out of my mind. In this last story, we come back to the sadness of the loss of "Kiss Me, Kill Me," 's Sandy

Bowman — the perfect marriage that ended because someone *outside* the couple fixated on the lovely wife. As long as I live, I will never forget Julie Weflen or give up hope that the answer to her disappearance will be disclosed. Someone fixated on Julie, and it was probably the death of her. Instant attraction is more likely to be sexual than an arrow in the heart from Cupid. I think the most frightening stories I ever have to tell are cases where someone waits and watches in the shadows because he has become obsessed with a complete stranger. This kind of killer isn't looking for romance or happy ever after; he wants instant sexual gratification or the thrill of capturing someone he finds attractive but unattainable without the use of force. I sincerely hope that some reader may hold the clue that will let those who still love her know what happened to Julie.

All of the cases in this book retrace the cataclysmic events that began with a kiss, a hug, or some other manifestation of affection or physical longing. Tragically, the time between kissing and killing wasn't very long in many of these true stories. Some of the killers were maddened by love, some by lust, and some appear to have been just plain crazy.

I must admit that when I finished *Kiss Me, Kill Me*, I was feeling sad. And then I thought, *Why not? Who wouldn't feel this way after thinking about all of these tragedies?*

These cases are interesting, yes, but they are also cautionary tales that every reader should take to heart, and use to arm herself against danger. Often, readers jokingly ask me to sign a book: "I hope I never have to write about *you!*" And I always refuse because it seems unlucky to say that. So please pay heed.

Kiss Me, Kill Me

Author's Note

Never is there greater need for rapid results than in a homicide investigation. If a murder is not solved within the first forty-eight hours, the chance that it will *ever* be solved diminishes in direct proportion to the time that passes. That is why detectives often work around the clock when they are called to a murder scene. It doesn't matter to them if it is day or night; they don't leave that scene unguarded for any reason until it has been thoroughly processed, right down to the most minuscule fleck of blood or hair that seems out of place. Although they might have to wait until sunrise to detect every-thing that might be there, they know they are working against an invisible stopwatch, mocking them as it tick-ticks the time away while the killer gains an advantage.

As unimaginable as it might sound, the true solution of the case that follows took almost *thirty-six years!* As I recall, it was the third case I wrote, far back in the beginning of my career as a true-crime writer. This was the tragedy that made me question whether my conscience would allow me to keep writing in the reality crime genre, and I almost quit right then. As I read the files on the death of a teenage bride, a girl who was totally happy with her new husband and looking forward to the baby they expected, I was saddened and heartsick.

I actually scheduled an appointment with a psychiatrist and told him of my doubts, explaining that I was alone with four children to raise and that having a steady assignment as the Northwest correspondent for *True Detective* magazine meant a lot to us financially. I only made two hundred dollars for an article, but in the late sixties that was enough for us to get by. At the same time, I wasn't comfortable with the thought that I was making a living from someone else's misfortunes.

The therapist smiled slightly at my question. He explained that half the population of the United States probably depended at least partially on the mishaps of others for their livelihood.

"*I* do," he said, "and so do insurance salesmen, doctors, police officers, firefighters, hospital workers, funeral directors, journalists, ministers, social workers. Well, you get the point. The list goes on and on. What really matters is how you *feel* about the people you write about."

"Then I think I can deal with that," I said. "I have no question about how I feel. I care a great deal for them. It's never going to be just a story for me. The victims are very real to me, and I want to do the best job I can to tell about their lives."

"Then you have your answer," he said. "You have no reason to feel guilty. If you ever stop caring about the victims, then you should write about something else."

I cared about Sandra Bowman then, and I still do now. If she were alive today, she would be fifty-two, probably a grandmother.

But she never got that chance.

The world went on for these thirty-six years without Sandra, and no one ever knew who had killed her. It was really a double murder because her unborn child died with her.

Ann Rule
August 2004

1

One of the reasons Sandy's — as she was called — murder disturbed me so much was because I knew her uncle. Her mother's brother, Jerry Yates, was a detective sergeant in the Crimes Against Persons Unit of the Seattle Police Department. His unit investigated homicides, robberies, sex crimes, and missing persons. Yates was in charge of the Missing Persons Division. He was an extremely kind man who worked hard to find loved ones other people had lost, and everyone who knew Yates was saddened that he would lose his own niece to an unknown killer. Although homicide investigators do their best to solve every case assigned to them, the men who had worked beside Jerry Yates for years vowed they wouldn't stop until they saw his niece's killer brought to justice.

But it would prove to be a baffling case marked by bizarre circumstances. In the beginning, the vicious senseless murder of a 16-year-old girl seemed to be only a slight challenge to experienced detectives. But so many suspects who might have killed Sandy Bowman emerged, clouding the probe with false leads that led only to frustrating dead ends.

Sandy Bowman was her maternal grandfather's favorite of all the offspring. Benjamin Yates was a hardworking Kansas native born around the turn of the century, and he had suffered many tragic losses in his life. His first wife, Ida Murphy Yates, died eight years after their marriage, leaving him with three children to raise. He was remarried to Neva Taylor Yates and they had eight more children. Sadly, their two baby sons, Earl and Donald, both died when they were only a year old, and another son, Ray, succumbed to leukemia at the age of 13. James, Jerry, Shirley, Dorothy, and Beverly grew to adulthood.

Every family deals with grief in its own fashion, and perhaps because Benjamin and Neva had to bury three of their children, they covered up their pain, kept their sorrow to themselves, and seldom discussed their losses.

Dorothy Yates married Roy Maki in 1947 three months before her sixteenth birthday. Dorothy was a native of Kansas who married a young Washington State man. Beverly Yates was 16 when she married Hector Gillis Jr.

Dorothy Maki was only 17 when her first son, William, was born, followed by Robert in just eleven months. Two baby boys in one calendar year meant that Dorothy had her hands full. Sandy came along four years later, and she was a sweet-faced baby girl with dark hair and huge eyes, someone her mother could dress up in frilly clothes.

Sandra Darlene "Sandy" Maki was born on December 3, 1952, the adored baby sister of her brothers William and Robert Maki.

The Yateses were a close family, and Dorothy's sisters, Beverly and Shirley, had children — who, along with Jerry's, played with their cousins often. When the children were young, they lived near each other in the Ballard section of Seattle, the neighborhood populated mostly by Scandinavians — Swedes, Danes, Norwegians, and Finns. Fishing ships docked in Ballard in between trips to Alaska and the Pacific Ocean, and both commercial and private boats had to move through the Ballard Locks to reach the open sea.

Ballard was a low-crime area and so was most of the near north end of Seattle in the fifties and sixties. Ballard was on the western end of 45th Street, and the University of Washington was on the eastern. In between were the family neighborhoods with Craftsman-style houses and local shops: Wallingford, Fremont, Green Lake. Decades later, they would be hip, then funky, and finally very expensive.

The elder Yateses, Benjamin and Neva, lived over in Port Orchard on Washington's Olympic Peninsula. Their grandchildren visited and Benjamin doted on freckle-faced Sandy. She was always laughing and she loved dogs.

Sandy's parents divorced in 1964 when she was 12 and her mother remarried later in the year. Surrounded by her large extended family, she seemed to handle the divorce well.

Sandy was always popular and dated often in junior high and high school. She was petite and wore her thick brown hair in a short bouffant cut with a fringe of bangs over her high forehead. Like most young women who followed the fashion of the day, she lined her blue eyes with a dark kohl pencil and applied several coats of mascara. Teenagers tried to emulate the English star Twiggy, and even though few of them were as sliver thin as she was, they all wore short dresses and go-go boots in 1968 and listened to recordings by the

Doors and the Beatles.

Sandy had gone steady with a boy named Lee Wilkins* for a while, but it was Tom Bowman who won her heart. She had never planned on going to college; so far all the women in her family dropped out of school to marry young, and she had looked forward to being married and having her own home.

She and Tom were very young. Sandy was only 15 when they were married on July 27, 1968, but her family saw that she had a lovely wedding. She was happy when her stepsister, Jo Anne Weeks, caught her wedding bouquet. The two young women got along very well.

Sandy and her new husband rented a small apartment, but something frightened her there and they quickly found another where she would feel safer. They were able to rent a second-floor apartment in the Kon-Tiki complex at 6201 14th Street N.W. for a reasonable price. They didn't have much furniture, but what they chose was Danish Modern.

She wasn't pregnant when she got married, but Sandy conceived two months later and both she and Tom were eagerly looking forward to the birth of their baby in June 1969.

Tom worked the three to eleven p.m. shift at the American Can Company, so Sandy was alone most evenings, but she had so many friends she didn't feel lonesome.

On December 3, Sandy celebrated her sixteenth birthday. She was excited about her first Christmas as a married woman.

Washington State had an extremely cold winter that year and Seattle's city streets were clogged with snow before Christmas, when usually it was only the mountain passes where snow was to be expected. In the Cascades, drifts towered over vehicles and the summits were often closed to traffic — and skiers — until the roads were cleared and avalanche danger was past.

Temperatures had dropped on Tuesday, December 17, and Ballard's streets were soon covered with snow.

That day, just a week before Christmas Eve, began happily when Sandy checked her mailbox and found a letter from a relative in New York with a twenty-dollar check tucked inside as a Christmas gift. Today, it doesn't sound like a lot of money, but it went much further in 1968. The average yearly income was about $6,400 a year, and gasoline cost only thirty-four cents a gallon. Tom was making a good living at the can factory, but the check was a wonderful surprise for Sandy. She smiled as she waved the check in front of her husband and told him she was going to buy more presents with it.

Snow fluttered past their windows as they shared a leisurely breakfast. It was the one meal of the day they could enjoy together without rushing. Then they listened to records on their stereo set — *Hey Jude* and *Green Tambourine*.

Two of Sandy's girlfriends who had attended Ballard High School with her dropped by to visit with them. The snow kept falling, making the apartment seem very cozy.

Early in the afternoon, Tom changed into his work clothes and Sandy asked if she could ride along with him as far as the bank. She wanted to cash the gift check, and then she planned to shop and visit some of her relatives who lived in Ballard. She promised him she would be home early; it would be dark well before five. The shortest day of the year was only four days away, and Seattle's winter days were almost as dark as those in Alaska. Tom didn't want her out after dark or walking alone on slippery streets when she was pregnant, even though she was six months from having their baby.

He grinned as he watched her walk away from his car toward the bank, enjoying the enthusiasm Sandy showed over even a simple shopping trip. Their marriage was still at the "playing house" stage and the newlyweds considered themselves very lucky.

2

It was 11:30 that night when Tom got home from work. Ordinarily, he would have finished his shift at 9:30 but he had a chance to work two hours overtime, and he took it. Without checking to see if the apartment's front door was locked, he automatically slipped his key into the lock. The door swung open. Later, he couldn't remember if the door had been locked or even if it had been ajar.

As he stepped into the living room an extra-long cigarette fell from the doorjamb above his head and dropped on the floor in front of him. It was a Pall Mall that had never been lit. That puzzled him slightly because Sandy smoked only occasionally, and then she chose Winstons. He didn't smoke at all.

The living room was a little messy, but Sandy wasn't a meticulous housekeeper so he didn't think much of it — until he noticed that her purse lay in the middle of the floor with its contents scattered as if someone had deliberately dumped it out and hadn't bothered to put the scattered items back in. One of Sandy's black pumps lay next to it. The coffee table was stacked with Christmas presents, along with some holiday wrapping paper and the daily paper. It had been read, its sections haphazardly stacked.

The lights in the apartment and the television set were still on. That was odd. Sandy usually turned off the lights when she left a room to save on their electric bill.

Tom saw that she had left a note propped up on the coffee table. Walking quietly so he wouldn't wake her up, he read it. "Tom," she had written, "I went to bed early because I didn't feel so good. The baby started moving tonight, it's not kicking yet, it squirms and moves. It moved up on my ribs. AND IT HURT. It must be a boy because it's strong. I got $23.00 left. I love you very much.

"Love, Sandy"

He doubted that she could actually feel their baby when she was only three months pregnant, but she was so thrilled about being a mother she probably had imagined she felt it inside her.

Tom walked toward their bedroom and saw that was the only room in the apartment where the light was switched off. He could make out Sandy where she lay across the end of the bed. His first thought was that she must have been so exhausted that she'd fallen asleep without even bothering to get under the covers.

And then he snapped on the light switch next to the door. He saw a silent tableau that he would never be able to forget. It was the most horrendous sight he would ever see.

Sandy lay in a crimson welter of her own blood, making him think at first that she had suffered a miscarriage and passed out from hemorrhaging. But as he dropped to his knees beside the bed, Tom saw that her hands were bound together with some sort of rope or cord. She wore the green dress she'd had on earlier, but now it looked as though it had been ripped almost completely off her body. The flowered sheets on their bed were soaked with blood, and the wall was spattered with scarlet droplets.

Someone had done this to Sandy. Tom looked at her closely, hoping to see that she was breathing and her heart was beating. But he *knew*. Even as he ran from their apartment, Tom Bowman knew it was too late to save Sandy. There was no dial tone on their own phone. Tom pounded first on the closest apartment, but no one answered. Then he ran to the apartment in the other direction. Mr. and Mrs. Wayne Brosnick* lived there.

Wayne Brosnick opened the door immediately, and saw an almost hysterical man with tears in his eyes. He blurted, "My wife's been raped and killed!"

The Brosnicks led Tom to their phone and helped him place a call to police. Then he muttered that he had to get back to his wife. Seattle Police patrolmen B. Mayhle and I. Citron, who were working out of the nearby Wallingford Precinct, responded to the call for help. As they ran up the steps to #203 of the Kon-Tiki, they found Tom Bowman sitting outside his apartment with his head in his hands. He pointed into the apartment as he sobbed, "My wife —"

It took the patrol officers only seconds to determine that homicide detectives were needed, and they hurried back to their squad car to notify the radio room. The Homicide Unit was on the fifth floor of the Public Safety Building in downtown Seattle. From midnight until seven a.m., it was usually empty and investigators were called at home when they were needed, but Sergeants Elmer Wittman and Cary Parkes, and Detective William MacPherson, who were just about to go off duty, were still there. They grabbed their homicide kits and ran instead to the police garage and leapt into an unmarked car. They asked radio to alert their command officers who *were* off duty. Lieutenant Dick Schoener and Captain Wayne Simpson said they would respond to the Bowmans' Ballard apartment.

While Tom Bowman sat in shock on the living room couch, the detectives entered the bedroom. They were all experienced officers, but the insane violence before them was almost unbelievable. If anything could make it worse, it was the sight of more Christmas presents that Sandy Bowman had stacked beside the bed.

The dead girl had obviously been stabbed, but it would be impossible to count the number of thrusts. It would take the medical examiner to determine the exact number if even he could do that. This was clearly a case of "overkill," usually the sign that the killer had known the victim and had some grievance to settle, some terrible rage to get out.

Sandy's panties, pantyhose, and bra had been ripped from her body and flung carelessly on the floor. The entire bed was stained with blood, but there were two distinct pools that appeared to have soaked through the bedding and into the mattress. It looked as if she had been stabbed and then rolled or moved to another part of the bed.

Her wrists were bound with cord, now tied loosely, although there were deep grooves there that indicated they had once been tightened cruelly. For some inexplicable reason, her slayer had loosened them before leaving the apartment.

A pair of black-handled household scissors and a butcher knife lay on the bedroom floor. At this point, it was impossible to tell if either — or both — had been used in the attack.

In the bathroom, the detectives checked the sink for signs that the killer had washed his hands. They would remove the P-trap later to see if anything of evidentiary value had been caught there. Glancing toward the toilet, they saw a gruesome mask fashioned from adhesive tape, a mask the size of a face. They didn't know yet whether the murderer had used it as a disguise or if he had put it on Sandy Bowman's face as some kind of blindfold or gag. Someone had tried to flush it down the toilet but it had been caught, too large to go down.

While Cary Parkes photographed Sandy's body, the obvious evidence, and then every room in the apartment, Dick Schoener called the "next-up" detectives — Wayne Dorman and Don Strunk — at home. They would gather any more possible or trace evidence, bag it and tag it, and take measurements of the rooms.

Schoener studied the cords binding Sandy Bowman's wrists and determined that they had been cut from the draperies in the living room. By measuring the cords on the opposite side of the windows, he was able to determine that all the cord cut was still in the apartment.

A search of garbage cans behind the apartment produced one knife. Upon autopsy, Dr. Gale Wilson would be able to tell if it matched any of Sandy's fatal wounds.

Detectives questioned the Brosnicks, whose apartment shared a common wall with the Bowmans: "Did you hear or see anything this evening which might have been unusual — anything at all?"

The couple looked at each other. Then Wayne Brosnick answered slowly, "Yes. We did. Now we realize what was happening, but at the time, I'm afraid we thought everything was all right. We heard a scream at about 7:30. I'm sure of the time because we were watching *The Jerry Lewis Show*, and it had just come on. We heard a male voice, too, but we couldn't understand what he was saying.

"Then we heard a woman's voice crying 'Oh, no. No. No!' I went to the bathroom and put my ear to the wall. But then I heard water running and we figured it was just a little family fight and that everything was all right. Sometime later — I can't say for sure how long — we heard their front door being slammed."

"Did you look out?"

"No, we had no reason to," Brosnick said. "We really believed everything was okay with them. If only we had —"

Clearly, the neighbors felt terrible that they hadn't run next door, but it was too late now.

Detective MacPherson approached the bereaved husband, who was calm but pale, and asked him gently if he could give a statement. Tom Bowman said he would cooperate any way he could. He explained that he had gone to work at two p.m., and taken a break at four for fifteen minutes. During that time, he was inside the plant, talking to the inspector in his section. His lunch break had been from 7:30 to 8:00 and he had watched fellow workers play cards. He had punched out at 11:12 p.m.

"If only I hadn't worked overtime," the anguished man murmured. "I should have been home with Sandy."

"From what we've learned so far, I don't think it would have made any difference," MacPherson reassured him. "Is there anyone you know who might be capable of this? Anyone have a grudge against you?"

Bowman considered that. "The only one I can think of is a guy named 'Nino.*' That's not his real name — just a nickname. But about five months ago, when we were just married, we lived in another apartment for a short time. Well, he dropped in on us one night unexpectedly. Just a few days after that, somebody broke into our apartment and burglarized the place. We always thought it was Nino, but we couldn't prove it.

"Sandy was frightened to stay there after that. That's why we moved here — so she'd be safe."

Tom dropped his head into his hands. Then he took a deep breath to steady his emotions. "I don't have any idea where to find Nino," he said.

"You told your neighbors that your wife was raped," MacPherson said slowly. "But you say you ran for help as soon as you found her. What made you conclude that so quickly?"

Bowman said the fact that Sandy's panties and pantyhose were tossed on the floor had just led him to assume that.

MacPherson made a note of it. It was probably nothing, but he would ask the pathologist who did the autopsy to validate if Sandy had, indeed, been sexually assaulted.

3

Working in the chilly wee hours of a December morning, MacPherson and Parkes contacted Sandy's aunt, whom she had planned to visit earlier in the day. They learned that she had gone shopping as she planned and then dropped in at her aunt's house. "But she didn't stay long," the shocked woman said. "She wanted to be home early so that she would be there when Tom got off work."

As the investigators continued to question Tom Bowman, they learned of another family with whom Sandy had close ties. Sandy had gone steady with a Ballard boy named Lee Wilkins for over a year before she broke off with him and became engaged to Tom. But she had remained on good terms with Lee Wilkins and his family. In fact, Mrs. Wilkins had been a kind of substitute mother figure for Sandy after her own mother moved to California.

It was 4:30 a.m. when detectives knocked on the door of the Wilkins home. Once again, they had to tell people who loved Sandy that she had been murdered.

Fighting to keep his composure, Lee Wilkins protested that that couldn't be true. "But I saw her at 6:30 tonight," he said. "She was fine. She wanted to go grocery shopping and the bags were heavy for her, so she asked me to go along and carry them and take them upstairs for her."

"And you did?"

"Sure, I carried them upstairs, put them down in the kitchen, and then left right away."

"Then where did you go?"

"I went over to a friend's house. There were several of us there. They can tell you I was with them."

Lee's mother, who was crying, too, spoke up, "There's a young married man living down the street. I don't quite know how to say this, but he's just funny, strange and kind of unstable. I think he knew Sandy before she was married. I know she's mentioned that he's been in their apartment."

"Do you know his name?"

"It's Rob Kinslow.*"

Back at the Bowmans' apartment, deputy medical examiners wheeled a gurney with a body bag containing Sandy Bowman's corpse from her bedroom. Tom

43

Bowman averted his eyes. He was still trying to cooperate with detectives, although he didn't know that homicide investigators almost always look first at the spouse or the lover of a victim as a possible suspect. They studied him carefully, trying to evaluate his emotional response. He appeared to be in shock and sincere in his grief.

Tom identified the purse in the living room as his wife's but he looked at the contents and said that Sandy's wallet and any money that might have been in it were missing.

Wayne Dorman and Don Strunk bagged a lot of evidence from the apartment: the black leather purse, a woman's shoe with a broken buckle, a writing tablet, a white flowered bra, a torn towel, panties and dark pantyhose, two short pieces of drapery cord, the wooden-handled butcher knife, the pair of black-handled scissors, the Pall Mall cigarette, the adhesive mask, dark red scrapings (of blood that had dropped from at least three feet above the bedroom rug), two small seeds — possibly marijuana — from the bathroom floor, one latent print from the medicine cabinet, two latent prints from doorknobs, scrapings from beneath Sandy Bowman's nails, and the bloodstained bedclothes.

All of this was placed at once in the Evidence Room of the Seattle Police Department.

At 6:00 a.m., the Bowman apartment was locked with police locks and secured against entry.

One hour later, King County Medical Examiner Dr. Gale Wilson performed a postmortem examination on Sandy Bowman. (Wilson had been a mainstay as a King County coroner and then as medical examiner for decades. When he testified in murder cases, he invariably took a small black book from his vest pocket and read the latest information on the number of autopsies he had performed. In 1968, he had more than 35,000!)

As Wilson studied the 16-year-old girl on his examining table, he saw that someone or some thing had spurred her killer into insane frenzy. There were close to sixty puncture wounds in her body, forty-five in front and twelve that had pierced her back.

Out of these five dozen wounds, Wilson estimated that thirty-seven to thirty-nine would have been rapidly fatal. There was no sign of strangulation in the strap muscles of Sandy's neck, the delicate hyoid bone at the back of her tongue, wasn't fractured, and her eyes, where blood vessels invariably burst when a person is suffocated or strangled, were clear.

Sandy's left lower jaw bore a deep bruise three by five centimeters in size, probably caused by a powerful human fist and sufficient, Dr. Wilson stated, to knock her unconscious. Some of the fifty-seven knife wounds had been made before death, but most of them had occurred after. It was quite possible that she had been unconscious from the blunt force to her head when the stabbing began.

One would hope so.

Surprisingly, none of the penetration wounds had been inflicted by either the scissors or the knife found in the bedroom where Sandy died. Detectives had thought they would turn out to be "weapons of opportunity": they belonged to the Bowmans, and the killer could have grabbed them as he began to attack Sandy. Apparently, he had brought his own knife with him.

The knife found in the garbage can behind the Kon-Tiki Apartments didn't match the specifications of the lethal blade either.

Sandy had had recent sexual intercourse.

Dr. Wilson took a swab of the semen in her vaginal vault. Tests available in 1968 would be able to establish if there were motile (live) sperm in the ejaculate, and possibly the blood type of the man who had put it there. She was a newlywed; it was likely she had made love with her husband earlier in the day of her death. Her undergarments had been ripped off. It was entirely possible that someone wanted the investigators to *believe* her death was motivated by a sexual attack, when the motive was something completely different. It was even possible that her killer was a female — although she would have had to have been a very powerful woman or one who had used a heavy object to strike Sandy that hard in the chin.

Detective Al Schrader joined the investigators on the Bowman case on the morning of December 18. He checked first on Rob Kinslow, the man mentioned by Lee Wilkins's mother. Kinslow was cleared almost at once. He had been working a 3:30 p.m. to 11:30 p.m. shift at the Boeing airplane company's plant in Everett, some twenty-five miles north of the death scene. Schrader verified that by talking to Kinslow's supervisors. They were positive that Kinslow had been on the job for the entire shift.

Kinslow might have struck people as odd, but he could not have been the person who murdered Sandy Bowman.

"Nino," the Bowmans' surprise visitor who they suspected of robbing them, was found to be Martin Simms.* He did have a record for auto theft and robbery in Seattle police files. Through informants, detectives traced him to his sister's residence, where he was living.

But Nino, too, had a solid alibi: he had been with friends all during the afternoon and evening of December 17. Questioned separately, all of his associates verified his account of that day.

Al Schrader then pored over records of assaults in the Seattle area whose M.O. resembled the Bowman slaying. He found one man who had been involved in several attacks on teenage girls in the Ballard area. They had been bound and stabbed although, luckily, the victims had all survived. Their attacker had been found to be psychotic and committed to the Western Washington State (Mental) Hospital in Steilacoom. And Schrader found he remained incarcerated under maximum security and could not have been in Seattle.

One statement "Nino" Simms had made stuck in the detectives' minds. Although Lee Wilkins had appeared genuinely shocked when informed of Sandy Bowman's death, Nino said he had heard that Lee had never forgiven Sandy for breaking up with him. He described one incident at a north end bowling alley. Sandy had announced to a group of friends that she was expecting a baby and Wilkins had become enraged. He had called Sandy a "bitch" and threatened to kill her. When he talked with several young people who had been at the bowling alley, Schrader found that Wilkins had indeed made these threats. However, his efforts to question Wilkins were thwarted by a lawyer hired by the boy's father. Wilkins promised repeatedly that he would come to the Homicide Unit for an interview, but he failed to show up for his appointment.

Schrader tried to impress upon the Wilkins family that it was vital for Lee to answer questions about Sandy — if only to clear his name.

Then an interesting phone call came into headquarters. Sandy Bowman had never lacked for friends; she had dozens of them, but only one particularly close friend: Bobbi Roselle.* Now, Bobbi's mother,

Mrs. Grace Roselle,* was on the phone. A man the Roselles knew only slightly had come to their home very early the morning after Sandy was murdered. He appeared to be extremely agitated.

"His name is Jim something," Bobbi's mother said. "It's something like Lofbrau or Leffler. No, wait — it's *Leffberg*. He's a wild-looking man. Made me nervous to have him here. You should check him out."

4

Jim Leffberg had been slightly acquainted with Sandy's mother, Dorothy, before she moved to California. Grace Roselle and Sandy's mother both described him as a kind of "hanger-on" person who attached himself to people he barely knew.

"Anyway," Grace Roselle said, "he just didn't seem right that morning. The girls don't like him — I know that for sure. He made a pass at my daughter, Bobbi, once. They've always called him 'the dirty old man.' Well, anyway, he was here bright and early this morning asking all kinds of questions. He talked in a peculiar, disjointed way — kind of rambling on and on.

"He kept asking, 'Do they have any clues?' and 'Was she stabbed in the back?' 'Did they find the knife?' His eyes kept rolling back in his head and he held his head funny. Then he'd say things like his daughter had been born on Sandy's birthday. None of it made much sense. And there were his clothes too. They were all covered with red, and he kept apologizing for getting red on my carpet from his shoes."

The detective was instantly alert. "*Red?* What do you mean by that. What did it look like?"

"Well, it looked like blood. But he said he'd been painting a house and it was stains from his work," Grace Roselle said.

Schrader checked Jim Leffberg's name against Seattle and King County police records. (It was long before police had computers for more thorough exploration.) He came up with a number of entries for Leffberg. The middle-aged man had been involved with the law on numerous occasions on charges ranging from minor offenses to grand larceny. Detectives contacted his parole officer, who told them Leffberg *had* shown tendencies toward sexual crimes of violence, and his folder noted that.

The Seattle police investigators expected that they would have a hard time locating Leffberg, but they needn't have worried. As Al Schrader and Detective Donna Brazel finished interviewing Bobbi Roselle and her parents, Leffberg approached their house and told the detectives that he had some important information for them.

Jim Leffberg was an interesting character

who looked as though he had just hopped off a freight car. He was about five feet eight inches tall and he had a wild bush of dark hair. His clothes were unkempt.

"Sandy told me that this magazine salesman was bothering her," he said. "If I was you, I'd go looking for him."

Leffberg himself had never seen the magazine salesman and Sandy hadn't described him or given Leffberg a name. All he knew was that the guy scared her. It sounded like a red herring, rather than a good tip. The man in front of them looked better to them as a suspect.

Leffberg willingly gave them his address in Kent, a small town fifteen miles south of the Ballard area. He assured them he would be on hand at all times to help in the investigation.

As the days progressed, every available member of the Homicide Unit pitched into the Bowman investigation. Sandy was like one of their own, the niece of Sergeant Jerry Yates. Both Donna Brazel and Detective Beryl Thompson were assigned to Yates's unit, and they canvassed every apartment in the Kon-Tiki complex, asking residents if they remembered anything even slightly unusual on the night of December 17 — particularly around 7:30 p.m.

It proved to be a fruitless effort. Many of the residents were unaware that there had been a homicide. Because of the cold and snow, most of the people who lived in the Kon-Tiki had pulled their drapes that night and wouldn't have seen anyone passing by. A few recalled hearing cars peeling out of the apartment complex's parking lot.

A couple of tenants who lived close to the Bowmans knew of them — mainly because Sandy and Tom entertained many of their young friends who were prone to run up and down the stairs of the generally staid apartment house. They didn't really mind Sandy and Tom, but they had been annoyed by all the pounding feet, shouting, and giggling.

The Kon-Tiki caretakers said that it was their policy *never* to give out duplicate keys to anyone other than the actual renters of apartments. There was no way a stranger could get through their doors unless he — or she — was invited in, or broke in. And, of course, the Bowmans' door showed no damage at all.

Donna Brazel and Beryl Thompson moved on to an almost impossible task: they wanted to contact the scores of teenagers and young adults who had visited the Bowman apartment. Indeed, they did find most of Tom and Sandy's friends. But not one of them described the Bowmans' marriage as anything but idyllically happy. Over and over the female detectives heard, "They were very happy, very much in love," and "Tom treated her so good."

Still, a few of Sandy's girlfriends remembered that she had been afraid of something. "She never left the apartment without peeking out of the door first," one said.

"Do you know what frightened her?" Beryl Thompson asked.

The teenager shook her head. "She would never say what it was — or *who* it was — that she was afraid of. We thought maybe she just wasn't used to being alone at night because she'd always lived home before she and Tom got married."

Several of the school friends said that Lee Wilkins had gone steady with Sandy for a long time — since junior high school — and admitted that he had been upset when they broke up, but they felt sure he had forgiven her for marrying Tom Bowman. Despite his occasional outbursts, the former sweethearts had ended up being only good friends by the time of Sandy's murder. Lee was happily dating someone else.

One ominous factor, however, began emerging as police personnel enlarged their picture of the Bowmans' habits: although Sandy herself would not touch narcotics, many of the young people who visited her apartment were suspected of experimenting with drugs to some extent. A lot of them smoked marijuana, and Bobbi Roselle was rumored to have tried LSD.

"Sandy was really a friendly kid," the teenagers said. "She wasn't flirtatious, really, because she was so in love with Tom, but she liked to joke around, and she let in almost anyone in our crowd who came over to visit. Her apartment was kind of a meeting place for kids."

Detectives wondered if Sandy might have opened her door to someone high on drugs or perhaps been naive enough to admit "a friend of a friend of a friend." But that warred with the information from her closest friends that she was afraid of something and always cracked the door to see who was there. Sandy had been only two weeks past her sixteenth birthday; she was caught between childhood and being an adult, and it was unlikely that she had been mature enough to use good judgment all the time.

The Pall Mall cigarette that had dropped from where it was wedged in the Bowmans' doorjamb remained a puzzle. That was finally explained when detectives received a phone call from a 24-year-old woman who said she and her husband were good friends of Sandy's. She had even lived with them briefly before she and Tom were married.

"I don't know why," she said, "but Sandy kept coming into my mind that night and we decided to drive over and see her. The lights were on but she didn't answer the door. We stuck the cigarette up over the door so she'd know we'd been there when she came home."

The couple weren't positive of the time they had knocked on Sandy's door, but they thought it was between eight and nine.

During subsequent reconstruction, the homicide investigators realized that Sandy probably wrote the note to Tom in the last half hour of her life.

The investigation, however, was clouded with almost too many clues and too many bizarre coincidences. Schrader, Dorman, and Strunk felt that both Wilkins and

Leffberg were prime suspects. And Al Schrader also felt that Bobbi Roselle knew much more than she was willing to tell officers. She, too, appeared to be afraid of something.

5

Every name of someone connected to Sandy or Tom Bowman was compared to Seattle Police records of people who had been the suspects, victims, or witnesses in earlier cases on file — for everything from purse snatching and window peeping to murder. One name started bells and whistles sounding. The detectives had found a strong connection to another unsolved murder. Two and a half years earlier, in June of 1966, two United Airlines flight attendants had been brutally bludgeoned in their Queen Anne Hill basement apartment. One of the flight attendants, Lonnie Trumbull, was dead of massive head injuries when officers responded to the frantic call from the apartment manager's wife. The other girl lay near death for two weeks after the attack. The only thing that had saved her, physicians surmised, were the big wire rollers in her hair. "The curlers absorbed a lot of the force of the blows," the ER doctor had told police. "But we won't know if she has permanent brain damage until she regains consciousness." Detective Joyce Johnson had been assigned to sit beside the injured girl's hospital bed in case she said anything that might lead them to the attacker. But the victim had mumbled only nonsense phrases and moaned. Although the young woman recovered completely, she was never able to tell officers anything about the events of the fatal night. She had a total blackout.

This attack took place several miles from the Ballard district. But there was a connection. The manager of the apartment house where the flight attendants lived had been Wayne Brosnick, who was, of course, the Bowmans' next-door neighbor. It was Brosnick who Tom Bowman had run to after discovering his wife's body.

Follow-up reports on the stewardess's murder indicated that Wayne Brosnick had been questioned extensively. He had submitted willingly to a lie detector test, which he passed completely. However, Brosnick was now interrogated about friends who might have visited him in either or both apartment houses. He acknowledged that one of his acquaintances had a record of sex offenses and had been questioned in the earlier case. Questioned and released.

"There's not a thing to tie Brosnick's friend to the Bowman case beyond simple coincidence," one investigator said. Still, the man was checked out and found to have been miles away at the time of Sandy Bowman's death.

In 2004, it is far easier to look back at Lonnie Trumbull's murder thirty-six years ago and even to name her killer. It was undoubtedly Ted Bundy, who was eighteen at the time and working at a Safeway store on Queen Anne Hill. The M.O. of the attack on the flight attendants had virtually the same scenario as Bundy's savage murders in the Chi Omega sorority house in Tallahassee, Florida, some fourteen years later. In the former, he picked up a piece of two-by-four from a woodpile outside the flight attendants' apartment; in Tallahassee, he used an oak log from another woodpile. But no one had ever heard of Ted Bundy in 1968, and he had not even been a suspect in the disappearance of 8-year-old Anne Marie Burr in Tacoma, Washington, in August 1962 — although he delivered her family's morning paper.

6

As the Sandy Bowman homicide investigation moved on, detectives fanned out in many directions. Detectives Nat Crawford and Wayne Dorman went over the Bowman apartment inch by inch with an iodine fumer, which could bring up latent fingerprints. Even the picture tube from the television set was removed and taken to George Ishii, the Seattle Police Department's crack criminalist, for print identification. There were prints there, but they didn't match any suspects. In 1968, the thought of a computer-generated fingerprint identification system would have been something straight out of science fiction. The FBI kept a full set of ten fingerprints only on their Ten Most Wanted felons, and they had no way to compare single unknown prints to the millions of prints on file.

Billy Dunagen, who was the Seattle Police Department's handwriting identification expert, determined that Sandy herself wrote the note found on the coffee table.

★ ★ ★

Sandra Bowman's funeral was held four days before Christmas. Detectives E. T. Mullen, Wayne Dorman, and Nat Crawford mingled with the crowd to observe those attending, and pictures were taken of the crowd. Lee Wilkins and Jim Leffberg served as pallbearers. There was a reason for that: the investigators wanted to keep track of them and have them out of the way so that their vehicles could be processed for evidence.

Sandy's uncle, Hector Gillis, recalled that he was asked to keep Leffberg close to him. "All of the pallbearers were in the same vehicle, and I was sitting right next to this weird guy. I knew that Leffberg was one of the prime suspects in my niece's murder, and it wasn't easy to make conversation with him. But we had to be sure that he was being watched all during the funeral."

Lee Wilkins, Sandy's former steady boyfriend, smiled a great deal during the services, and one of the detectives who had questioned Wilkins recalled that he hadn't seen Wilkins smile at all during previous contacts with him. Other than that, nothing unusual transpired at the final rites and interment of the lovely teenager who had so looked forward to Christmas and to motherhood.

On the same day as Sandy Bowman's funeral, two mortuary attendants transported a corpse to another Seattle funeral parlor. It was not Sandra Bowman's body, but the attendants called police about a macabre incident. As they wheeled the corpse from a hearse into the establishment, a wild-eyed young man approached them, demanding to know, "Is that the body of the 16-year-old girl? It better not be!"

The attendants ordered the man to leave the mortuary, but one followed him and memorized the license number of his car as he drove hurriedly away. He reported this intelligence to homicide. A license check with auto records gave them the name of the registered owner, a Seattle woman.

Two homicide detectives drove to her address at once. The door was answered by a distraught older woman, who admitted that her son had been driving her car that day. She explained that he was a former mental patient. "He was traumatized when my husband was murdered ten years ago," she said. "It upset my son so much that any murder he hears about seems to send him into a psychotic state. There's been so much about that poor girl in the newspapers, and I'm afraid the publicity about her death has disturbed him a great deal."

When the investigators talked with the woman's son, he gave them an erratic account of his activities on the night of December 17. "I had the car and I went out to the country club because that's the only place in Seattle where the water isn't poison," he said. "When I got there, I had an accident. Another car hit me by the entrance gates."

They checked and found that the deranged man had, indeed, been involved in a minor accident near the guard station at the entrance to the posh grounds of a north end country club. The accident took place at 7:35 in the evening.

The unfortunate woman had her hands full with her psychotic son, but he wasn't Sandy Bowman's killer.

7

Lee Wilkins and Jim Leffberg remained the top suspects, even though their cars hadn't held a smidgen of evidence linking them to Sandy's murder. Keeping an eye on Jim Leffberg was no problem: he seemed always to be underfoot, pestering the dead girl's relatives, repeating his story of the magazine salesman, and demanding to be allowed to attend all family functions. At the funeral parlor, he had insisted on sitting with the family as if he truly did have close connections to them.

Leffberg answered questions easily at first, and then became more and more evasive as detectives interviewed him. He refused to take a polygraph test. He said that he had been painting a home in North Seattle until 7:00 or 7:30 on the night of the seventeenth. Then he had gone to a bar in South King County where he played pool with a friend and drank beer. He chided the investigators because they weren't looking hard enough for the magazine salesman.

Detective Al Schrader had already made every attempt to track down Leffberg's theory on the elusive magazine peddler but he had found no one in the Kon-Tiki complex who remembered seeing such a salesman within the six months preceding the murder.

Obtaining a search warrant, Schrader searched Lee Wilkins's room. The boy was advised of his rights and he offered no objection. Schrader was looking for a knife — *the* knife, because the butcher knife found on the floor of the murder bedroom wasn't the murder weapon.

Now, in Wilkins's room, Schrader found three knives. All of them were hunting knives, but all of them were also rusty from disuse. Still, Lee Wilkins, like Jim Leffberg, refused to submit to a lie detector test, which was his right.

After conferences with his lawyer and his parents, Lee Wilkins finally agreed to take a polygraph. Investigators had already checked out his alibi, but they did it again. He insisted that he had spent the entire evening of December 17 with three friends in the basement recreation room of one of the boys' houses. Each boy still verified that Wilkins had been with them from shortly before seven until eleven o'clock.

Lee continued to deny that he had borne Sandy any grudge at all. "She was my good friend," he sighed. "Why can't you believe that?"

Dewey Gillespie was the most experienced polygraph expert in the Seattle Police Department, known nationwide for his accurate readings. Gillespie had never met Lee Wilkins and would have no preconceived notions about his guilt or innocence. He was chosen to administer the lie detector test to him. After hooking Wilkins up to leads that would register respiration, blood pressure, heart rate, and galvanic skin responses, Gillespie began by asking the teenager innocuous questions to establish his normal responses. His name. His age. Where he lived. Only gradually did he begin to ask questions about Sandy Bowman and her murder, all the time watching the pens that moved along the graph in front of him. There were no high spikes that indicated Gillespie's subject was being deceptive.

"He doesn't have any guilty knowledge of the girl's murder," Gillespie told the detectives who waited anxiously for the test results. "He passed without a hitch. I don't believe he's the guy you're looking for."

That left Jim Leffberg as the top candidate among the suspects. He was placed under even more intense surveillance than he had been before. He was a strange man, indeed. Why had he insinuated himself into Sandy Bowman's circle of young friends? He was twenty or thirty years older than most of them, and had nothing in common with them. Leffberg had known Sandy's mother since she babysat for his children before his divorce. When she moved away and the children no longer needed day care, Leffberg had attached himself to Sandy and Tom.

He always seemed to be somewhere around them and their extended families. One of Sandy's cousins recalled, "Jim wasn't invited to Sandy and Tom's wedding — but he came anyway. He got drunk and obnoxious and we finally had to ask him to leave."

Friends remembered an incident when Leffberg approached Sandy in a local restaurant and insisted that he accompany her home. "Sandy kidded him along, but she didn't really want him around."

Jim Leffberg had been anxious to be part of the homicide investigation in the beginning, but now with every police request he became more defensive and evasive. He wasn't stupid — just peculiar — and he knew they had switched their suspicions from Lee Wilkins to him. On December 30, Al Schrader talked to him and asked him to take a "routine" polygraph. As he had told Lee Wilkins, it was the best way for Leffberg to eliminate himself from consideration as a suspect.

"Don't you want to clear your name completely?" Schrader asked, "so we can get on with this investigation? You'll be able to help us solve it — but we have to wonder now why you won't agree to take the lie detector test."

Leffberg agreed only to think it over and call back.

There was no physical evidence linking the bushy-haired handyman to Sandy's murder. The red streaks on Leffberg's clothes that had seemed so telling proved to be only Rustoleum paint, just as he had claimed. Cary Parkes and Bill MacPherson had talked to the couple whose home he had painted on December 17. They verified that he had, indeed, been there painting until well into the supper hour, although they could not give the exact time he left.

Leffberg had claimed that he was in the south end of King County after work that day, drinking and playing pool at the Sand

Dunes Restaurant next to the Green River in Kent. Jorge Guerraro,* his drinking buddy that night, had given detectives what seemed to be a "well-rehearsed" verification of Leffberg's alibi. Just to be sure, Bill MacPherson talked with a waitress at the Sand Dunes. She said she knew Guerraro and Leffberg as regular customers.

"Were they here on the 17th — the night the girl was murdered in Ballard?" MacPherson asked.

"What day of the week was that?"

"It was a Tuesday."

"I can't be sure. They usually came in on the weekend. I don't remember seeing them on the 17th."

MacPherson was elated; maybe he'd found the first flaw in Jim Leffberg's alibi.

But a few days later, another waitress from the Sand Dunes called him and asked him to come back to the restaurant. She had some information for him. She had been off duty when MacPherson questioned her co-worker. "I remember them, and they were both here on the seventeenth. They hung around from about 6:30 p.m. until 10:30 p.m."

"How can you be positive about that?"

"Well, that was the first night it really

71

snowed, and we were all talking about it, wondering if we'd be able to get our cars out of the parking lot and if the roads would be dangerous. But I *particularly* remember because Jorge Guerraro borrowed some money from me. See here: I marked it down — with the date."

She showed MacPherson a notation in a small notebook she carried in her purse. Sure enough, the date was December 17, and her loan to Guerraro was marked there.

"And you're sure that Jim Leffberg was here with him that night?"

"I'm sure. They always came in together. They nursed beers and tried to hustle pool players, but they weren't very good."

8

The case with too many clues was rapidly turning into an almost impossible maze. When detectives tried to find Bobbi Roselle to question her again, they discovered that her parents had spirited her out of the state on a plane to California under an assumed name. As they questioned teenage friends who hadn't been as close to Sandy Bowman, they met with more frustration. So many of them had been involved with drugs that they were afraid to talk to police, even when they were told, "We're not investigating marijuana. We're trying to solve a murder."

One girl finally told them, "You should really try to find Bobbi. She was supposed to be Sandy's best friend — but if that was true, she didn't need any enemies. Bobbi liked Tom way too much. She used to go around telling us places she'd gone with Tom. She never mentioned that Sandy was along at the time. Bobbi's a troublemaker. She likes to start rumors to mess people up."

"You aren't saying that Tom Bowman

was interested in Bobbi, are you?"

"No way. He loved Sandy, but Bobbi had a crush on him. I don't think he even knew it. Bobbi just made stuff up."

That made sense. Their investigation so far had involved statements by dozens of people, and not one of them had ever even hinted that Tom was unfaithful. He had been cleared as a suspect almost from the beginning. But Bobbi Roselle wasn't a likely suspect, either: she was a tiny girl who could never have overpowered Sandy. She wouldn't have had the strength to plunge a knife into the victim.

Bobbi Roselle returned from California in January 1969. The diminutive girl assured detectives that she had been Sandy's friend and would never do anything to hurt her. They weren't so sure about that, but again, she was just too small to do any physical harm to Sandy. Although she was chagrined to be asked, Bobbi Roselle grudgingly agreed to take a lie detector test. Once more, the results were negative. Bobbi may have been a rumormonger but she passed the polygraph examination easily.

Where there had once been so many likely suspects in Sandy Bowman's murder, they had been winnowed out until there were none at all. There was a substantial reward offer put out to urge anyone with information on Sandy's murder to tell the police about it. Several King County commissioners contributed to it and Tom Bowman added every penny he could.

No one came forward.

In the late sixties and early seventies, *True Detective Magazine* had a series called "Number One Mysteries," and a year later I wrote Sandy Bowman's story, entitling it "Washington State's Number One Mystery" and asked anyone who might have information leading to her killer to contact Detective Al Schrader at the Homicide Unit of the Seattle Police Department.

Schrader received a few letters, but none of them contained useful information. They were filled only with theories that would-be sleuths who didn't know Sandy or Seattle had come up with.

Al Schrader had a theory of his own, gleaned from scores of interviews he had had with LSD users. Rarely seen today, it was a popular drug of the era, mind altering and unpredictable, and the story persisted that Sandy had known people who experimented with the hallucinogenic once espoused by Dr. Timothy Leary, Cary Grant, and even the Beatles.

"Many users have told me that LSD can bring on a kind of compulsive behavior," Schrader said. "That is, once an idea forms in a drug-induced state, they must complete the whole sequence. It is possible that could account for Sandy Bowman's being stabbed almost sixty times. The killer, once started, may have had some drug-charted pattern to complete.

"Maybe the murderer himself doesn't know he is a killer. Or it may be that deep in the subconscious of that person's mind, the memory of that 'bad trip' lies buried and could surface at any time. We don't know. It's only a theory."

That theory seemed to be a much more viable possibility in 1969 than it did as time passed.

The Seattle Homicide Unit has had an enviable closure record on murder cases for decades, successfully charging suspects in over 85 per cent of their investigations. Back in the sixties and seventies, there were usually between forty-five and sixty homicides a year within the city's borders, a figure that hasn't changed over the years. Like most major cities, suburbs have attracted massive migrations. When I began as the Northwest correspondent for fact-detective magazines in 1969, King County, excluding Seattle, rarely had more than one or two murders a year. Today, the county homicide rate keeps pace with the city's.

In the Seattle Police Department, unsolved cases were worked and reworked until there were no more avenues to explore, and then they tended to drift to Archives, where they were seldom read. That wasn't the case with Sandy Bowman's unsolved murder. Although most of the detectives who tried to find Sandy's killer retired over the years, younger investigators coming into the unit were briefed on the case. Still, as years — and then decades — passed, it seemed as though Sandy's murder would never be avenged. As they worked beside Jerry Yates, the veteran detectives and the young men coming up were continually reminded of their failure to bring some kind of justice to this man who was their coworker, whom they admired as a good cop who had comforted so many other families, but who could not tell his own parents and sisters why someone would kill his sweet teenaged niece.

Sandy's family dealt with losing her the best way they could. Her mother did her crying in private; she refused to discuss Sandy at all. Losing her beloved daughter and the grandchild she had hoped for was too painful to talk about out loud.

The family decided not to tell Sandy's grandfather about Sandy's murder. He was elderly and frail and they were afraid the truth would kill him. "When she was killed," her cousin Rita Gillis recalled, "no one was allowed to talk about her. To my knowledge, no one ever told my grandfather she was dead. They told him she got married and moved away."

Benjamin Yates died in 1977 without ever knowing that his favorite granddaughter had been murdered.

Inevitably, the names of newer cases were written on the charts in the captain's office, a little cubicle in the northeast corner of the cramped Homicide Unit. Although I wrote factual articles about almost every case listed, I never forgot Sandy Bowman.

9

Shortly after Sandy Bowman's name faded from the headlines and slipped to the back pages of *The Seattle Post-Intelligencer* and *The Seattle Times*, and finally vanished completely, a series of abductions of young women captured the public's interest. In a sense, they were more baffling than Sandy's murder because no one knew *what* had happened to them for a long time.

Mary Annabelle Bjornson was 21 years old when she disappeared on January 4, 1969, only two and a half weeks after Sandy's death, but the circumstances of her vanishing were unlike the M.O. in Sandy's case.

The relatively new I-5 freeway was the direct route from downtown Seattle to the University of Washington and then north to Everett, Mt. Vernon, Bellingham, and Canada. It crossed over the University Bridge above the Lake Washington Ship Canal. As cars approached the north end of the bridge, they could look down and see two rectangular apartment buildings that sat side by side on N.E. 42nd Street below. Painted beige and brown since they were built in the twenties or thirties, the twin structures each had several apartments on three floors. They were stodgy compared to newer buildings that featured brick or sandstone and individual balconies and patios, but the apartments had big, airy rooms and lots of windows. Their location beneath the bridge was handy for residents, close to the University, the shores of the ship canal, and to bus stops. And the rent was a bargain. Few units were empty for long.

Mary Annabelle wasn't a student; she had an entry-level job. She was an extremely attractive young woman, quite tall and slender with lovely features. But it was her hair that people remembered: it was dark brown, long, very thick and wavy, and she parted it in the middle so that it framed her face like a cloud.

In one of the bleak coincidences that often mark homicide cases, Mary Annabelle was also the niece of a Seattle police detective. Her aunt "B.J." Bjornson was one of the last of the oldtime policewomen who had been hired early on to act more as matrons who dealt with women prisoners than as investigators. B.J. was tall, too, and stocky, with several feet of braids wound around her head. She may have been Mary Annabelle's great-aunt because she was well into her sixties when her niece disappeared, but they were very fond of one another.

B.J. Bjornson worked in the Crimes Against Persons Unit, as Jerry Yates did, but her assignment was "Mental Cases," as they were called then. She had a steady, calm presence and she could make even the most disturbed person brought in by the uniformed officers feel safe.

Mary Annabelle had plans for the Saturday night of January 4, 1969. She had invited her date for a home-cooked dinner and then they were going dancing at the Civic Center, where a West Indies band was playing. She loved calypso and reggae, and her date, Duane Thornton,* was one of her favorites.

Duane was due for dinner between 8:30 and 9:00, and Mary Annabelle had dinner in the oven and simmering on the stove while she changed into her pink chiffon dress and white high-heeled shoes.

She had made a lot of friends in the apartment house under the bridge and Mary Annabelle dropped in to see Don Simmer about 8:00 that Saturday night.

He was expecting dinner guests himself — three friends.

"Some guy came by my place a few minutes ago," she said. "He was looking for Steve. He must have meant Steve Shelton, Linda Williams's friend."

Linda lived in an apartment a floor above Mary Annabelle's and Don's floor, and she dated Steve Shelton. "I told him how to find Linda's apartment," Mary Annabelle said, "and he went up there and came back and said Linda wasn't home."

The stranger had asked for a pencil and a piece of paper so he could leave a note on Linda Williams's door, and Mary Annabelle had given them to him. Within a few minutes, he returned yet a *third* time to tell Mary Annabelle that he had left the note and would be back in about an hour.

Don Simmer said that she didn't seem concerned about the stranger, but thought it was a little odd that he kept coming back. When Simmer asked what the man looked like, she said he was young and quite "husky." He had worn a blue Navy pea jacket.

Mary Annabelle had visited with Simmer until about 8:30 and then she left, telling him she had things cooking on the stove that she had to check on.

About fifteen minutes later, he heard someone knocking on her door. She must have opened it because he heard it closing. And shortly after, he heard it close again.

Since Mary Annabelle had been expecting Duane Thornton for dinner, Simmer thought nothing of it. But when Thornton arrived for his date with Mary Annabelle at five minutes after nine, she wasn't there. Her door was unlocked, the curtains were open, and there was food cooking on the stove. Three of the burners and the oven were on, and some of the food was beginning to stick to the bottom of the pans.

He turned the burners down and sat down to wait. Then he assumed that Mary Annabelle must have gone next door to visit with Simmer, so Duane went over there.

"She was here," Don Simmer said, "but she left about 8:30 to finish cooking. She's probably close by."

Duane Thornton went back to Mary Annabelle's apartment to wait for her, listening to music on the stereo. When minutes passed with no sign of her, he walked nervously around her kitchen. He noticed a piece of note paper with a sketch on it on her kitchen table. It looked like her writing and he could tell it was a drawing of her building with an upstairs apartment marked. He recognized the location as Linda Williams's apartment.

But Mary Annabelle *knew* where Linda lived. Why would she need a map to it? When Duane asked Don Simmer about it, he told Duane about the stranger who had made three stops at Mary Annabelle's apartment looking for a "Steve."

The minutes stretched into an hour. When there was no sign of Mary Annabelle by 10:30, Thornton and Simmer were very concerned. They looked through every room in her small place and found her purse was still in her bedroom. Her cigarettes were on the kitchen table along with the diagram to Linda's apartment. Even her coat was still there.

But Mary Annabelle was gone. The two men called Seattle Police.

The missing young woman had probably been in her apartment, safe, until at least 8:45, when Simmer heard her door shut for the second time. Why she had left on a winter's night without her coat, purse, or cigarettes was the baffling question. She had no plans to go anywhere without her date, and at 8:45 he was due any moment. Whoever had knocked on her door, she would have expected to see Duane Thornton.

As for the husky young man in the Navy peacoat, no one other than Mary Annabelle had seen him.

"Would she have left with a stranger?" the patrol officer asked her friends.

"I don't think so," Simmer said. "She's the kind of a girl who will go out of her way to do a favor for someone, but she was pretty trusting. She opened her door several times when that guy knocked on her door. She just assumed he was looking for a friend of ours. I wish now that I asked her if she knew his name or if he had a car — or something. But it seemed like such an ordinary thing, except that he kept coming back."

It would have been easy for Mary Annabelle to feel secure. Simmer was right next door, and his friends would be coming down the hall at any moment, along with her own date.

But something must have happened to her. A search of the two apartment buildings came up empty. Nobody had seen her. She wasn't locked in the basement, or in any storage area.

Her disappearance was reminiscent of a scary movie where a secret door opens in a wall and an arm reaches out and pulls a beautiful young woman inside. Mary Annabelle was just *gone*.

Music still played in her apartment and the smell of the meal she had been cooking lingered.

Because she was an adult and because there was no sign of foul play, the police couldn't take even a missing-persons complaint until forty-eight hours had passed. Maybe she had had her own reasons to stand up her date, although Simmer and Duane Thornton were sure she wouldn't have done that.

Maybe a friend with a problem had called her and she had rushed out to comfort them.

And there was always the possibility that she had staged her own disappearance, setting it up by telling Don Simmer about the "stranger" in the peacoat. As I write this, there are scores of young women missing all over America, but there are also several who vanished on purpose, faking an "abduction" to get attention from a reluctant boyfriend or because they were failing their college classes and wanted to avoid final exams.

People sometimes behave in strange ways.

Again, a Seattle Crimes Against Persons detective had close ties to a young woman who was almost certainly in danger. Investigators had to wonder if there was someone out there with a grudge against their unit. But who would even *know* all the relatives of the detectives? Mary Annabelle had the same last name as B.J. Bjornson, but it would have taken someone intimately acquainted with the Yateses' extended family to know that Sandy Bowman was Jerry Yates's niece.

It had to be simple tragic coincidence.

Mary Annabelle didn't show up at her job on Monday morning, January 6, 1969, and she never came back to her apartment. No one who knew her ever heard from her again. She became one of the dozens of missing persons in Jerry Yates's files, and both his crew and the homicide detectives continued to work on the mystery of her disappearance.

10

Lynne Tuski was 20 in January 1969, and a junior at the University of Washington. Her shining blond hair was cut short and framed her face. She wore glasses with oversized tortoiseshell frames. Like Mary Annabelle, Lynne was very attractive, but she was a totally different type, studious looking when she wore glasses, but with a model's slim figure. Lynne worked part-time at the Sears department store on Aurora Avenue in the north end of Seattle.

She worked on the snowy Saturday evening January 25, exactly three weeks after Mary Annabelle's disappearance. Lynne had her own car, and after the store closed at nine, she was last seen walking toward it in the Sears parking lot. The lot was well lighted but relatively empty. Lynne usually walked out with other employees, but on this Saturday night she was anxious to get home. She carried her car keys in her hand so she could open her door quickly and hop in.

The temperature was dropping rapidly

and more snow was piling up. Although Aurora Avenue is one of Seattle's main arterials, the hills on the side streets quickly become treacherous when it snows.

Lynne Tuski disappeared from sight as she walked into the swirling snow.

No one ever saw her alive again. No one heard a cry for help or a sudden scream. Her car was in the parking lot when her friends and family started looking for her. It was still locked, just as she had left it.

Neither Mary Annabelle nor Lynne was the kind of girl to run away. But they were gone, nevertheless, and as the weeks went by, both the police and the news media spoke of them in the same breath.

Whom had they encountered on two Saturday nights in January? Both had gone missing about nine o'clock at night. Neither had ever spoken of being afraid of anyone. Intense questioning of their friends and family by Seattle Police investigators failed to turn up a suspect or suspects.

Or an eyewitness.

Or a motive for their disappearance.

There were no ransom notes.

That left the dread conclusion that a complete stranger had watched and waited for a pretty girl who suited his purpose, and that purpose was almost surely rape.

While it was true that the young women who were missing had disappeared in the same general area of Sandy Bowman's violent murder, there were many dissimilarities too.

The most glaring difference was that Sandy was killed where she lived and the scene was very bloody. Someone had obviously rifled through the contents of her purse, dumping it on the floor. Mary Annabelle's purse hadn't been touched. There was no sign of a struggle in the Bjornson apartment, or in the Sears parking lot where Lynne Tuski was last seen.

Until the missing girls were located, there was no way to compare their fates with that of Sandy Bowman.

11

On February 21, another University of Washington student disappeared. Connie Stanton* had agreed to meet her brother, John, who was a Navy officer, at her apartment. They planned to leave that Friday afternoon on a trip to their hometown of Leavenworth, Washington. Leavenworth is a quaint small town where tourists come to see the Bavarian buildings along its main street. It is apple country, close to Wenatchee on the eastern side of the Cascade Mountains. The northern approach to Leavenworth is over Stevens Pass or it can be reached by crossing Snoqualmie Pass and then Blewett Pass. But either way drivers chose, they needed chains for their tires and experience driving in snow and ice. Connie would never have attempted the trip without her brother as the driver.

Still, when John Stanton* and his wife arrived to pick his sister up between three and four in the afternoon, she wasn't in her apartment. She was a predictable, punctual, and considerate young woman, so much so that her brother and sister-in-law were instantly alarmed. Connie was *always* where she said she would be.

Stanton knocked on the doors of neighboring apartments and learned from a man who knew Connie that he had seen her leave the day before with a man driving a white station wagon.

"Did she come back?" Stanton asked.

"I don't know. We haven't seen her since then."

"What did he look like?" Stanton asked, immediately concerned.

The neighbor said that the man was about 25, broad shouldered and strong looking, with a haircut that failed to tame several cowlicks. "He looked like he'd just walked through a high wind," the man said. "I got the impression your sister knew him. She called him John."

That was enough for John Stanton and his wife. He had to be talking about a casual friend of the Stantons who had attended high school with them in Leavenworth: John Canaday. Canaday had been a sports hero in high school. He had recently been divorced from one of Connie's closest friends, and he wasn't taking it well. He and his ex-wife had two small children, but they hadn't been able to hold their marriage together after Canaday returned from serving in the Navy in Vietnam.

Connie had mentioned that Canaday was living with his parents in the north end of Seattle, and working for the Seattle Water Department. He had called her to talk a few times. He had even visited her, and she felt sorry for him because he wanted to reconcile with his wife, and Connie knew that wasn't likely to happen.

John Stanton knew his sister: Connie was naive, too sympathetic, and very inexperienced with the world. As far as he knew, she had never dated anyone seriously. If Canaday was using her as a sounding board or as a way to get his wife back, Connie's natural kindness would have kicked in. But *leave* with him, and be gone all night? That didn't sound like Connie.

As the Stantons waited for her to come back to her apartment, John and his wife were frightened for Connie. It had been dark for two hours and there was no sign of her.

Stanton called his family in Leavenworth on the slight chance that Connie had decided to ride over there with John Canaday instead. Maybe she had tried to get a message to him that he hadn't received. But his heart sank when he learned she wasn't with their parents.

John Stanton called the police and insisted on making a missing-persons report. Two patrolmen agreed to take the information since the neighbors had said his sister had been gone for more than twenty-four hours. He also called a mutual friend of his and Connie's to see if he had heard from her. Joe Sternholm* said he hadn't talked to her at all, but he was so concerned that he drove at once to Connie's apartment to wait with Stanton and his wife.

Early the next morning, John Stanton and Joe Sternholm phoned Canaday's ex-wife. She hadn't heard from Connie, either, although she'd expected to see her during her weekend visit in Leavenworth.

"What kind of car does John drive?" Stanton asked.

"It's a white station wagon. I'm not sure of the make but it's small, and it's either a '65 or a '66. Why?"

"I think he has Connie with him. She wasn't at her place when I came to pick her up."

"Oh dear."

"What's the address in Seattle where his folks live?"

She gave him an address near 125th and

Dayton Avenue North. It was almost impossible for either of them to imagine that Connie would have gone willingly with Canaday, not when she had promised to wait for her brother. And John Canaday had changed since he'd come back from the service. He wasn't the boy they had known in high school.

When the landlord let Connie's worried brother and his wife into her apartment, it was perfectly neat — as it always was. It was so completely normal that, like Mary Annabelle Bjornson's, it looked as if Connie had only stepped out for a moment. The two women had lived only a few blocks from one another.

12

The difference between the two disappearances was that John Stanton *knew* whom his sister had left with. At least, he had some place to start looking for her, and the police had run John Canaday's name through the Department of Motor Vehicle Registration so that they had a license number. Stanton enlisted Joe Sternholm's help so that one of them was watching either Connie's apartment or John Canaday's parents' house around the clock. As close as they could determine, Connie had been missing from her apartment for more than two days without contacting anyone. She was an adult, and it was her own business whom she chose to be with, but they all knew she would never have left with Canaday without notifying someone.

Still, the Vietnam vet had no police record, so it was difficult to explain to the missing-persons detectives why they were so worried. Had they known the hidden side of Canaday's life, they would have been frantic — but only he held those memories. As it was, the Stantons and John Sternholm shared a presentiment that something awful was going to happen — or had already happened — to Connie.

The two men and the Stantons' uncle not only kept watch, they also continually scanned the streets between Connie's place and John Canaday's current residence for a small white station wagon.

Late on Saturday night, February 22, Joe Sternholm drove past the house on Dayton Avenue North. As he circled the block, he spotted a white station wagon driving toward him. Because the nearby streetlight cast a glow over the vehicle, he was able to see that there were two people in the car — and he was quite sure he recognized Connie sitting in the passenger seat. But then the station wagon passed him, and Sternholm had to make a U turn to catch up with it. As he drove past the elder Canadays' house again, he saw that the station wagon was now parked in the driveway, and he caught a glimpse of a man and woman on the porch, just entering the house.

Sternholm looked for a phone booth and called John Stanton. "I think it's Connie, and it must be Canady I saw," Sternholm said. "Get here as soon as you can. I'll sit on the house and block the driveway until you can get here."

Stanton immediately dialed the number at the Dayton Avenue house, where there had been no answer for two days. Now a man picked up the phone.

"Is this John Canaday?" Stanton asked.

"Yes," a cautious voice answered.

"Well, this is Connie's brother. I understand you have my sister with you?"

"No — no," Canaday stammered. "I dropped her off in the University District last night."

"You're a liar," Stanton said evenly. "Someone just saw you take her into your house."

"Just a minute —" Canaday said. John Stanton could hear the sound of voices in the background, but he couldn't tell who was talking or make out their words. It sounded as if Canaday had put his hand over the receiver.

Finally, Canaday came back on the phone. He admitted that Connie was there with him.

"Let me talk to her — *right now!*"

"Just a minute." There was another long stretch of waiting while the voices murmured somewhere in the room. "Okay," Canaday said. "Here's your sister."

And then Stanton heard Connie. She sounded frightened and she spoke very softly. He asked her if she was all right, but before she could answer, John Canaday grabbed the receiver away from her and said roughly, "She's okay."

Stanton was not at all convinced of that. "I'm coming out to get her," he told Canaday.

"Okay — but be sure you come alone."

John Stanton had no intention of coming alone. Joe Sternholm was already there, watching the house, and Stanton brought his uncle with him. They had no idea what condition they would find Connie in as they sped north. It took them only ten minutes to get to the house where she was.

As they pulled up, the front door burst open and Connie came running toward them. She was crying, her eyes were red, and as she got closer they could see that she had purple bruises on her mouth and face, and rope burns around her neck.

"Be careful," she warned them. "He's got guns and rifles in there."

She was so close to hysteria that the men who rescued her didn't bombard her with questions, but they all feared she had been raped. Connie told her brother that Canaday had held her prisoner for two nights in a mountain cabin at Rainbow Springs up on Stevens Pass, and that he had then forced her to come back to Seattle with him to his parents' house. John and Joe helped her into John's car. It was well before cell phones were invented, but one of the men sprinted to a phone and called the Seattle police to report that they had found Connie and she had been kidnapped and was injured.

Within minutes, they heard the sound of sirens. Patrol officers Robert Bender and Charles Lindbloom listened to Stanton's explanation of his desperate efforts to find his sister. They could see the bruises around Connie Stanton's mouth and noted her disheveled appearance. She wasn't able to tell them much more about what had happened, but she warned them that the man inside the house had guns.

If John Canaday did have weapons in the house, he hadn't fired at Connie's relatives and Joe Sternholm. He'd simply slammed the door behind Connie as she fled. She was still sobbing so much that she couldn't give her brother or the police any information about where she had been since Thursday or what had happened to her.

John Stanton had the feeling that if they hadn't found her just in time they might never have found her alive. Canaday had abducted her — for whatever bizarre reason. Why, then, would he have taken the chance of bringing her back to his parents' house? He must have known that she would tell them what had happened to her.

Maybe he hadn't meant to let her go at all, but Canaday had little choice once he realized that there were witnesses who knew that Connie Stanton was with him. They had feared that he might try to kill her. Now that they saw how battered and bruised she was, and the ugly rope burns on her neck, they realized that their worst imaginings probably weren't far off. She was shivering, not from the bitter cold, but from shock.

They watched tensely as Bender and Lindbloom approached the house, expecting to hear the sound of a gunshot inside, convinced that Canaday's behavior had turned irrational enough that he would either kill himself or the policemen. But there was only quiet — until the two officers pounded on the door and then stood back, one on each side, guns drawn.

And then the front door opened and they saw Canaday's silhouette outlined against the lights inside. He wasn't holding a gun. Instead, he stood aside as he let the two officers in.

John Canaday put up no resistance when he was informed that he was under arrest for assault and for suspicion of kidnapping. They advised him of his Miranda rights and handcuffed him.

He watched silently as Bender and Lindbloom searched his station wagon. Under the front edge of the driver's seat, they found a trench knife and two pairs of gloves. They found several lengths of rope on the backseat and on the floorboards in the rear. They moved into the house, where he showed them his room. Canaday did not object to their search or demand to see a search warrant. They found another glove there, a gray blanket that was identical to one in his vehicle, and a Navy peacoat with his name sewn inside. The actual crimes where he was a suspect — kidnapping, abduction, and assault — had ended only a few minutes earlier and the possible evidence the two officers found was fresh and connected to the charges. If they didn't seize it and mark it into evidence, it might very well disappear.

The battered young woman with recent rope burns around her neck waited just outside. If the crime had been in the past, the officers would have had to get a search warrant, but when a law officer literally steps into the middle of a crime that, in essence, *continues*, a search warrant is not required. Thanks to the stubborn efforts of Connie Stanton's brother and her friends, she was alive.

The consensus was that she surely had suffered a sexual attack, but she denied that she had been raped. And when she was taken to a hospital emergency room for treatment of her injuries, doctors verified that Connie was still a virgin, and she didn't have the bruising on the inner sides of her thighs commonly found in women who have been forcibly raped.

She was, however, in deep shock and seemed very confused. She asked what was going to happen to John Canaday. Connie remembered him as the top athletic star of her high school. He had gone with one of the most popular girls in school for a long time, and then been morose and inconsolable when the girl broke up with him. Connie had known nothing at all about his secret side — at least, not until he'd forced her to go to the cabin with him. Sometimes it seemed to her as though she might have agreed to go with him. Her mind would not focus.

Connie Stanton had, in all likelihood, been subjected to brainwashing. First, John Canaday had been her friend in high school, and then her good friend's husband, and recently a heartbroken divorced man — or at least he had told her that — and then her captor. But he hadn't killed her. She kept reminding herself that he could have killed her while they were alone up in that isolated cabin, but he hadn't done it.

She thought that he must be a decent person underneath all the violence and anger.

But that was part of the brainwashing. Although in the sixties few laymen understood what would later be called the Stockholm syndrome because the most infamous case where it was employed — the kidnapping of Patty Hearst — was years in the future, it was a potent psychological technique. A captive must pass through four phases of terror before he or she begins to be confused about who the "good guys" and who the "bad guys" are. And Connie Stanton had done that. She had been ripped from the place and the people where she felt safe; suffered a profound psychological shock when her "friend" became her captor; been programmed to believe what he told her because he repeated what he wanted her to believe over and over and over; and, finally, been promised a "reward." In her case, as in most cases of deep programming, John Canaday had held out the promise that he would spare her life if she did what he told her to do.

While Canaday was incarcerated and questioned by detectives, Connie Stanton struggled to cope with what had happened to her. She was physically exhausted and emotionally damaged. It was probably fortunate that she had no idea of the depth of Canaday's depravity.

Even Seattle police detectives had no idea what a big fish they had caught when they responded to John Stanton's call for help on February 22. Canaday admitted taking Connie Stanton away from her apartment against her will and holding her captive in the mountain cabin, although he denied raping her. He surprised detectives, however, when he suddenly admitted to raping another young woman. To protect her privacy, she would be known in court files only as "B.B." He had used a knife to threaten "B.B." into submitting to a sexual assault, but he had let her go.

This, he said, had occurred a short time

before he kidnapped Connie Stanton. The difference between "B.B." and Connie was clear: he *knew* Connie, while the other girl had been a stranger. Charges for rape and assault were filed against John Canaday in the attack on "B.B." on March 1, 1969.

His life was rapidly collapsing around him. He wasn't the first man who longed for a wife and children and the home where he was no longer welcome but Canaday seemed to have been the kind of guy who could snap back. He had been a football hero in high school, he was tall and husky and quite handsome in a rugged way. There were many young women who would have been pleased to go out with him, but he had become morose and sorry for himself.

Now his secret life was being revealed. Detectives working on the disappearances of Mary Annabelle Bjornson and Lynne Tuski only a month before Connie was abducted certainly noted where John Canaday had been living: he was very close to the Sears store on Aurora Avenue and only a few miles north of the University District, and when he visited Connie, he had been just a few blocks from Mary Annabelle's apartment.

But she and Lynne Tuski were still

missing. If they were indeed dead, their bodies might be found one day. For the moment, there was absolutely nothing in the way of evidence that would connect Canaday to either of them. Yes, Mary Annabelle had described a man in a pea jacket and one had been found in Canaday's room — but a lot of men who had been in the Navy had pea jackets.

Rapists are violent criminals, but the majority of them don't move on to commit murder.

13

On March 13, a Seattle Community College student named William Kramer was walking alongside the Index River Tract Road near the hamlet of Index in Snohomish County, the county that lies north of King County. The region, an hour's drive from Seattle, is in the foothills of Stevens Pass on the west side of the mountains. After one of the stormiest winters in years, the deep winter snowbanks had just begun to melt a little on Washington's mountain passes. As Kramer glanced at the diminishing drifts beside the road, he saw something that didn't compute in his brain, and he couldn't identify what he saw. The hairs stood up on the back of his neck as he moved closer to get a better look.

At first, he thought someone must have tossed a store mannequin into the snow, and yet the part of it that he saw was so lifelike, even though it was marbled and blue. He gasped as he realized that he was looking at a human body.

Lynne Tuski was no longer lost. Her nude body was perfectly preserved, frozen solid in the snowbank where she had lain for almost two months. Although Snohomish County and King County authorities were able to move her body from her icy grave, any postmortem examination would have to wait until her remains slowly thawed out. None of her clothes were retrieved from where her corpse had lain.

It took several days before the medical examiner was able to do an autopsy on the body of Lynne Tuski. He found that she had died of strangulation by ligature, the weapon obviously a rope. She had been raped. Her forehead was bruised and there were abrasions on either side of her mouth, as if she had been gagged.

Because she had been left in the snow, it was impossible to tell how long Lynne had been dead. And, in 1969, only the blood type of her rapist and killer could be identified from the semen left behind, and that depended upon whether he was a secretor — someone whose blood type could be gleaned from body fluids such as blood, saliva, and semen.

Lynne's body had been found in the same general vicinity of the cabin where John Canaday had held Connie Stanton captive, close to Highway 10, where motorists headed east from Monroe, through Sultan, Startup, Gold Bar, and Index. And Canaday had used a rope around Connie's neck to control her. He had actually come close to strangling her with it before he loosened his grip.

On March 17, Donald Priest, who was a Snohomish County deputy prosecuting attorney, interviewed John Canaday in the King County jail. Initially, Canaday denied that he had any knowledge about the murder of Lynne Tuski or the disappearance of Mary Annabelle Bjornson. Two days later, Canaday had a change of heart after he spoke with his attorney, Phil Mahoney. Through Mahoney, he sent a message to the Seattle homicide detectives and to the King County Prosecutor's Office that he might be able to shed some light on what had happened to the two young women who had vanished in January.

On March 20, the first day of spring, John Canaday gave a detailed oral confession to Seattle Police Lieutenant Dick Schoener; Captain T. T. Nault, head of the King County Sheriff's Office's Major Crimes Unit; and deputy prosecutors William Kinzel and Patricia Harber of longtime prosecutor Charles O. Carroll's staff.

As Mahoney witnessed this meeting, Canaday told them what had happened on the nights of January 4 and January 25. He also admitted that he had raped the girl known only as B.B. at knifepoint two days before he encountered Lynne Tuski.

The group of investigators from the Seattle Police Department and King County Sheriff's Office and prosecutors followed Canaday's directions to the icy foothills of Stevens Pass. He knew exactly where he was going and directed the driver of the lead car about where to turn and what markers to look for.

As they approached a bridge, he said, "Turn left before you cross this bridge, and you'll be on Garland Hotsprings Road. Go past the gravel pit where there's a shed in the middle. You'll find another body on the north side of this road, just past that big mound of snow there."

They did. Mary Annabelle Bjornson, gone from her apartment even as she was dressed in pink chiffon for an important date and stirring dinner on the stove, had been there in the snowbank since January 4. The pink dress was gone, and so were her shoes and undergarments.

She, too, had been strangled, and autopsy results indicated that rape had been

111

attempted but not consummated.

The three cases involving Lynne Tuski, Mary Annabelle Bjornson, and Connie Stanton were "similar transactions" under the law, with so many commonalities. Canaday had many charges hanging over him:

> Count One: Attempted Rape of Mary Annabelle Bjornson.
> Count Two: Murder in the first degree of Mary Annabelle.
> Count Three: Rape of "B.B."
> Count Four: Assault with a deadly weapon in the second degree during the rape of "B.B."
> Count Five: Rape of Lynne Tuski.
> Count Six: Murder in the first degree of Lynne Tuski.

John Canaday pleaded not guilty by reason of mental irresponsibility that he claimed had existed at the time of his crimes.

His trial was set for the summer of 1969. He would be defended by the well-known Seattle criminal-defense firm Whipple and Mahoney, and prosecuted by Patricia Harber and William Kinzel, under the direction of the new prosecuting attorney of

King County, Chris Bailey.

The prosecution team had decided not to seek the death penalty, should Canaday be convicted.

Just before his trial began, his attorneys notified the Court that he wished to withdraw his not-guilty plea in the rape of "B.B.," and he was allowed to plead guilty to that specific charge.

It was an odd situation — as if John Canaday was admitting that he was eminently sane only a few days before Connie Stanton's abduction but was insane at the time he took her to the mountain cabin, and also insane when Mary Annabelle and Lynne were killed.

I attended John Canaday's trial when it began on July 8, 1969. It was, in fact, one of the first murder trials I have ever covered. I found it both disturbing and fascinating. Ever since then, I have said I would rather go to a trial than a Broadway play. Until the advent of television documentaries and Court TV's live coverage of trials, my friends were baffled by my enthusiasm for watching cases unfold and listening to witnesses. Since John Canaday's trial, I have sat on the hard benches familiar to courtroom devotees in dozens of jurisdictions from Florida to the Northwest, and watched a hundred or more cases move through our American justice system.

They have all been memorable in some way, but Canaday's trial taught me so much about human nature that I could never have imagined. I remember sitting in the second row of the gallery, not that far from the defendant. Even after months in jail, he looked very strong, with huge shoulders.

There was a quiet, rather plain young woman sitting beside me, observing the trial. It was several days before I realized that she was Connie Stanton, one of the alleged victims who survived being abducted by John Canaday.

During subsequent courtroom breaks, Connie told me that she was grateful to be alive. John Canaday, whom she had known for many years, had convinced her to leave her apartment with him on Thursday night. It was supposed to be a quick errand, and she didn't have to meet her brother until Friday afternoon. All he asked for was her help as a driver. He said he had to pick up a second car a short distance away, and needed Connie to drive one of the cars back to his parents' house. It hadn't seemed like that much of a favor to ask of her, and he assured her that it wouldn't take long.

Once Connie was in Canaday's car, however, he hadn't driven very far before he pulled over to the side of a country road, where he tied her up with ropes that he had precut and hidden in the backseat of his station wagon.

Connie told me she had kept her wits about her during the forty-eight hours he held her captive. She had kept him talking, reminding him that they were old friends from the same town and bringing up happy memories of the old days. When he began to talk about sex, she impressed upon him that she was a virgin and that she had always wanted to save herself for the man who would one day be her husband.

According to Connie, Canaday understood that and respected her wishes. "He did try to have intercourse with me, though," she confided, "but I was always able to stop him before he penetrated me. In a way, I'm grateful to him for that."

Sometimes, Canaday had been gentle with her. "He even cooked chocolate pudding for us," she told me.

But there were other moments when she feared for her life. He had tried to strangle her and she had passed out from lack of air a couple of times, although usually she had talked persuasively enough to snap him out of it. And it was Connie who had convinced her captor to bring her back to his house. She thought she would have a better chance of survival if she was around other people.

That certainly made sense.

Connie Stanton was still somewhat confused about her feelings. Given the four criteria for brainwashing, she had endured them all: she was shocked when she realized her friend's ex-husband meant to kidnap her and tied her up with ropes; she was far, far, away from home and the people who meant the most to her; Canaday had warned her often that he might kill her — "do to you what I'd like to do to [my ex-wife]"; and yet, he occasionally told her he might let her go without hurting her any more. That would be her reward, and she had wanted to live so much that she finally came to think of him as being a good person because he didn't kill her.

"Sometimes he was so nice to me," she murmured. "I'd like to just give him a note to thank him for not killing me, but they won't let me talk to him."

As she tried to catch his eye, she seemed to bounce between her fear of Canaday and her concern for him as a troubled person whom she had tried to help. He never glanced in her direction.

I'll admit I was baffled that she seemed so sad for his current predicament, but I could see she was a really kind person. I asked her if she had romantic feelings toward the defendant, and she denied that vigorously. It was more that she had had preconceived notions of what a kidnapper would do to his victim, and once John Canaday had promised not to rape her and that he would bring her back to Seattle, he had kept his word.

Now he sat at the defense table, his sports jacket too tight for him, his shaggy head hunched forward, and he surely looked like a man who had run completely out of luck. It was very easy for me to remember that he had made his own luck, and that he had probably destroyed two young women's lives absolutely. I didn't feel at all sorry for him.

Finally, Connie Stanton prevailed upon me to at least give the short note she had written to John Canaday to one of his defense attorneys. If it made her feel less sad, I didn't see that it would hurt anything, although I doubted the attorney would pass the note on to the defendant.

At the noon break, I ended up giving it to the bailiff. I have no idea if John Canaday ever saw it. I spent the rest of the trial urging Connie Stanton to talk to a counselor about her feelings. She had done nothing wrong. She was a victim who had come closer to dying than she realized, and she was the last person who needed to be concerned about what was going to happen to a man who had tightened a rope around her neck until she passed out. Had her neck muscles or arteries been configured in a slightly different manner, she probably would have ended up in a snowbank too.

That was the odd thing about strangulation — and another thing I learned from sitting in on murder trials: some people died within a minute of having their airway cut off; some survived for several minutes. By ligature or manually, strangulation is an iffy thing, and many people have become murderers when they didn't intend their actions to go that far.

But *they* are construed by the law to have planned to kill from the moment they grabbed someone by the neck.

"Accidental strangulation" is not an adequate defense in a homicide trial.

14

John Canaday wanted to testify and tell his story to the jurors. Defense attorneys appear to be unanimous in their hesitancy to allow their clients on the witness stand. They know that the defendant immediately opens himself up to cross-examination by the prosecution.

And anything can happen. Few murder defendants are adroit enough to joust with trained prosecutors, and they are likely to blurt out answers they never meant to give. They may think they are giving the appearance of innocence — or, in John Canaday's case, insanity — that will sway a jury.

At this point, Canaday didn't need to fear the death penalty because the State had not asked for it. But the jurors could do whatever they wanted and *they* might invoke it.

Canaday was adamant. He was going to speak for himself.

The jury had heard many witnesses who recalled their last moments with Mary Annabelle and Lynne, and the testimony of investigators, forensic pathologists, and relatives of those who had been sexually attacked and/or murdered. Now they stared at the man who had already confessed to many of the charges against him.

Jurors are notoriously hard to read, but, to me, none of them looked friendly as Canaday took the stand. He said he was 24 years old, a high school graduate, an honorably discharged Navy veteran, and that he and his ex-wife had two small children.

He agreed with his defense team that he had asked that the investigators be contacted so that he could tell them about Mary Annabelle Bjornson and Lynne Tuski.

"Now, it is not your desire to be turned loose at this time, is it?"

"No."

"Do you feel that you are dangerous to be at large at this time?"

"Yes."

". . . Do you have a clear recollection of the incidents?"

"If I sit down and think about."

So far, the defense wasn't making a very strong case. Pat Harber rose to cross-examine Canaday. The slender blond prosecutor was adept at pulling out statements that made defense attorneys cringe. She began by showing premeditation on Canaday's part. He admitted that he had burned the ends of the lengths of rope the patrolmen had found in his car after Connie Stanton was rescued. He had done it, he said, to keep the ends from unraveling. It seemed glaringly obvious that he had prepared his garottes carefully so that they would be ready when he spotted a woman he wanted.

Canaday said he remembered the night he went to Mary Annabelle's apartment house, but denied that he had ever seen her before and gave no reason for choosing her apartment. He was just "looking for a girl."

"And you had your pea jacket on when you knocked on her door?"

"Yes."

When he was asked how he got Mary Annabelle to leave her apartment with him, he replied that he told her his car wouldn't start and asked her to help him.

"At the time you went up to the door, do you recall what was wrong with your car?"

"Nothing was wrong with it."

But he had raised the hood and asked her to get behind the wheel, and he told her when to turn the key. The engine started. Then he had slammed down the hood and walked around to the driver's-side door. Mary Annabelle was still sitting behind the steering wheel.

To Harber's questions, he said repeatedly, "I don't remember." He didn't know if she had worn a coat or a scarf. He claimed not to remember her pink party dress.

"Now, at this point, did you just get into the car, or what did you do?"

"I pulled a knife. It was in the automobile, somewhere on the floor . . . Most of the time I used to keep it under the seat."

"When you used the knife, did you hold it in your hand — how did you use it?"

"I had it in my hand."

"Close to her?"

"I think so. Yes."

"In other words, she couldn't have run away the way you were holding her. Is that right?"

"I believe so . . . She started screaming and I put my hand over her mouth and told her to be quiet and she did."

"Did she appear to be scared?"

"Yes. I think anybody under that situation would," he answered calmly. He denied that he was angry at Mary Annabelle for screaming.

"Didn't you feel that someone might

come running if they heard the screams? Is that why you put your hand over her mouth?"

"It didn't bother me."

"At the point that you put the hand over her mouth, were you able to control her in any way?"

"Yes. I just put my hand over her mouth and dropped the knife and she shut up."

"What did she do with her hands?"

"Nothing. She was more scared of the knife than anything else."

Canaday described how he had entered the station wagon by forcing Mary Annabelle to slide over. He had taken his hand away from her mouth, but he had the knife very close to her body at this point. He then tied her hands with rope.

"Where did you have the rope?"

"I always have rope in the automobile. I've always had rope since I owned it — for about a year."

He explained that he had tied his captive's hands in front of her and driven away immediately. The nearest entrance to the I-5 freeway was right there. He said he found it "quickly, very quickly."

Mary Annabelle wasn't screaming any longer but she was "still scared. She was shaking."

Canaday explained that he took the first off-ramp he came to, one that passed houses and led eventually to a wide body of water. That would have been Lake Washington, along Lake Washington Boulevard. The defendant recalled that he had driven to the Stan Sayres hydroplane pits.

No place in Seattle would have been more deserted in January; the powerful hydroplane races took place during Seafair in July, and tens of thousands of fans jammed the beach and the green sweeps of lawn then, but it was very dark and cold and completely deserted in the winter.

"I parked and told her I was going to rape her . . . She started screaming."

"Did you react to this in any way at all?" Pat Harber asked.

"Yes — I put my hands around her throat."

John Canaday testified that he believed Mary Annabelle was facing away from him, trying to roll down the windows with her hands, which were still bound, as he closed his huge hands around her throat. "I told her to stop screaming. It just disturbed me. I don't like people screaming in the first place."

"Did it make you angry?"

"In some ways, yes."

"Did your wife used to scream at you?"

"No."

Canaday's answers came out in a stilted way. He remembered what had happened, but he seemed determined to keep his affect stolid. He described how he had "squeezed" Mary Annabelle's neck until she made no more sounds.

"Did you think there was something wrong with her when she stopped screaming?"

"I thought maybe she'd be dead."

"Did you, at this point, feel something had gone wrong? I mean, that you had done something wrong?"

"In a way, yes."

The jurors' faces were pale and their expressions set as John Canaday told of driving away from the hydroplane pits with the dead girl in the front seat of his car. He said he had headed north because he knew he couldn't leave her body within the city limits of Seattle. He was afraid someone might find it.

He was heading for the road to Stevens Pass. He said he wasn't concerned at all about needing snow tires because the tread was good on his tires, and he had driven in snow for many years. He had been skiing since he was ten and was a ski jumper.

Leavenworth had several steep jumps. "I [never jumped off] the large one, no," he said.

Oddly, John Canaday insisted he had never been to Index, and he had only accidentally found the road where he left Mary Annabelle Bjornson. He described laying her body on the ground and then taking off all of her clothing. She *had* grabbed a light coat as she followed him out of her apartment, and he had used it to carry all of her clothing like a "laundry bundle." He could not recall if she had worn jewelry.

"And now what did you do with her?"

"Threw her over the snowbank."

"How deep was the snowbank?"

"Shoulder high."

"Was she heavy?"

He could not remember. Taking her clothes with him, Canaday had driven directly back to Seattle. His parents weren't home that night, so it had been easy for him to burn the pink chiffon dress, her coat, and other garments in the fireplace. He had started newspapers burning and thrown Mary Annabelle's clothes in, watching them in the flames until there were only innocuous-looking ashes left.

So little time had passed since she was waiting happily for her boyfriend to arrive.

As the last ember faded, she should have still been dancing to Jamaican music. She had been kind to a stranger who came knocking on her door three times. Was it true that John Canaday had never seen Mary Annabelle Bjornson before? That seems doubtful. He didn't approach any other apartments in her building; he came straight to her door with his made-up story about looking for "Steve." There was no Steve; Linda Williams's friend, Steve Shelton, had told police he didn't know Canaday. Neither did Linda.

It is far more likely that Canaday had spotted Mary Annabelle in the neighborhood and scoped out which apartment she lived in, and that he had gone there expressly to lure her outside with him.

15

Canaday returned to the witness stand after the lunch break. So far, he was strengthening the prosecution's case far more than he was making points for the defense. His coldly matter-of-fact recitation of the details of Mary Annabelle's abduction and murder was shocking to listen to — worse coming from his own lips than from Pat Harber's or Bill Kinzel's presentation for the State.

Although it seemed that he must have stalked Mary Annabelle, his first January victim, after having seen her and become obsessed with her, Canaday's recall of Lynne Tuski's disappearance made it sound as if *her* fate had resulted from a spur-of-the-moment decision. She was far more a victim of opportunity.

He admitted that he was looking for a girl again on Saturday night, January 25, three weeks after he killed Mary Annabelle. He described driving slowly through the Sears parking lot shortly after closing time. Once again, it was around nine p.m. on a Saturday night. He spotted a blond girl, he testified, who held her car key in her hand and who was just about to unlock her driver's door.

Lynne Tuski had been only seconds away from safety when John Canaday stopped and asked her for directions. She had explained how to get to the road he asked about, and she was very nice to him as she did so, even though it was very cold and she was standing in a heavy snowfall.

"And then what did you do?" Pat Harber asked.

"I started to drive off — but then I backed up. I think I got out . . . I think she was walking away."

Canaday said he had approached her and said, "Come on. You're coming with me."

"At that time, did you have anything in your hand?"

"Yes. The knife." His recollection was that Lynne had been "scared" as he hooked his hand round her arm and pulled her to his vehicle. He had then pushed her into the driver's seat. She had not screamed. "I think she was too scared to scream."

"Did you have your knife in your hand at the time you pushed her into the car?"

"Yes."

Canaday said he had repeated what he had done to Mary Annabelle and tied Lynne Tuski's hands in front of her. He looked at a piece of rope that had been entered as an exhibit in his trial, and said he couldn't identify it.

Harber pointed out that it had been found in his station wagon under the dashboard near the air conditioner. He acknowledged then that he had put it there because "the air conditioner squeaked."

"Is there any reason why there should be any hair on any of this rope?" She held it toward him. "See?"

"I don't want to talk about that."

"In other words, you knew there was hair on one of these pieces of rope?"

"Yes." Canaday said that he had driven Lynne Tuski to Golden Gardens, a waterside park in the Ballard district of Seattle.

"Did Lynne Tuski say anything to you as you were driving to Golden Gardens? Do you remember that?"

"She was talking about something, but what, I can't remember."

"Do you suppose that she was wanting to know what was going to happen to her?"

"If I was in the same situation, I would, yes."

Once at Golden Gardens Park, Canaday

had parked. Lynne's hands were still tied, but he denied that she had a gag in her mouth. He testified that he didn't know why she would have had marks at the corners of her mouth. He remembered that they talked a little bit, but, true to form, his memory was clouded — up until the point where he told her he was going to rape her. "I told her to get in the backseat."

How his victim had managed to do that with her hands tied, he could not say. But he had followed her into the backseat.

"What happened then?"

"I raped her."

"Did she fight you?"

"She pushed me away."

"Do you know if she was a virgin or not, John?"

"I think she was. Yes."

Just as he could not say how Lynne had suffered the abrasions on her mouth, he insisted he had no idea how she could have gotten bruises on her forehead. He did recall that she had crawled into the front seat after her rape.

"What did you intend to do at that point?"

"Let her go."

"You were going to let her go?"

But Lynne Tuski had made the mistake of screaming for help. And, of course, John Canaday hated to have anyone scream. He had just happened to find another piece of rope in the front seat of his car as Lynne, like Mary Annabelle, managed to roll down the passenger window and scream.

"Just an odd piece of rope?"

"Yes."

"There was no loop in either end?"

"No."

"Now, when you put the rope around her neck, what did you say to her?"

"I think 'Stop screaming' or something to that effect."

"Did she stop screaming?"

"Yes, she did."

"How did that happen, now?"

"When I let go of the rope, she was dead."

Mary Annabelle's body had not been discovered, so John Canaday stayed with his body disposal plan, taking Lynne's corpse up to the Index area. She, too, was stripped of her clothing and tossed over a snowbank. And, once again, he testified that he had burned her clothing in his parents' fireplace.

"Do you remember taking anything off her finger?"

"No, I don't."

"Was it because the ring wouldn't burn that you didn't burn it?"

"I didn't realize I had a ring."

"How did you think it got in your drawer?"

"I don't know."

"How about the contact lenses?"

"Not unless I had them in my pockets and I took everything out and threw it in the drawer."

"Now, did you feel at the time you had strangled Lynne — did you feel that this was the wrong thing to do?"

"Yes."

"Are you sorry for what you've done?"

"Taking any human life, anybody should be sorry."

"*When* did you become sorry, John?"

"When?" he answered, considering. "Maybe right after I did it — or soon after."

"Did you ever think the police would catch up with you concerning this?"

"Yes."

Although John Canaday's answers during cross-examination were given in a flat tone and showed little emotion, his efforts to appear insane weren't very convincing. Under the M'Naghten Rule, a criminal must have known the difference between right and wrong at the time he committed the act. When a defendant has planned ahead and armed himself with weapons, and *then* taken great pains to hide his victims' bodies and any evidence connecting him to the crimes, the M'Naghten Rule test almost always indicates that he was fully aware that what he had done was wrong.

John Canaday had his knife, his ropes singed on the ends so that they would not unravel, his ruses to put his intended victims at ease, and he certainly covered up evidence after Mary Annabelle and Lynne died, burning their clothing to ashes.

His own brother and a boyhood friend testified for the defense, but neither of them claimed that he was insane or even mentally irresponsible. He had held down a job and been a satisfactory employee.

Dr. John Riley, a psychiatrist testifying for the defense, deemed Canaday to be a sexual psychopath, a category of personality disorder, but one that excludes insanity, mental deficiency, or irresponsible behavior. On cross-examination, Dr. Riley agreed that Canaday's conduct and personality were consistent with sanity.

Two other forensic psychiatrists — Dr.

Richard Jarvis and Dr. George Mac-Donald — who had also examined Canaday concurred.

The jury retired to debate, and returned in less than two hours. To the shock of almost everyone, including the prosecution team, they not only found John Canaday guilty of the murders of Mary Annabelle Bjornson and Lynne Tuski, but they recommended the death penalty, even though the State had not sought it.

The laws regarding capital punishment in Washington State in 1968 at the time of Canaday's crimes were confusing. Had he chosen to plead guilty to two counts of murder, he would have avoided the death penalty — imposed by hanging. A confession with a sure death penalty punishment would have been construed as the defendant committing suicide. However, since he had pleaded not guilty (by reason of insanity), and the jury hadn't believed him, they had the right to impose the death penalty.

In September 1971, John Canaday's appeal to the Washington State Supreme Court asked for a new trial. The appeal was based upon alleged "newly discovered evidence." His attorneys put forth their belief that Connie Stanton would testify that

Canaday had demonstrated "an almost un-controllable anxiety" during their time alone in his parents' cabin.

At other times, the defense counsel's affidavit submitted that he "would become kind and considerate."

While it was evidently true — at least from what Connie Stanton had told me — that Canaday occasionally seemed to consider her feelings as he tried to convince her that they were two lovers enjoying a weekend in a cozy cabin in the snowy mountains, he had also strangled her unconscious. Would the supreme court consider that an indication of "uncontrollable anxiety"?

It would seem more a sign of frustration and, most of all, rage. Moreover, Connie Stanton's affidavit that accompanied Canaday's appeal for a new trial recalled how he had tied her with rope and taken her against her will to the cabin where she was held captive. She stated that she had no opinion about his sanity during her captivity, during his trial, or in the two years since.

I realize now that when I talked with her during Canaday's 1969 trial, she was only four or five months past one of the most terrifying experiences a woman could endure. She would still have been suffering from post-traumatic stress, and inordinately thankful to be alive. Because he had brought her down from the mountain, she wanted to think that, in a sense, he had saved her.

By 1971, Connie had allowed herself to face the very real possibility that — if it were not for her brother's rescue efforts — she might well have died too. She remained a captive in the house where Canaday lived, he still had the knife and the rope garottes, and she had had no idea what he intended to do to her next.

Faced with an angry John Stanton, Canaday had released her. Now she saw the truth clearly.

The Washington State Supreme Court denied John Canaday's appeal for a new trial. In 1972, however, Canaday got a reprieve from the death penalty when the U.S. Supreme Court ruled against capital punishment in thirty states — and Washington was one of them. But he was facing sentences that would undoubtedly keep him behind prison walls for the rest of his life.

He would first serve fifty-five years on one murder conviction, and only when the Washington Indeterminate Sentence Review Board approved the decision would he begin a consecutive sentence of forty-five years, followed by sentences for his lesser crimes.

16

Certainly, Seattle Police homicide investigators had noted that John Canaday's stalking rapes and murders of young women in the early months of 1969 had occurred in the north end of the city, and not too far away from where Sandy Bowman died in December 1968. There were some similarities, and detectives weighed them against the differences among the cases.

Canaday's victims had been single girls living alone, and he had abducted them, killing them in his vehicle. Although he had used a knife to threaten them, he had not stabbed them — and Sandy had been stabbed at least fifty-seven times. The knife Canaday had used to threaten his victims was *not* the knife that killed Sandy. He had left his victims' bodies in isolated places while Sandy was found in her own bed.

Sandy's hands *had* been bound, however, although her murderer had loosened them, but the bonds had come from her own apartment, cut from her living room drapes.

There was no physical evidence linking Canaday to Sandy Bowman's murder. His fingerprints were not among those lifted in her apartment. No one who knew her had ever described anyone who looked like Canaday, and he was memorable looking — big, hulking, with his rough, spiky haircut.

Who had Sandy talked about who might have come back to kill her? It seemed as though every man in her life had been cleared through alibi and/or lie detector tests. She had told Jim Leffberg, according to Leffberg, that she was afraid of a magazine salesman, but the investigators had never been able to find him.

John Canaday had used all manner of ruses to coax his victims out of the safety of their apartments or their cars: the broken-down car lie; the asking for directions ploy to bring Lynne Tuski close to his car so he could grab her; the lie about needing Connie Stanton to help him pick up a car. Was it within the realm of possibility that he had pretended to be a magazine salesman to get Sandy to open her door? Had he returned more than once?

He had used "granny knots" to tie the wrists of his victims, and Sandy's bonds were also tied that way, but it was a common knot that any Boy Scout or serviceman might use.

In the end, John Canaday had confessed to his crimes, but he had never mentioned Sandy Bowman. With the forensic science tools available in the late sixties, there was no place else to go to try to link him to the murder of the teenage bride.

Throughout 1969, Al Schrader had continued to get leads on Sandy Bowman's murder, but most of them came from high-school students who had heard a rumor that came from someone who had heard a rumor from someone else. Many of these rumors were traced back to Bobbi Roselle and none of them shed even a sliver of light over the investigation.

Only the bare facts that detectives began with remained. Sandy Bowman was alive and happy at 6:30 on December 17 when Lee Wilkins carried her groceries up the stairs to her second-floor apartment. She wrote her husband Tom a note — probably shortly before 7:30. She told him she planned to go to bed at once, but she hadn't had time to change into nightclothes before someone came to her door.

She had time to cry out, "Oh . . . no, no, no!" before she was struck on the chin and probably knocked unconscious. According to the Brosnicks next door, they had heard her say that just after 7:30. Within the next hour, her friends had come by and knocked on her door, but she failed to answer and they left the cigarette in the doorjamb. It was conceivable that her killer was still in the Bowmans' apartment when they had done that.

Was Sandy killed by someone she felt was safe to admit to her apartment, or had she carelessly left the door unlocked? That seems unlikely because she was afraid to leave her home until she peeked out the door to check the walkway first.

Somewhere, someone knew who destroyed two lives — Sandy's and her baby's — on that horrific night. The Seattle Homicide Unit initially contacted several hundred people in the investigation, and continued to follow up on the diminishing leads that came in. The file on Sandy Bowman grew thick and unwieldy, but it remained close at hand in the "Open" section.

In time, every detective who had worked on the Bowman case in 1968 retired, including Jerry Yates, Sandy's uncle. Inevitably, some of them passed away. Even the Public Safety Building where the Homicide Unit was housed for decades was scheduled for demolition.

And years went by. More than thirty-five years. I would write about more than a dozen unsolved "mysteries" in my *True Detective* territory. And most of them, like Sandy's story, remained in the "loser" file, a self-deprecating term homicide detectives themselves used to describe what the media now call "cold cases."

Either term meant that they had tried every avenue available to them, followed every lead — no matter how obscure — and still failed to arrest a suspect, much less see one convicted.

Over the last thirty-five years, I have read hundreds of homicide files. The unsolved cases are invariably many times thicker than those that can be tied up neatly. They represent frustration and even despair on the part of the investigators who worked many, many hours of overtime as they strived to find a killer who remained free to roam and, perhaps, to destroy more lives.

One case I remember clearly was the murder of a young flight attendant whose name was Eileen Condit. She rented a small house not far from Madison Park near the shores of Lake Washington, some miles east of Seattle's downtown section.

The houses were built very close together there because it was a very desirable location, and her next-door neighbors could see into her living room area if her drapes weren't pulled, which she seldom did during daylight hours. She was a gaminelike girl with a short "pixie" haircut, friendly and approachable.

But no one saw who attacked Eileen on May 28, 1970. Someone murdered her with several thrusts from a butcher knife — a knife taken from her own kitchen. One neighbor caught just a glimpse of a man running between the two houses, and could remember very little about him except he seemed to be in his early twenties and wore tennis or boat shoes.

Like Sandy Bowman's murder, Eileen Condit's was still unsolved as Seattle rolled over to another century.

Although neither Sandy's nor Eileen's investigations fell into the category, some of the cold cases are marked "Exceptional." That is a term Seattle homicide detectives use when they refer to murders where they *know* in their minds and in their bones who the killer is — but they can't prove it. These are probably the most disheartening challenges of the many they face.

When 5-year-old Heidi Peterson vanished in a matter of a few minutes from the sidewalk in front of her house in February 1974, Seattle's heart broke. No child could disappear so fast, but Heidi had. Police and volunteers combed the neighborhood. I remember riding all night with a K9 unit, hoping desperately that the German shepherd accompanying us would help us find her.

But we couldn't find Heidi along her tree-lined block of comfortable Dutch Colonial homes with children's tricycles and bikes on their porches. I remember that it was raining hard and the thought of one little girl lost somewhere close to us was frightening.

There were rumors and tips. Someone said they had heard a child screaming in a house one street over. But when detectives investigated, there was no indication that Heidi had ever been there.

It was the next winter when the snows came before anyone knew where Heidi was. On the corner a half block south of her house there was a vacant lot where wild blackberries had towered eight feet or more over the ground for years. But this snow was heavy enough to make the vines break and flatten to the earth. Heidi's skull was there, and the fractures in it showed the cause of her death — bludgeoning with some heavy object. There was no other evidence left. No clothes. No weapon. Nothing at all that the killer might have left behind.

The homicide investigators continued to check residents in an ever-widening circle with Heidi's house in the center. They found men with records for sexual crimes and younger men whose answers to their questions didn't quite add up. They had a suspect in mind, but they could never link him to Heidi's murder.

One of the things detectives count on is that even the most secretive murderer usually has to tell *someone*, either to brag about what he has done or because he feels guilty and is compelled to talk. Allegedly, Heidi Peterson's killer told the woman in his life, and when they broke up, she told someone else. Eventually, word reached Seattle detectives. They were sure they knew the killer's name.

They looked beneath a house where the suspect said he had left evidence, but too much time had passed. It was gone. They could not arrest him.

Heidi's case is a classic example of a case closed "Exceptional." But someday the person who killed her will pay for the horrendous crime against her. One way or the other.

Through the seventies, eighties, and nineties, forensic science leapt ahead and techniques were developed that even expert criminalists could never have imagined: computerized fingerprint systems, hair and fiber identification, scanning electron microscopes, spectrometers with laser probes, surveillance cameras that were almost infinitesimal, and — probably the biggest boon to detectives in a century or more — DNA. Other than identical twins, each human being in the world has his or her own DNA profile, detectible in body fluids, bones, the tags (roots) of hairs.

And DNA would revolutionize homicide investigation.

Fittingly, as the world moved on to another century, the Seattle Police Department initiated a speciality "squad," although it was made up of only two detectives: Richard Gagnon and Gregg Mixsell. It would be known as the "Cold Case" squad. They would concentrate on cases long unsolved, some of them in dusty files, some almost lost in the past because even those closest to the victim were dead, and the murderer himself — or herself — might also be deceased. The original investigators were gone, too, in many cases. And, predictably, more recent cases grabbed the headlines and the public's interest. Gagnon and Mixsell began poring over the old cases. In some instances, there *were* no police files on them any longer, and they found the details in the King County prosecutor's paperwork.

Gradually, the two investigators became as familiar with many of the unavenged victims as the detectives who initially worked the cases. Luckily, they discovered that some of those investigators had preserved physical evidence that had been virtually useless decades before — hoping that there *would* be scientific advances where the fingerprints, bloodstains, and body fluids might be the one key to solve a murder case.

The comparison of DNA profiles was first used to find and convict a killer in the mid-eighties. But it took a substantial amount of the sampler to make that comparison, and often the test matter itself was destroyed in the DNA process.

Still, it was a whole new way to catch a killer. The FBI got AFIS (Automated Fingerprint Identification System) operational nationwide about the same time. With only *one* fingerprint — and not all ten that had been required before that — the computers could spit out the name of a suspect who had left that print at the scene of a crime. Before, human beings had studied the ridges, loops, and whorls of the prints submitted.

Out of the almost three hundred unsolved murders in the annals of crime history in Seattle, some will never be solved. But many long since written off as cold as death itself will be. Gregg Mixsell and Dick Gagnon began to get results. By 2004, after only three years, they had solved twenty of those homicides.

The newest DNA tests use a process known as STR-PCR (short tandem repeat polymerase chain reaction) requiring only minuscule amounts of the test material. As many seminars as I have attended on DNA, I still can't explain exactly how it works — I got a D in most of the science courses I took in high school and college. However, it *does* work. Our DNA profile is the blueprint of who we are.

Seattle's Cold Case Squad had more success with homicides that involved a sexual attack because semen is the most likely body fluid a killer leaves on his victim. Because rape is sometimes the motive behind murder, Gagnon and Mixsell had a plethora of cases to reexamine.

17

As several cold case squads began to get results in the Northwest, I was surprised that some of my own long-held theories on suspects had been wrong. I wasn't alone.

In 1988, the Thurston County Sheriff's Office detectives took another look at the murder case on a young woman that would go unsolved for twenty-eight years.

After her sister saw television coverage of the then unidentified victim in December 1973, she recognized the clothing she had worn. It was Katherine Merry Devine, who had last been seen hitchhiking north of the University District in Seattle on the Sunday after Thanksgiving — November 25. She was only 14 years old, but she could pass for 18. She was slender and had long brown hair parted in the middle. Like many teenagers, Katherine Merry had had an argument with her mother about dating, and took off to visit relatives on the Oregon coast, more than two hundred miles south of where she was last seen.

Two friends had seen her accepting a

ride with a man driving a small white pickup truck, and she had waved to them as the truck pulled away. Invariably, Kathy called home to let her family know that she had arrived safely and that she was sorry for leaving in a huff. But this time she didn't. Her parents, Sally and Bill Devine, reported her as a runaway.

Eleven days later — on Thursday, December 6 — a worker picking up trash in the Margaret McKenny Campground near Olympia, Washington, came across her body in a depression in the forest floor next to Campground Space #1. The campground was close to the I-5 freeway and about sixty miles from Seattle.

A week after that, I got a phone call from the then sheriff of Thurston County, Don Redmond. Because I had written several articles about Thurston County homicide cases and he knew that I had once been a police officer, he asked me if I would attend a briefing with him and his top detectives, Dwight Caron and Paul Barclift, about the Devine case. As a "special deputy," I would also look at the files on this fresh case and view slides of the crime scene. Redmond wanted my take on the investigation, but more than that he needed a comprehensive summary of the case — at least thirty pages of narrative. Time was of the essence, or so it seemed in mid-December 1973.

None of us could have realized just how long it would be before this case would be solved.

Sheriff Redmond said he would have a deputy pick up my finished document on Sunday afternoon so that he could present it to the Thurston County prosecutor.

The winter of 1973–1974 was unseasonably warm, and Kathy's body had decomposed more rapidly than one might expect in December. She had been found lying facedown in the forest undergrowth of ferns, salal, moss, and a low meandering shrub Native Americans call *kinnickinik*. Kathy was fully clothed in blue jeans, a white peasant blouse, a mock suede coat with fur trim, "waffle stomper" boots, and some costume jewelry.

But her jeans had been slit from waist to crotch down the back seam, indicating that her assailant had probably had a sharp knife. However, small animals had ravaged her corpse, entering at her neck. That suggested that Kathy had either been strangled or had her throat cut because damaged tissue decomposes more rapidly than skin with no trauma. A postmortem wasn't very satisfactory; her heart, lungs, and liver had been carried away by animals. However, investigators Caron and Barclift asked the pathologist to take a vaginal swab so that semen found in her body could be preserved. Considering the era, that in itself was almost miraculous.

The timing of Kathy's murder and the places where she had last been seen and where her body was found would make one man highly suspect: Ted Bundy.

For almost thirty years, I believed that Katherine Merry Devine was one of Ted's victims, and pondered the synchronicity of that weekend in December 1973. As most readers know, Bundy was my partner at Seattle's Crisis Clinic in 1972, and I spent two nights a week alone with him as we answered calls from people in deep emotional distress — people who were considering suicide. On Saturday night, December 15, 1973, I attended a Crisis Clinic Christmas party, and I spent most of the evening talking to Ted Bundy. He was, at that point, a fair-haired boy in the Republican party, assistant to the Washington State party chairman, and he had been active in helping Dan Evans's successful election campaign for governor. Everybody liked Ted.

I was no more likely to consider him as a murder suspect than I would Santa Claus himself.

When a man named "Ted" surfaced as the prime suspect in the serial murders of perhaps a dozen young women in the Northwest in early 1974, forensic psychiatrists and psychologists took educated guesses about what he would be like.

Although no one thought he was really named Ted, and that that was only a name he had given to prospective victims, Dr. Richard Jarvis drew a verbal picture of "Ted." Ironically, Jarvis compared the still unknown "Ted" killer to John Canaday — although he didn't use Canaday's name. "He is probably between 25 and 35, mentally ill in a sense, but not the type who will draw attention to himself," Jarvis told reporters. "The man I'm thinking of is currently serving life in prison. He changed after his longtime high school girlfriend rejected him. He married someone else later, but he began his sexual prowlings after his wife filed for divorce. Like 'Ted,' he is not legally insane, but he is a sexual psychopath, with no deficiency in intelligence, no brain damage, and no frank psychosis."

John Canaday was safely in prison, but

Ted Bundy was still free and hiding behind a perfect mask when Kathy Devine was murdered.

We know now that Bundy was not what he seemed to be. It has been documented for decades that Ted Bundy's trail of serial murders began in the winter of 1973–74. On January 4, 1974, Bundy left one girl for dead after a savage sexual attack, and then moved on to take the lives of eight young women before he moved to Utah in the summer of 1974.

During this time, he was either attending the University of Puget Sound about thirty miles south of Seattle on I-5, or working for the Washington State Department of Emergency Services in Olympia. He lived within two miles of where Kathy Devine was last seen and he regularly drove I-5 between north Seattle and Olympia. While Ted drove a tan Volkswagen "bug," his brother was said to own a white pickup truck.

There seemed to be too many coincidences not to believe that Ted Bundy had picked up the hitchhiking Kathy Devine, raped and killed her, and left her body in an isolated area as he allegedly did his other Northwest victims, one of whom was a coed in Olympia.

Although Bundy was executed in Florida on January 24, 1989, Kathy Devine's murder was not one of those he admitted to committing. Even so, many people who had studied Bundy's crimes for many years — including myself — were convinced that it was he who had killed her. Even her parents believed that Ted Bundy had murdered Kathy. Only Paul Barclift suspected a local man, whose family suffered an unusual number of suspicious fires.

Cold case detectives, a new crew of Thurston County sheriff's detectives, and DNA proved me wrong. It had been twenty-eight years since Kathy Devine's death when Thurston County Sheriff Gary Edwards announced on March 8, 2002, that she was not one of Bundy's victims after all. Rather, DNA test comparisons of a vaginal swab taken from Kathy and a blood sample from a convict at the federal prison on McNeil Island, Washington, matched.

William E. Cosden Jr., now 57, was found not guilty by reason of insanity in the rape slaying of a young woman in Maryland in 1967. Deemed sane, he was released four years later. He moved to Washington State, where he worked at a truck stop owned by his father. It was near an I-5 off-ramp in Tumwater, just south of Olympia, and the truck stop was a popular place for hitchhikers.

Kathy Devine hadn't been murdered by the man who gave her a ride in Seattle. She almost certainly reached Olympia safely, hopping out at the truck stop, where she hoped to catch another ride south to Portland.

A witness with a long memory belatedly told Thurston County investigators that he recalled Cosden's having dark reddish-brown stains on his shirt on the morning of November 26, 1973. Another observer said that he had seen what appeared to be bloodstains in Cosden's truck.

Coincidentally, his truck caught fire at midnight on the twenty-sixth and was completely destroyed. Except for Barclift and Dwight Caron, Cosden had escaped scrutiny by detectives for a while, but he was arrested on rape charges involving another woman in 1976 and sentenced to thirty-two years in prison. That didn't mean *real* time, however, and he stood a chance of being paroled as early as 1990, but he was not a cooperative inmate. His temper got him tossed out of two pre-release housing units and he was returned to more secure facilities.

In 1986, Detective Mark Curtis of Thurston County obtained a court order and took a blood sample from Cosden. State-of-the-art DNA testing wasn't yet precise enough to risk losing the precious swab sample taken from Kathy Devine, and investigators forced themselves to wait. And Cosden apparently forgot all about having had his blood drawn.

But he would be reminded. Curtis was offered some grant money through the Washington State Attorney General's HITS program, and in 1988 he was able to pay for DNA testing. As he, Caron, and Barclift suspected, the DNA on the swab was a likely match to connect Katherine Devine to William Cosden. They didn't want to use all the sampler, however, for fear of losing that vital piece of evidence.

Detectives Joe Vukich and Brian Schoening visited Cosden at the federal prison on McNeil Island. He was adamant that he didn't know anything about Kathy Devine, had never even seen her, and that there was no way he could be connected to her.

But the Thurston County Sheriff's Office didn't give up. In 2002 there was no question at all that the DNA left by Kathy Devine's killer belonged to Cosden. Detectives David Haller and Tim Rudolf confronted Cosden again. There was no arguing with DNA results, and he now recalled having sexual relations with her, but insisted that he had not killed her. His denials didn't help Cosden, not when the circumstantial evidence of the blood on his clothes and his truck fire the day after Kathy vanished were weighed. Arrested in prison, Cosden was furious that he was being charged with Kathy Devine's murder.

William Cosden remains in prison. He has failed to convince the Indeterminate Sentence Review Board that he is a likely candidate for rehabilitation, particularly after they read a disjointed, pornographic "essay" he wrote in his cell. And, of course, because of the new information they learned about Cosden's deadly connection to the 14-year-old runaway whose murder had been a tragic mystery since a foggy, rainy night in November 1973.

The slight indentation in the forest floor where Kathy was left is still there, more than thirty years later. Dwight Caron has retired, and Paul Barclift passed away shortly after his "bulldoggedness" came to successful fruition with Cosden's arrest. Mark Curtis will retire in a little more than a year.

18

The murder of Katherine Merry Devine appeared to be the oldest unsolved case to be closed in Washington State. But the investigation into Sandy Bowman's death predated Kathy's murder by five years. With every positive DNA match between long-dead victims and suspects who had been free to move about in society when Sandy died, there was always the question "Could this have been the one who killed her?"

In 1975, Seattle police investigators tackled another homicide that was as baffling as Sandy's. It was April 30 when a noontime jogger found the body of a dark-haired woman lying faceup in blackberry brambles beneath the I-5 freeway near the Roy Street exit. The first officers responding saw that she wore a gray, yellow, and pink striped dress and a lightweight tan coat. Her panties were missing, and one leg of her pantyhose had been sliced away by something very sharp — a knife or a razor. The other leg of her pantyhose with the attached panty section had been pulled down over her left leg inside out so that her stacked-heel black sandal was still caught inside.

Detective Sergeant Bruce Edmonds and detectives Don Strunk and Benny DePalmo weren't even aware of the perfect spring day as they stared down at the dead woman. The sight before them was too graphic and too sad. Even in death, they could see that she had been classically attractive, with clear gray eyes and thick chestnut hair parted in the middle and pulled back into a single thick braid that wound two feet down her back.

Someone had stabbed her viciously in her abdomen and her back, and on both sides of her torso, cutting right through her clothing in many instances. The detectives had no help at all with clues that might identify the dead woman. She looked to be in her mid-twenties, possibly as old as 30. But she had no purse, there were no labels in her dress or coat, and she wore no jewelry. All they knew about her at the beginning of their investigation was that she had certainly been dead for more than a dozen hours.

Rigor mortis had frozen her body completely, and the lividity that occurs after death when the heart ceases to pump blood through veins and arteries appeared as purplish striations along the *front* of her corpse. She had to have lain facedown somewhere for many hours before she was left on her back as she was found.

The dead woman was immaculately clean, right down to her unpolished fingernails. She wore little if any makeup. She was just over five feet nine inches tall, and weighed 148 pounds. She would have been able to put up a good fight, and she obviously had: her arms bore many defense wounds.

The King County medical examiner, Dr. Patrick Besant-Matthews, pointed out that the knife that had pierced the unknown victim's liver, stomach, lungs, and the main artery of her body — the aorta — had been fairly small. But she had been stabbed eleven times with a blade somewhere between two and a half to three inches long. There was even a wound below her right knee. Her murderer must have been in a frenzy; it was the kind of violence found after an attack by a sexual sadist or by someone who hated his victim with seething anger.

The young woman was still a "Jane Doe." An anonymous woman called detectives after she heard a request on television news for anyone who might possibly have information to come forward. Although she had no idea who the dead woman might be, and was afraid to give her own name, she wanted them to know what she had seen the night before: she thought she might have witnessed the victim's abduction.

"I was driving home when I saw something very, very disturbing," she began. "It was near the University at the corner of N.E. 40th and 8th N.E. I saw an older white station wagon. It might have been a Ford — I don't know cars that well. There were two men in it. The passenger had dark hair and the driver had long, curly blond hair."

Wayne Dorman, the detective on the other end of the line, waited patiently for something that might be connected to the unidentified woman.

"But before they drove away," the caller continued, "I saw the driver outside the car. He was loading this girl into the back seat, and, ah . . . she looked like she was unconscious or maybe even dead."

"What makes you think that?"

"Well, her legs were spread wide, so wide I could see her panties. They were multicolored and she had on black sandals with two- or three-inch stacked heels. I *wanted* to stop and try to help her, but the people with me said *we* could be in danger if we tried to get involved. At least, I talked them into driving around the block to get another look — but by the time we circled back, the white wagon was gone."

"Could you identify the men you saw?" Dorman asked.

"I don't know. Maybe the blond one. They were under the street light."

But when Dorman tried to persuade the woman to give him at least a phone number, he heard the empty click of the receiver falling back on its cradle.

The victim remained unidentified until May 2. And then a University of Washington professor in the School of Architecture called to voice his concerns about a graduate student. "She hasn't been to class for two days, and her description would be pretty close to the 'Jane Doe' in the papers and on television," he said. "Her name is Hallie Ann Seaman. She's 25 years old."

His worries turned out to be well grounded. Hallie Seaman's sister and Hallie's boyfriend, a dentist, identified her body. The Seaman sisters had come to Seattle from Idaho, where their father was head of the University of Idaho's philosophy department.

Hallie was an outstanding student, according to her professors, and she had been given her own "studio" in the basement of the architecture building. It was more of a cubbyhole, really, than a studio, but it gave her her own space where she could complete her designs for her thesis; she was convinced that it was possible to build quality low-cost housing. That was her dream: to provide homes for people who weren't yet able to afford them. Hallie had been just two quarters away from her master's degree.

The last person to see her alive had been a fellow student who saw her talking on the phone in her studio at twenty minutes to ten on April 29. She had already put on her light-colored raincoat as if she was on her way out. When he passed her door ten minutes later, she was gone.

There was no sign of a struggle in her workspace. Anyone could have looked in the well window above her drawing board and watched Hallie as she bent over her work. But if he (or *they*) planned to confront her, it would have been a lot easier to observe her until she left. Other students came and went continually, and there was a popular cafeteria in the basement of the architecture building. Any attack would not go unnoticed. No, it would have been smarter to lurk outside the building. Hallie had to walk a dark path lined by evergreen shrubs to get to her car in the lot outside.

All he would need to do was wait for her. But Sergeant Mike Mudgett of the University of Washington Police Department doubted that the person who killed Hallie Seaman would have done that. To exit the parking lot, he would have had to drive by a security guard kiosk. At that point, she could have cried out for help — unless, of course, someone was holding a knife against her.

Hallie's apartment was only 1.7 miles north of the campus, but her sister looked around the empty rooms and said she didn't think Hallie had ever come home that night. It was possible that she had been abducted from the parking lot there.

"She told her boyfriend she was coming over to see me that night," the girl said softly. "He talked to her at 7:30 and she said she had a class that evening, and then she was coming by my place — but I never heard from her."

A canvass of people who lived near Hallie's apartment and the adjacent parking lot — and of the few residents who lived near where the witness had seen the white station wagon — failed to elicit any information at all about screams they might have heard in the night. Whoever Hallie had left with had either taken her off guard or he was someone she knew and trusted.

Hallie's dentist boyfriend told detectives that she had been known to pick up hitch-hikers. A lot of people did in the seventies.

"Yes, she picked up hitchhikers," he said sadly. "But only a certain type — the student type. She was independent and confident and not likely to be talked into any type of potentially dangerous situations. There weren't many situations Hallie couldn't handle."

That white vehicle turned out to be Hallie's own car. "She drove a 1965 Ford Fairlane station wagon," the dentist said. He gave detectives the license number.

The witness who had seen the lifeless-looking woman being loaded into the backseat of the white station wagon had observed that within a half hour of the time Hallie Seaman left the architecture building, and within a few blocks.

But the vehicle itself wasn't located until May 2. It was three miles south of where

Hallie's body was left, near a storage lot for over-the-road containers owned by the Sea-Land Corporation. The huge containers with foreign products came in on ships and were then loaded onto trucks or railroad flatcars.

But even though the Burlington Northern railroad line kept a switch engine with a 24-hour crew in the area where Hallie's car had been abandoned, none of them had seen who left the car there.

And it was useless in terms of evidence. Someone had torched it the night Hallie was murdered. It had been fully engulfed in flames when Seattle Fire Department firefighters arrived in response to a call at 2:40 a.m. the morning of April 30.

Jack Hickam, one of the legends of Marshal 5, the Seattle Fire Department's arson unit, processed Hallie's car. He determined that the fire hadn't started in the engine compartment, but rather in one of the seat cushions, and he got a "probable" reading for flammable liquid when he used a hydrocarbon indicator.

Someone wanted to be very sure that detectives would find no damning physical evidence in Hallie's car.

And they didn't, even though criminalist Ann Beaman from the Western Washington State Crime Lab literally sifted through the ashes. She found Hallie's other shoe with a nylon stocking melted into it, a small charred coin purse, and part of a key chain. The driver's door handle, thrown clear when the gas tank exploded, was tested for fingerprints but nothing identifiable was found on it.

Although the Seattle Homicide Unit detectives followed dozens of possible leads, they have never been able to find Hallie Seaman's killer, and thirty years later her murder is still a cold case.

One of her relatives described her as she recalled what a great loss her death was to so many people: "She was a bright, dynamic girl. She was the most dynamic creature I've ever seen. Suggest something and it would be done. She had tremendous drive."

"Hallie was one of the most brilliant students we've had," her professor remarked. "We'll never know how much she could have done to help low-income families have decent housing."

But, three decades later, Gregg Mixsell and Dick Gagnon are working on Hallie's case. They are inventive detectives, and they employ whatever means it takes to gather DNA samples and fingerprints. In many instances, the unsolved homicide cases involve prime suspects where there was never enough physical evidence to arrest them. In others, there were virtually no suspects.

Sylvia Durante was 21 on December 14, 1979. She was a beautiful brunette with huge dark eyes who lived alone in a small apartment in the Capitol Hill district of Seattle. She worked as a waitress in the popular Red Robin tavern, which was located on the Washington Ship Canal beneath the *south* end of the University Bridge. Mary Annabelle Bjornson's apartment house had been just across the water beneath the north end of the bridge. In this case, the proximity of the two structures was surely only grim coincidence, because John Canaday had admitted to Mary Annabelle's murder and detectives who checked found he was still locked up in maximum security in the Washington State Penitentiary in Walla Walla, and had been for eight years, when Sylvia Durante was killed.

When Sylvia failed to show up for her shift at the Red Robin, concerned friends went to her apartment. She lay partially clothed on her bed. She had been strangled, and both her wrists and ankles bore indentations showing that she had been tied up before that occurred, although the ropes were no longer tight.

A single long-stemmed red rose rested nearby.

Seattle homicide detective Gary Fowler was assigned to be the lead detective on Sylvia's case. In the beginning, there were several factors that might explain motives behind Sylvia Durante's murderer.

There was the obvious, of course. She was such an attractive young woman that a stalker might have become infatuated with her. She met scores of men in her job at the Red Robin, and her friendly, vivacious personality could have given false encouragement to someone off balance enough to think she wanted to date him.

Or it could have been a much more sinister motive. The Red Robin had been robbed a night or two before Sylvia was killed. It was a daring robbery, and Sylvia was one of the waitresses who had seen it happen. She would probably be a witness against the thieves if they were found. Would they have followed her to see where she lived so that they could be sure she would never point a finger at them? Maybe — but hardly with a rose in hand.

Unless they were devious enough and clever enough to use that ploy to get into her apartment.

The Capitol Hill neighborhood where Sylvia lived drew people from every stratum of society with its booming, lively main street: Broadway. Rockers, singles, gays, and a myriad of alternate lifestyles abounded on Broadway. There were restaurants and clubs where music boomed until two a.m., and sometimes long after. Bronze "dance steps" were embedded there, encouraging pedestrians to literally dance down the sidewalk. Nobody seemed like a stranger, but it could also be a high-crime area. Seattle Police patrolled it on foot and in squad cars.

Would Sylvia have let a stranger into her apartment? Probably not, but she might have welcomed a man she considered a friend — especially one holding a long-stemmed rose.

There was no one special man in her life, although she hoped to find one. And perhaps she had. In early November, Sylvia had written to her cousin that she had recently met an "interesting" man in Portland, Oregon, and hoped to see him when she visited friends there at Thanksgiving. Maybe he had decided to visit her in Seattle.

There was a man who lived near Portland who matched Sylvia's preferred type: handsome, dark-haired, and muscular. And that man was Randy Woodfield, 28, former Green Bay Packers draft choice, former pinup in *Playgirl* magazine, former bartender, former president of Christian Athletes on Campus at Portland State University, and an ex-convict who had been arrested on oral-sodomy and robbery charges. He had been paroled in July 1979, only five months before Sylvia Durante's murder.

Randy was a smooth ladies' man, who would be convicted of the January 1981 Salem, Oregon, rape/murder of a young female janitor and the rape/attempted murder of her best friend. He would also be a suspect in a half dozen other homicides and many, many sexual attacks along the I-5 corridor from Redding, California, to Lynnwood, Washington, from July 1979 to early 1981.

Woodfield encountered most of his victims where they worked in fast-food franchises near off-ramps of the freeway, and the Red Robin fit generally into that pattern, although it wasn't as easy to get to as the other restaurants he'd invaded.

Later, investigators tracking Woodfield

174

on other cases found traffic violation records that confirmed he had been in Seattle during the week before Sylvia Durante was murdered. In fact, he had played "Sir Galahad" to a nurse who worked at the University of Washington Hospital, which was located a scant half mile from the Red Robin. When the nurse came off a late shift to discover she'd allowed her gas gauge to drop below empty, Randy Woodfield had driven by in his gold "Champagne Edition" Volkswagen and given her a ride home. He'd asked for a kiss in thanks, and she gave him one, unaware that she was alone with an extremely dangerous predator.

For some reason, Randy didn't attack the nurse. The question was whether he had been to the Red Robin or ever even met Sylvia Durante.

There was never one iota of physical evidence or a witness who could link them. Randy Woodfield has been in the Oregon State Penitentiary since 1981 and the search for Sylvia's killer moved on, although it eventually ended in the cold case files when there were no other avenues to pursue.

Gregg Mixsell and Dick Gagnon wondered if there was any connection between

Sandy Bowman's murder in 1968, Eileen Condit's in 1970, Hallie Seaman's in 1975, and Sylvia Durante's almost exactly eleven years later: Sandy's murder had been committed on December 17 and Sylvia's on December 14, 1979. If they caught the killer of one of them, might they also have the answer to the other mystery?

Solving homicides can be all about parallel patterns and coincidences, but those phenomena can also lead the way down a garden path to a dead end.

And then suddenly, amazingly, all the pegs fell into the proper holes and what once seemed impossible was revealed.

19

I had been wrong on Ted Bundy's connection to Katherine Merry Devine, and I was wrong again when I wrote a book about Randy Woodfield, *The I-5 Killer*, and noted that Woodfield had been so close to where Sylvia Durante worked at the Red Robin during the week she was murdered. A long time ago, I came to understand why homicide detectives have to fight to avoid tunnel vision. When proximity, timing, and circumstantial evidence all seem to link a known predator with a murder victim, it's difficult not to leap to conclusions because they want so much to tell the victims' friends and families that they have, indeed, found the person who killed someone they love.

It is doubtful that Randy Woodfield ever met Sylvia Durante, although he is serving life plus 125 years in the Oregon State Penitentiary for crimes against other women.

The clue to who *really* strangled Sylvia Durante was there at the homicide scene twenty-five years ago, but there was no way detectives could know how important it was. As they processed her apartment, they dusted furniture, light switches, the undersides and tops of counters and any other surface that might hold the finger-prints of the person who killed her. One of the more innocuous items in her living room was a half-finished project. Sylvia was taking a class in stained-glass art. A lot of people were making lamp shades, vases, framed plaques to hang in windows so that sunlight would catch the colors and shapes, and jewelry. Her latest attempt was there in plain sight.

Its pebbly surface yielded little in the way of fingerprints. It was just something in her living room, something sad because now she would never finish it.

Gregg Mixsell and Dick Gagnon in-cluded Sylvia's murder in their cold case files as one that might be solvable *if* they could match DNA saved from the 1979 in-vestigation with that of a known sex of-fender. When you are looking for sex offenders, you don't begin by getting blood samples from people with no criminal rec-ord — although that is not to say that they *aren't* sex offenders who have never been caught.

The natural place for the Cold Case

Squad to look was among the Level 2 and Level 3 sex offenders in Washington State. Computers cross-indexing their names with lists gleaned from the victims' associates and activities can pop up red flags too.

William Bergen Greene, 49, would have been 24 in December, 1979. Whether he and Sylvia Durante ever had a dating relationship — which is unlikely — he had the look she preferred: dark, handsome, and well built. He had thick, wavy brown hair, a mustache, and a "puppy dog" look in his eyes that hid what he was really thinking. He was also intelligent and charismatic — and artistic. Greene was in the same class in stained glass that Sylvia was attending that Christmas season in 1979.

Long after Sylvia was dead, William Greene's penchant for tying up women and sexually assaulting them resulted in several arrests and confinement in the Washington State Sexual Offender's Unit at the Monroe Reformatory. He had an explanation for his behavior — he was suffering from MPD: Multiple Personality Disorder. One of the prison's psychiatrists diagnosed him as having MPD, and he was given a female therapist to help him cope with the two dozen "alters" who kept him confused about who he was.

Most "multiples" have both good and bad personalities, often alters of both sexes and ages ranging from tiny children to adults. Greene said that "Sam" was one of his honest, caring personalities and that "Tyrone" was only four and did pretty much what he wanted to do. He also sometimes came through as a dragon named "Smokey."

While there probably are people who have correct diagnoses as MPDs, it is also a category of mental illness that is easy to fake, and a favorite with antisocial personalities, sociopaths and psychopaths. People for whom lying is as easy as breathing and who feel no guilt about it are very good at *being* whoever they choose to be at any given time.

Dr. L.,* Greene's therapist while he was incarcerated in the early nineties, believed him to be a true multiple, and she was sympathetic to him. Most of the personalities she saw were gentle, dependent, and confused. It was hard for her not to care about Greene; he didn't seem at all like some of the hardened sexual offenders who ended up in the Monroe program. He did so well in therapy that he was released from prison in 1994. He moved to a small apartment near Everett, a city twenty-six miles north of Seattle.

As it happened, Dr. L. resigned her job at the prison soon after and opened a private practice in Everett. She continued to treat Greene. He came to her office for therapy sessions. However, in 1994, she became concerned when he threatened to commit suicide. Thinking that he might have to be hospitalized, she went to Greene's apartment to evaluate his condition.

By this time, Dr. L. was sure that Greene was a classic MPD and she wasn't afraid of him. She felt she recognized all the characters who moved in and out of his conscious mind and knew how to deal with each of them.

She was wrong. Alone with Greene in his apartment, she became the target of a three-hour sexual attack. He ripped off her blouse, tied her up, and fondled her sexually. She assumed that it was the unpredictable 4-year-old *Tyrone* who had taken control, but she could not dissuade him.

Once, *Sam* appeared and Dr. L. was sure he would protect her, but he disappeared quickly. Finally, she was able to break free of her bonds after Greene stole her car and drove off. She wasn't able to call for help because he had ripped his phone out of the wall before he left.

Dr. L. went to a nearby hospital emergency room to be treated for her cuts and bruises and called police from there.

William Greene was arrested and went to trial on charges of kidnapping and indecent liberties. He was found guilty in 1995, but that judgment was set aside on an appeal by Greene's defense team. They asked for a new trial because the original judge refused to allow the MPD defense into the trial.

In November 2003, Greene's second trial, which lasted five weeks, also ended in a guilty verdict, even though William Greene said he couldn't be held legally responsible for something one of his personalities had done.

Snohomish County Prosecutor Paul Stern and his deputy prosecutors put forth their belief that Greene wasn't crazy at all, but a charismatic psychopath who had manipulated Dr. L. into providing him protection for his crimes.

The jury agreed, and found Greene guilty of kidnapping and indecent liberties once more. He also faced what convicts call "The Big Bitch" — life in prison — under Washington State's "three strikes, you're out" statute. He was subsequently sentenced to life.

Dr. L., while grateful that her long ordeal was over, was heartsick about the sentence. She still believed Greene to be mentally ill and felt he should be in a mental hospital, rather than in prison. Other experts disagreed, especially after William Bergen Greene's DNA profile was compared to the semen left at Sylvia Durante's murder site. There was no longer any question about who had raped and killed her. Nevertheless, he pleaded not guilty to her murder on December 2, 2003.

Would Sylvia have let William Greene into her apartment on that other December twenty-four years earlier? Probably. She knew him from the stained-glass class, and he had never seemed at all dangerous.

Sylvia's parents had waited a long time for some kind of justice for her. Her 77-year-old mother, Joan Durante, said, "She's never been out of our minds, of course. We've never been able to put this to rest. We didn't know who or why, but we never gave up hope."

20

The balance of the scales of justice was shifting, ever so gradually, and the "good guys" now had the tools they needed to crack cases that no one ever believed would be solved.

Thirteen-year-old Kristen Sumstad was long thought to be a victim of the elusive Green River Killer, largely because her murder occurred during his prime killing time — in November 1982. She had been strangled just as the first Green River victims were in July and August. But Kristen was so young and so small that she seemed a child. She weighed only eighty-seven pounds. Her body, nude from the waist down, was discovered in a large cardboard box behind a Magnolia Hi-Fi store.

In the beginning, hers was a murder case that seemed easy to solve. Her circle of friends were from her neighborhood, and she was usually with them, close to home. The pretty little girl with her shag haircut and undeveloped figure didn't match the Green River victims at all, but her name stayed stubbornly on the list of victims for a few years. One or two of those dead girls had been almost as young as Kristen was, but none of them had vanished from the Magnolia neighborhood.

Kristen had been seen and then she was gone in the flicker of a smile or the blink of an eye. Years later, when they were adults, I met women who had known Kristen when they were girls. They said, "We think we know who killed Kristen, but we can't prove it. It was this boy who liked her."

The Cold Case Squad had heard the same thing, but they couldn't prove it either — not at first.

Although criminals are known to tell all manner of lies and devise hoaxes to trick the innocent, detectives aren't usually expected to pull tricks. They have, always, the need to avoid the accusation of entrapment. I have written about wives who hired hit men to kill their husbands, who screamed "Entrapment!" when they learned that they had really "hired" detectives who turned around and arrested them after money changed hands. Police officers pretend to be prostitutes and arrest johns, and detectives who don't even smoke shave their heads, grow beards, get fake tattoos, and become "drug dealers."

One of the best ways to cast a net out for scofflaws who owe big money for back traffic tickets or who evade arrest warrants has been for police departments to send them letters saying that they have won money or vacations or television sets. The idea is designed to get them all together in a warehouse or office building.

And it works, although those felons and miscreants who show up are very, very annoyed when they get arrested instead of winning prizes.

When Cold Case Squad detectives Dick Gagnon, Gregg Mixsell, and Linda Diaz needed to get DNA from a likely suspect in the rape and murder of Kristen Sumstad twenty years after her death, they came up with their own variation of creative approach.

They had looked at statements given by teenagers in the Magnolia neighborhood and found several mentions of a 14-year-old boy who'd been seen several blocks away from the television/radio store pushing a hand cart — a dolly — the night before Kristen's body was found.

Some of those interviewed said he had a cardboard box on the hand cart. Detectives had talked to the boy — John Athan — and asked him about it. He looked nervous, but he explained why. "It wasn't a box — I've been stealing firewood from the neighbors."

Athan was a friend of one of Kristen's sisters, and he'd been part of the gang of kids who knew the four Sumstad girls. Some of them said he'd had a crush on Kristen and he stared at her all the time. But he was just a kid. And so was she. His story about the hand cart was suspect, but John Athan stuck to it doggedly. Detectives couldn't picture a boy that age being capable of the violence done to Kristen. And even if they could, they had no way of proving it.

But someone had raped Kristen and left body fluid in the form of ejaculate behind.

Several years later, criminalists in the Washington State Patrol Crime Lab took some of the semen and attempted to isolate DNA from it. But it was too soon, and the process wasn't refined enough yet to risk destroying all the semen. But, on their second try in 1992, they succeeded.

Now Gagnon and Mixsell went looking for a way to get John Athan's DNA. His DNA profile was entered into national data banks in computers that held DNA information on thousands of state and federal felons. But apparently he hadn't been arrested, at least for anything more than a misdemeanor. Moreover, the detectives weren't even sure where he was. He would be an adult — almost 35 years old.

The Cold Case Squad investigators found John Athan. He was living in Palisades Park, New Jersey, where he ran a contracting business. They had his address, but the question was how were they going to get his DNA? They didn't have probable cause to obtain a search warrant to demand a blood sample.

Criminalist Bev Himick of the State Patrol lab assured them that while a blood sample would be ideal, all she really needed to test against the DNA in the semen left behind by Kristen Sumstad's killer was some saliva. Just a little spit, basically.

Gagnon and Mixsell came up with a marvelously devious plan. If John Athan didn't use one of those little damp sponges to moisten a stamp and seal an envelope, they thought of a way they could get their DNA sample.

They had to offer him something tantalizing enough to use as bait in a solicitation by mail. A simple advertisement wouldn't do it. Athan would probably toss out a consumer survey questionnaire. Most people did. But millions of people entered sweepstakes come-ons that came in their mailboxes, hoping they would be the one who got flowers, balloons, *and* a check for a million dollars. There were commercials about that on television all the time. Forget that there is no free lunch.

What could they offer John Athan that would make him write back to them? Not a million dollars. It had to be something more believable.

Using the letterhead of a nonexistent law firm, Mixsell and Gagnon informed Athan that he was eligible to join a class-action lawsuit against the City of Seattle by people who had been overcharged for parking tickets. Everyone had a parking ticket or two in their history. With interest and other money the city owed, the "law firm" suggested that Athan could benefit handsomely.

All he had to do to join in the lawsuit was send back a letter saying he wanted to participate.

It took a few weeks, but the letter from New Jersey came in. Now Bev Himick had plenty of saliva from which to extract a DNA profile. When she looked at the blurry dots on the printout, she saw that they lined up perfectly with the sampler that had been preserved for twenty years.

John Athan's DNA matched the DNA left in Kristen Sumstad's body.

The odds against the match being absolutely accurate, Himick said, were "One in fifty-nine quadrillion."

Gregg Mixsell and Dick Gagnon went to Palisades Park and talked to Athan. Knowing that they could ask only a few questions, they planned their interrogation *very* carefully. To get the answer they needed, they proceeded cautiously.

When they asked Athan about Kristen Sumstad, if he denied having had intercourse with her, they had him — because they knew his semen had been in her body. Athan could defuse that easily, however. All he had to say was that he and Kristen had experimented with sex, and their case against him would be weakened. If he had ejaculated into her vagina with her willing cooperation, they wouldn't have a motive for murder.

But when they asked Athan about Kristen Sumstad, he said, "I know very little about her." He said he had no idea whom she might have had sex with.

Dick Gagnon recalled, "He played right into our trap. If he'd have said, 'Oh yes. We were boyfriend and girlfriend and I'd had sex with her once a week,' it would have been difficult at that point. But he says, 'Barely know her.' "

If Athan had reacted like most suspects who had just been arrested, he would have shown some emotion. They expected him to question why they were there talking to him after two decades. But he didn't. John Athan was angry, but he didn't make any attempt to explain or deny what had — or not — happened in 1982. He didn't say he was innocent.

Returned to Seattle for trial, John Athan hired one of the city's outstanding criminal-defense attorneys: John Muenster. Muenster attacked the two Cold Case Squad detectives for tricking his client, insisting that they had only proven Athan had sex with the petite seventh-grader — not that he had strangled her.

But the jurors were more impressed with Bev Himick's testimony on the DNA match than they were put off by how the defendant was caught.

In spring 2004, after only four hours of deliberation, they found John Athan guilty of second-degree murder in the case of Kristen Sumstad, and he was sentenced to ten to twenty years in prison. Because he had been only 14 at the time of Kristen's murder, his sentence was relatively light.

21

The years were passing, a torrent of time that left Sandy Bowman further behind. But she was not forgotten; Gregg Mixsell searched for every FIR (Field Investigation Report) of people who had been interviewed in connection with her death, and combed files to find any information that might have been lost. The Cold Case Squad was unaware that I still had the article I had written about Sandy way back in December 1970, and I didn't know that her case had been reopened. I was sitting in trials in Orange County, California; Olathe, Kansas; Wilmington, Delaware; and San Antonio, Texas. And even if I had known, I'm not sure that what I had written would have helped them much, beyond giving them an overview of the case as it unfolded. I knew what the physical evidence was on December 17, 1968, but it had been tested then and found wanting.

But the original case file on Sandy Bowman was being meticulously rebuilt so that Mixsell and Gagnon would have every bit of information they might need to finally solve a case that had gone so long without a last chapter.

They were also working on a more recent case, one that made headlines all over America: the murder of 27-year-old Mia Zapata on July 6, 1993. When Mia was killed, Mixsell and Gagnon had just been promoted to detectives, but the Cold Case Squad was still a long way in the future.

A lot of people who have never visited Seattle still picture it as the farthest outpost in the United States, half forest and orchards, part rodeo, part Boeing, and a lot of Microsoft, a place where it rains all the time. And, of course, the center of the universe for serial killers.

It is all of those things and none of them. Still, it did seem an unlikely city to become the jumping-off place for the "grunge" movement of popular music, negative caterwauling to those born before the sixties, but inspiring and connecting to the angst of younger fans who understood the message sent by Kurt Cobain and his group Nirvana and by Pearl Jam, and Alice in Chains.

Mia Zapata was the lead singer in a punk rock band called the Gits, and while they weren't as big as Nirvana and weren't really grunge but rather punk rock, the Gits had first a huge local following, then wildly enthusiastic fans who crowded their concerts on the road, and soon a lucrative record deal looming ahead. By 1993, they were on their way, about to finish their second album and preparing to leave on a European tour. That spring and summer their tour of the West Coast exceeded even Mia's expectations.

Seattle was home to Mia Zapata, and Capitol Hill was her stomping ground. She had never had it easy, and she worked at Piecora's, a pizza restaurant there, to get by until the Gits began to succeed. At 16, she probably couldn't have visualized that her name and the band's name would be familiar to punk rock devotees in countries far across the sea.

Mia wasn't classically pretty. She had a *real* face, a slim figure, and wore her light hair in dreadlocks. She once told a reporter for *The Seattle Times* that she strived to make her song lyrics appeal to everyone. "When people twice my age and half my age can relate to us, we must be doing something right."

In early July 1993, Mia confessed to one of her band members that she had a premonition about returning to Seattle. She considered herself intuitive, someone who got psychic feelings both good and bad about the future, and what she was feeling was something dark looming ahead.

One of the songs in the Gits' new album had lyrics that were eerily prophetic: "Go ahead and slash me up / Throw me all across this town / Because you know / You're the one that can't be found."

Mia was a feminist who lived her life independently, fearlessly — just as she seemed in her music. She was strong, flawed, sometimes a little over the edge, good-hearted, beloved by her fans, and full of deep emotions. She often walked alone through dark streets, almost daring anyone to bother her or endanger her.

On July 6, Mia attended a gathering of friends at the Comet Tavern, located up one of Seattle's steep hills from the downtown area, near 9th and Pike. It was Tuesday night, after the long Fourth of July weekend. The Comet was one of Mia's favorite hangouts and she had lots of friends there. July 6 was the one-year anniversary of the death of a musician friend, and the mood of the crowd was somewhat reflective and nostalgic as they raised their glasses to the memory of old friends.

Mia was a little intoxicated when she left

the Comet Tavern. She was upset about an ex-boyfriend that night and muttered that she was going to find him and have it out with him. He lived nearby and it would have been like her to walk farther into Capitol Hill. She was at home there day or night.

She didn't find her ex. He was with another woman in the early hours of July 7, a woman who would supply him with a solid alibi — which he would soon need.

Mia went to another friend's apartment and hung out there until around two a.m. She said she was going to look for a cab, but she left walking. An hour and ten minutes later, Mia's body was found near a curb in a dead-end street more than a mile away. She had been strangled with the cord of her Gits sweatshirt.

Her body was "staged," according to some who saw it, in the shape of a cross, arms extended, feet together.

Mia Zapata, who had both distrusted the world in her lyrics and *trusted* her fellow man enough to walk dark streets alone in the wee hours of the morning, had met someone monstrous. She had suffered internal injuries severe enough to be fatal even if she hadn't been strangled, and she had been raped.

Thousands of people, many who had never known Mia Zapata, mourned her death and demanded justice for her. The Gits broke up soon after her death. Fellow feminist musicians raised money to found Home Alive, which offers affordable self-defense classes for women.

In 1996, a benefit concert was held to help fund the classes and to hire a private investigator who might help unravel the mystery of Mia's unsolved homicide. Members of Nirvana, Soundgarden, Foo Fighters, and Pearl Jam were among the headliners.

There were many theories and many suspects between July 1993 and June 2004. Some made sense. Others seemed unlikely.

A Seattle clinical psychologist announced in 1999 that he believed Mia Zapata had been killed by the Green River Killer, who was, of course, believed to be responsible for more than fifty murders in the eighties. No one knew who the Green River Killer was in 1999, so linking him to Mia's death wasn't particularly helpful to the investigation.

The psychologist guessed that the Green River Killer might well be obsessed with religion and acquainted with Bible lore. He claimed that Mia had been killed exactly eleven years to the day after the first Green River victim, Wendy Coffield, disappeared in July 1982. Since Mia had been found near a Catholic church and her body was allegedly arranged in a crucifixion-like position, the psychologist felt her injuries resembled instructions from the book of Hosea on how a sinful woman should be punished. Many of the Green River victims, the expert said, had been teenage prostitutes, and he claimed they were also placed in the same position.

His information was wrong and his theories strange, indeed. But they garnered some press because Mia Zapata's name had never faded from the headlines. Nor had the hopes of her friends, who continued to remind the world that Mia's killer was still out there somewhere, walking free to kill again.

Seattle homicide detectives didn't need to be reminded; they had simply come to the end of the possibilities open to them. It would be eleven years before Mia Zapata's murderer would be identified. When he was, it was through forensic procedures that once again used DNA comparison.

Gregg Mixsell and Dick Gagnon studied Mia's case file, reading it over and over. They noted that their fellow detectives who had processed the crime scene the night Mia's body was found had routinely used cotton swabs on various spots on her corpse — in the pubic area, on her belly, in her mouth, on her breasts. Those swabs still existed — preserved, hopefully, so that any material left on them would not break down. There wasn't much, but there was possibly enough for the Washington State Patrol Crime Lab's forensic scientists to work with.

In June 2003, Jodi Sass analyzed the swabs and found that one swab, taken from Mia's breast, held saliva. She was able to isolate *two* DNA profiles from the minuscule amount of human fluid left behind. One was Mia Zapata's own. The other belonged to an unknown male.

The unknown DNA profile was entered into the FBI's computers to be compared with the two million profiles in the database.

There was a hit. But it was a hit that seemed too incredible to be true. The man whose saliva had been smeared on the breast of a beloved singer in Seattle, Washington, was Cuban-born Jesus Mezquia, now 48. He lived in the Florida Keys and he was a fisherman. He was married and had a family.

But Jesus Mezquia had a long rap sheet in Florida and in California. In Florida, he had been convicted of the battery of a pregnant woman in 1997 and possession of burglary tools in 2002. He had also been arrested for soliciting, kidnapping, false imprisonment, and indecent exposure.

Florida authorities had entered his DNA profile in the FBI computers in November 2002. Seven months later, Jodi Sass's submission from the Mia Zapata case matched it.

In Palm Springs, California, Mezquia had been convicted of battery and assault and battery of a spouse, and had been arrested for rape, robbery, and indecent exposure.

Somehow, this violent man's path had to have crossed Mia Zapata's during the early-morning hours of July 7, 1993. It was up to Seattle's Cold Case Squad detectives to place Mezquia in Seattle on that night.

They did. Like so many killers, Mezquia was tripped up by police stops for relatively minor offenses. He was a lousy driver, and Gagnon and Mixsell found traffic citations that proved he had been in Seattle at the time of Mia Zapata's murder.

A Seattle woman came forward to say that she recognized photos of Mezquia as the man who had exposed himself to her five weeks after Mia Zapata's murder. She had jotted down his license number.

Mezquia was extradited to Seattle in January 2004 and went on trial in March. Jesus Mezquia does not speak English, so a translator was provided for the hulking defendant. He glowered at the witnesses and the jurors, but he never spoke and did not take the witness stand. The trial lasted eight days, and the jury deliberated for three days.

In the end, they announced that they had found Mezquia guilty of the murder of Mia Zapata. Superior Court Judge Sharon Armstrong's courtroom was packed with emotional friends and fans who remembered Mia as vividly as if they had seen her only the day before.

Jesus Mezquia was sentenced to thirty-seven years in prison.

"He was always looking for a victim," Dick Gagnon said to *48 Hours* producers later. "He was a predator."

22

The biggest hurdle for a homicide detective is a case where the killer and the victim were complete strangers until the moment that the murder took place. Gagnon and Mixsell believed that Mia Zapata had never seen Jesus Mezquia until shortly before she died. He would never talk about the murder, and yet, there was reason to believe he had been trolling on Capitol Hill to find a woman alone — *any* woman.

Mia might have accepted a ride, but that wasn't likely. She would have stepped close to a driver who claimed to be lost, though, so she could give him directions. Her death was clearly a stranger-to-stranger situation.

From everything the Cold Case Squad detectives could deduce from Sandy Bowman's 35-year-old case file, her death had also been the work of a stranger. The investigators who had worked Sandy's case over the years had done a thorough job of eliminating dozens of suspects that Sandy *knew*.

They had employed every forensic science technique available to them in 1968. They had canvassed the neighborhood around the Kon-Tiki Apartments, interviewing every neighbor.

It wasn't for lack of trying that Sandy Bowman's homicide was still unsolved. But in June 2004, it was finally Sandy's turn.

Gregg Mixsell and Dick Gagnon had concentrated mainly on homicides where the motive had probably been sex. Killers don't usually bleed at a scene themselves unless the victim manages to wound them. Sometimes the killer's skin cells *do* end up under a victim's fingernails if she has been able to scratch him deeply enough before she succumbs. That is why homicide detectives put bags around the hands of the dead before they are removed by deputies from the medical examiner's office.

Sandy Bowman had been taken by surprise and had had no chance to fight. Her nails had been clean and unbroken. There was blood in her apartment but it was all her own type. If Sandy's killer had had the same type, the state of forensic art in 1968 wouldn't have been able to differentiate between the two.

But some evidence remained — even after thirty-five years. Dried semen. Finding Kristen Sumstad's killer had seemed impossible — but it wasn't. Finding Sylvia Durante's killer seemed just as unlikely. And using only a trace of saliva to find a man who lived as far from Seattle as he could be — in the Florida Keys — who had killed Mia Zapata, seemed miraculous.

Gagnon and Mixsell weren't batting a thousand, but their score was climbing: twenty cases closed and still going up. They still didn't know who Hallie Seaman's murderer was — or Eileen Condit's. There were other young women lost to unknown killers in the files: a little girl named Gwen, drowned near a dock in Ballard; Rogena Switzer, killed as she walked home from school; a beautiful teenager named Sarah Beth, followed home from a bus stop and stabbed in the bathroom of an abandoned gas station; Carmen Campbell, who simply disappeared.

I wrote about every one of them, and sometimes I come across their photographs as I sort through the thousands of pictures I've saved from my days as "Andy Stack," the *True Detective* writer, and wonder where their killers are now. Are some of the unknown murderers responsible for *other* unsolved cases? Are they dead or alive? Or in prison?

On June 15, 2004, I was reading my morning *Seattle Post-Intelligencer* when my jaw dropped: "Seattle Police on Verge of Solving '68 Murder."

It was a story about a "pregnant newlywed" whose long-unsolved case was about to be connected, at last, to the person who had killed her.

It was Sandy Bowman.

King County deputy prosecutor Tim Bradshaw, who has handled a number of the old cases, would not comment on who the suspect was. However, a search warrant had been issued after Gregg Mixsell submitted an affidavit seeking a DNA sample from a man confined in prison. It would be the second DNA test — only to confirm the match that had already been made.

The first results had linked Sandra Darlene Bowman's murder to a man who wasn't going anywhere. He still had decades to serve on his sentence for his crimes in early 1969.

It was John Canaday. John Canaday, who left the frozen bodies of Mary Annabelle Bjornson and Lynne Tuski in the snowdrifts of Stevens Pass a month after Sandy was stabbed sixty times just before Christmas 1968.

Although he admitted to killing them,

and to raping "B.B.," he never mentioned the petite 16-year-old pregnant girl, surprised as she wrapped presents.

But he left something of himself behind, something that would come back to connect him to her so many years later.

Canaday is 59 years old now, locked up for most of his life. One can only be relieved that he was caught before he continued to kill at the pace he had set for himself. He might well have rivaled Ted Bundy — who came along six years later — in terms of the loss of innocent human lives.

On September 2, 2004, John Dwight Canaday was formally charged with murder in the death of Sandra Bowman. When Gregg Mixsell and Dick Gagnon told him that his DNA profile in the nationwide database matched the sperm found in Sandy's body, he reportedly sighed and threw up his hands, admitting, "I attacked her. I stabbed her."

Canaday insisted that he hadn't known Sandy Bowman before the attack, and he had "randomly knocked on her door." He blamed his actions on "a lot of anger at myself and immaturity."

King County Deputy Prosecutor Tim

Bradshaw filed the charges, and said that Canaday could receive a third life sentence. In the end, though, it wouldn't extend his time in prison. But it will serve as long-delayed justice for Sandy Bowman.

John Canaday has grown old in prison. His shaggy head is bald now, his face etched with deep wrinkles.

His "immaturity" and rage destroyed many lives, and it is a positive thing that he will never be free to hurt anyone else.

The Postman Only Killed Once

The murder of another 16-year-old wife had a few similarities to Sandy Bowman's case.

This case was solved within a short time, possibly because Pam Carrier's killer was not a stranger to her. And the romance that had begun with love and promises ended with what can only be called lust.

The Carrier case stunned jurors in a friendly hometown community in Eastern Washington, a town I visited initially to research the Carrier case, and many years later for my 2003 book *Heart Full of Lies*. Actually that title would have fit either case, although the details were not at all similar.

The sexual fantasies of human beings are as diverse as any other appetite. If private and unspoken secrets could be read, some eavesdroppers would be shocked, many titillated, and a few might just laugh out loud. While both men and women may *pretend* to have tremendous interest in sex, a lot of them do so only because they think it is expected of them. In reality, they couldn't care less.

Others put on a facade of morality, but what lies beneath their saintly masks is pagan and ravenous. Most humans fall somewhere in between, but trying to peg an individual's true sexual appetite by the way he or she talks, dresses, or looks is apt to be way off the mark.

That was certainly valid in the case of the pivotal figure in one of the most shocking homicides ever to surface in the prison town of Walla Walla, Washington. He didn't appear to fit the role of the classic satyr. Actually, he looked more like a studious candidate to become a certified public accountant than he did a dedicated student of sex. Yet, as an intensive investigation by the Walla Walla County Sheriff's Office poked into the dark corners of his life, this man's activities in and out of bed began to read like a modern-day Boccaccio's *Decameron*.

And if no one had died, his amateurish approach to homicidal violence might well have been laughable. As the story played out, it became increasingly peculiar.

The case began on August 7, in a ditch southeast of the Walla Walla city limits. Two teenage boys who were looking for a way to beat the pervasive August heat that blankets Walla Walla when the sun is high in the sky had set out on their minibikes long before six in the morning. It was a beautiful morning, and they encountered little traffic as they buzzed along the Russell Creek Road. Fields of grape arbors, pea vines, and popular "Walla Walla Sweets" onions edged the parched ditches on each side of the road.

The teenagers had already whizzed on past the still, pale form in the ditch before they realized what it was. At the same moment, they hit their brakes and skidded to a halt.

"Hey . . . ," one teenager began. "I saw something."

"Me too. We'd better go back."

What had registered in their mind's eye had been correct. A woman, completely naked, lay on her back amid the dry weeds of the ditch. She did not appear to have any injuries, but her complete stillness frightened them. Later they would tell police, "We both knew she was dead, and we tore out to get some help."

The bikers rode hard until they found a farmhouse. When they told the farmer what they had seen, he called Sheriff Arthur Klundt's office and reported what might be a dead body to the radio dispatcher. It was also possible that it was just a matter of two kids with active imaginations, but someone in authority had to check it out.

Klundt was out of town on business on that early Friday morning, so the dispatcher called Chief Criminal Deputy Scotty Ray at his home. Ray recalls the morning wryly: "I'd been up all night with an acute kind of flu and wasn't even sure I could make it into the office when the call-out came."

However, manpower in a small law enforcement department is limited. At the time, the Walla Walla Sheriff's office had only ten deputies to handle any problem that might come up in the 1,267 square miles of the county. Ray, a ten-year veteran in the sheriff's office, was one of the most respected crime scene processors in Washington State — he'd had a lot of practice. He fought back his queasy stomach and instructed the radio operator to send patrol deputies Frank Lucas and Frank Nemec to the body site. "I'll be there as soon as I get dressed," he said with resignation, hoping devoutly that it would turn out to be only a scarecrow or a deer lying in the ditch so he could turn around and go home.

But it wasn't.

Noting the location of the alleged body, Ray realized that it had been located a mile and a half *outside* of Walla Walla — but the possibility existed that she had actually been killed inside the city limits. He had called Walla Walla police chief A. L. Watts and asked that their two departments cooperate in the investigation. The chief had agreed and directed Captain Alex Dietz to Russell Creek Road. Washington state trooper Roger Gerow was also on hand to aid his fellow lawmen.

There was no question that the young bike riders had, indeed, come upon the corpse of a naked woman — a teenage girl, probably, from the way she looked. How she came to end up there was a puzzle for all of them.

Even as the investigators meticulously worked to gather evidence and photograph the crime scene at 6:30 in the morning, the promise of blistering heat as the day progressed hovered. It had been eighty degrees at nine the night before, so the sun already had a head start.

Ray looked at the dead woman. She was young, perhaps early twenties — probably even younger. She was not a small woman, however; he judged her to be about five feet seven and thought she probably weighed about 140 pounds. Young and strong. She looked healthy enough, but he knew you couldn't determine that just by looking.

And that raised a question: If she had died of natural causes, why on earth would her body have been disposed of this way?

And, if she had been murdered, why hadn't she resisted? Even if she hadn't succeeded in saving herself, surely a woman of this size would have inflicted some marks on her killer. And, in resisting, it would seem that she would have defense wounds on her own body. Torn fingernails. Scratches. Bruises. Something.

Ray and Dietz were in agreement on one point: the dead woman had not been killed where she lay. The field grass in the ditch was two or three feet high and dry as dust. Had there been any struggle there, the grass would be broken and trampled. But this wasn't the case. The only crushed vegetation was underneath the body and along a path from the road.

"Something bothers me," Ray mused. "I get the feeling that the killer wanted us to find her here. Look. There's a culvert running under the road only a few feet from the body. If he wanted to hide her, the obvious thing would have been to put the body in there. Then we might not have found her for weeks, or even months."

The other officers nodded. Certainly, putting a nude woman beside a well-traveled road could not be construed as hiding the body.

Something else nudged at Ray's mind. The position of the girl's sprawled body and her nakedness suggested that the motive behind her murder had been sexual. Again, he wondered if that was what her murderer wanted him to think. At this point, it was only a hunch. It would take a postmortem exam to know whether she had actually been raped, or if rape had been attempted.

One thing was certain: the young woman who lay before them in death had been alive the night before. Rigor mortis, the rigidity that seizes the body's muscles soon after death, was almost complete. Full rigor generally begins in the jaw and shoulders and grips the entire body within six or seven hours after death, keeps the corpse frozen for a time, and then gradually recedes.

Ray, Dietz, and the men helping them secured the area and combed the roadside inch by inch. There was a chance that the killer — or killers — had dropped something, perhaps something very small, that could be traced.

Near the body itself, they found nothing. However, the deputies spotted some beer cans and pieces of female lingerie about a hundred yards away. The beer cans still had a trace of liquid in them, and appeared to have been deposited there recently. All the items were bagged separately and labeled as possible physical evidence.

When they felt that they could learn nothing more from the body site, Ray and Dietz released the body to the county coroner. An immediate autopsy was scheduled, to be performed by Dr. Albert Kroll. The pathologist concurred with the detectives' supposition that the woman in the ditch had succumbed near midnight of the previous night. He removed the small silver earrings from the victim's pierced ears and they were bagged and kept, in the hope that they might help in identifying her.

The dead woman had worn a ring on the third finger of her left hand; there was a light groove from pressure on the skin there, but the ring was gone. Either her killer didn't want her to be identified through her jewelry or the missing ring was so valuable that it might even have been the motive for her murder.

Dr. Kroll guessed that she was in her early twenties. She had borne at least one child. She had not, however, engaged in sexual intercourse, either willingly or by force, within a day or so before her death, or been sexually assaulted after her death.

The only marks the pathologist found on the body were some scratches on her back, which he felt had occurred postmortem. "If the body had been dragged over a rough surface — say, concrete — these scratches would have occurred. And there was virtually no bleeding."

Why, then, had she died? Toxicology screens would show there were no drugs in her system, or any alcohol. There were no bruises on the strap of muscles of her throat, and the hyoid bone at the back or her tongue — which is often broken during strangulation — was intact. Her eyes and face didn't reveal any petechial hemorrhage — tiny pinpoints of dammed blood which bursts during strangulation or suffocation.

However, Dr. Kroll *did* find some petechiae in the brain and internal organs. "It was a matter of suffocation more than any other way," he stated firmly. The woman's airway had been effectively shut off, possibly by a pillow being pressed over her mouth and nose.

Shortly after the autopsy was completed, when embalming fluid was injected, hemorrhages *did* appear in the victim's face. They tended to confirm Dr. Kroll's suffocation diagnosis.

Both the police investigators and the pathologist agreed that it would have taken a very strong person to suffocate the victim. Normally, she would have fought hard to get a gulp of air. Yet, scrapings of her fingernails showed no evidence of flesh from her killer's hands. Why? She had been neither drunk nor drugged. She hadn't been struck or rendered unconscious that way.

There were no hidden brain injuries beneath her skull when the top of the calvarium was sawed and lifted off. Why didn't she fight?

Chief Criminal Deputy Scotty Ray, who'd grown up in Walla Walla and who had seen a succession of shocking homicide cases in his years on the department, was about to enter into a contest of wills with a man who would, in time, threaten not only Ray but his family.

Ray learned that a Walla Walla resident had reported his wife missing at 8:45 that Friday morning. Ray talked to the man, a 24-year-old postman named, fittingly, Carrier: Dale Carrier.*

The worried young husband said that his wife, Pamela, 16, had vanished from their home the night before. Tall, awkward, and bespectacled, Carrier explained that he and his wife had been out the evening before. At eleven p.m. they had picked up their two youngsters, age eight months and 2, from a sitter's house. Then they had driven to the small house they'd rented recently on Isaacs Street, one of the main thoroughfares in Walla Walla.

"Pam put the kids to bed," Carrier recalled. "But then she got to worrying about two kittens we had that were missing."

Carrier said that his wife had gone to their door many times to call the lost kittens, and looked for them all around the yard, all to no avail. She had been worried that they would wander into the busy street and be hit by a car. Finally, he recalled, she had informed him that she was going to sleep in their car because she was afraid that she wouldn't hear the kittens if they came home.

"What?" Ray asked incredulously.

"Yeah, she said that she couldn't hear them on the back step if she slept in the bedroom, so she went out to the car."

At that moment, Ray was suspicious. He had heard of animal lovers, but he found it hard to believe that a young mother would chance missing her children's cries to hear those of kittens.

Of course, he didn't know at this point that the dead girl was Pam Carrier. But the physical description given by Dale Carrier for his missing wife was hitting awfully close to that of the nude corpse found in the roadside weeds. Same height. Same weight.

The sheriff's investigators contacted Pam Carrier's relatives, as well as her dentist. When he furnished them with her dental records, there was no question that the nude girl found in the ditch was the 16-year-old Pam. At least her husband and relatives wouldn't have to go through identifying her body.

After getting the verification that it *was* Pam Carrier who had been left beside the country road, Scotty Ray returned to his office, where the tall mailman waited. When Ray confirmed that the dead woman was Carrier's wife, Carrier broke down and sobbed for several minutes.

When he was finally able to talk, he agreed to try to help in the investigation of his wife's killing. Although he couldn't imagine who might have wanted to kill her, he would tell them everything he could about her.

Dale Carrier said that he and Pam had been married for two years. She had been only 14 at the time of the wedding, but she was pregnant and it seemed the best choice they had to give their baby a chance and save Pam's reputation. Their first son was born a few months later. And then Pam had conceived again while Dale Jr. was just a baby.

In answer to Ray's questions about their marriage, the lanky widower admitted that things hadn't been going too smoothly. Not surprisingly, his young wife had found herself too tied down for a girl in her mid-teens. She had confessed to him, he said, that she wanted to date boys her own age, and that she felt she had missed out on an important part of her life. That desire on her part had hurt him but he had tried to understand. There had been talk of a divorce, and the couple had gone so far as to visit a lawyer a few weeks before.

Carrier agreed to let detectives search his home and yard. He didn't think they would find anything, however, as he himself had looked for any sign of Pam earlier and found nothing. He told Ray that he had started to look for his wife around one a.m. He was so concerned about her when he didn't find her in the car or the yard that he drove to several locations looking for her. When he'd been unsuccessful in his search, he had gone home to bed and awakened at five to look for her again.

Detectives at the Carriers' modest home on East Isaacs Street noted, first of all, no cats or even any signs that cats had lived there. There were no cat dishes, cat food, litter box, or even cat hairs on any of the furniture pieces upholstered in dark fabric.

"Kittens haven't come back?" Ray asked.

Carrier shook his head. "Nope."

Pam Carrier's purse still rested on a

table in her home. With Dale Carrier's permission, they looked inside. They found her glasses, and they were thick, extremely strong glasses prescribed for someone who was very nearsighted. Later, an optometrist would estimate that the person needing those glasses would be unable to see clearly any object more than twenty feet away without the corrective lenses.

Ray and Dietz were curious about why she would have left after dark without her glasses to search for kittens. They could have been on the other side of the backyard and she wouldn't have been able to see them if she didn't have her glasses on.

The fireplace in the postman's home showed signs of being used very recently. During a week when temperatures reached almost a hundred degrees and cooled down to a mere eighty degrees at night, most people in town weren't lighting logs in their fireplaces.

They sifted through the ashes and found remnants of purple cloth. Dale Carrier had an easy explanation for that: "Those were a cheap pair of purple pants of Pam's. They were damaged in the dryer and one of us threw them in the fire last night."

Carrier said that he and Pam had

planned to sit by the fire the evening before, but that she had vetoed that plan when she decided to sleep in her car.

Ray said nothing at this point but, remembering the steaming evening of the day before, he doubted that a roaring fire in the fireplace was called for.

Pam Carrier's relatives identified the bra and panties that investigators had found a hundred yards up the road from her body. Whoever had dumped her corpse in the ditch had apparently thrown them from a moving car almost as an afterthought.

A homicide detective works with a basic formula: Motive-Opportunity-Means. In the case of 16-year-old Pam Carrier, motive was a mystery. She hadn't been raped; she didn't have anything to steal — unless they could count a modest wedding band. Questioning of her family, friends, and neighbors failed to turn up any enemies.

As far as opportunity went, the last person to be seen with her was her own husband — a husband who told them that she had indicated that she wanted to leave. Still, the possibility existed that some man had seen the young woman sleeping in an unlocked car late at night and decided to take advantage of a vulnerable target.

But then, she hadn't been raped. And if

she had cried out for help — as surely she would have — it would seem that her husband would have heard her.

No matter how they approached the case, Scotty Ray and Alex Dietz kept coming back to Dale Carrier. His story of leaving their two babies alone while he went driving around looking for Pam just didn't make sense.

The "means" — or weapon — had probably been a pillow — something readily available in any home. However, looking at the bone-thin nonmuscular Carrier, the two detectives wondered how he could have suffocated his husky young wife with no signs of struggle and no scratches. If it had been the other way around, *maybe*. . . .

A week after Pam's death, Scotty Ray had a visitor. It was Dale Carrier. He handed the detective a crumpled note. It was signed "Pam" and it said she'd "gone for a walk."

Carrier said he had found it on the back porch of his home a few days before. He hadn't brought it in sooner because he didn't know how long it had been there.

If it had been on the back porch, Ray was pretty sure that he and the other investigators would have seen it when they checked the Carriers' house right after

226

Pam Carrier's body was found. Still, he accepted it without comment.

But a check into Dale Carrier's background failed to reveal any criminal record whatsoever. The postman was an ex–Navy man with an honorable discharge. Before that, he'd spent his childhood and youth in many different areas of the United States, as his parents had moved from place to place. He was employed by a federal agency, the U.S. Postal Service, which didn't hire convicted felons or those with suspicious backgrounds.

Scotty Ray noted a keen native intelligence in the young widower, although Carrier lacked much formal education. He also found that, after his first dramatic sobs, Carrier demonstrated a rather flat emotional response to the death of his wife, the mother of his children. Although Carrier seemed to be cooperating with Ray, there was a certain wariness on his part, as if he were somehow jousting with the detective in an intricate game.

All through August, Ray worked on the Carrier killing. In September, he had to diminish the intensity of the probe because another Walla Walla County woman had been murdered. Dolores Wilson, a beauty parlor operator, was found dead, and it took several weeks of investigation until a suspect in her death was arrested and charged.

On September 14, Scotty Ray received a letter purportedly signed by Dale D. Carrier. It was a strange letter, smacking of protesting too much. The message, marked to be opened "only in the event of my death," began: "I want you to know that I did not kill my wife." It went on to say how much Carrier had loved his wife and what a wonderful girl she had been.

If Dale Carrier thought the letter would persuade Scotty Ray to drop his investigation, he was sadly mistaken. Actually, Ray had questioned Carrier himself only infrequently; it was Carrier's friends and acquaintances who were questioned. And, of course, the word got back to the mailman. That's the way Ray wanted it.

Just how nervous Carrier was beginning to feel about Scotty Ray wouldn't be revealed until much later. Dale Carrier was playing some mind games himself.

Scotty Ray and his partner, Ron Kespohl, worked carefully, tying up dozens of loose ends. They wanted Dale Carrier and, with each new phase of their investigation, they wanted him more — but they had to build an almost perfect case. They had virtually no physical evidence, the backbone of a detective's ideal case, and they wanted to be sure that, once charged, Carrier would not slip free through an unforeseen legal loophole.

It was December 9 when Ray, Kespohl, and Alex Dietz secured an arrest warrant for Dale Carrier, charging him with murder in the first degree in the death of his 16-year-old wife. They weren't convinced that he would go easily when he learned he was being arrested, so they waited for the right moment.

The next day, Scotty Ray spotted the cagey postman in a gas station where he was talking to a couple of buddies. The chief criminal deputy knew that Carrier was always looking over his shoulder for some sight of him, so Ray radioed Deputy Frank Nemec and Kespohl that he had located Carrier.

It was fortunate that he had backup when he walked up to Carrier. The man who appeared to be a mild-mannered widower was armed with a .38 pistol with a four-inch barrel in a shoulder holster at the time of his arrest. However, he didn't reach for it.

If Walla Walla citizens were surprised at

Carrier's arrest, they were in for a lot more surprises at trial time. It was a trial that seemed a long time coming. First slated for the following June, it was delayed until the fall calendar, more than a year after Pam Carrier's murder.

Although the Washington State Penitentiary is located in Walla Walla, Washington, most of the citizens there have come to see it as a familiar background to their daily lives. They rarely lock their cars or homes and know little about the truly dangerous convicts in the maximum security units there. Crimes committed in their town and county are relatively rare. But they would be shaken by the many shocking revelations to come in the murder trial of Dale Carrier.

On November 8, a jury was picked. On November 9, Walla Walla County deputy prosecutor Jerry Votendahl outlined the prosecution's case. Votendahl first assured jurors that he would present witnesses to back his statements about Dale Carrier's motives to want his wife dead. He suggested the defendant was bitter about her alleged unfaithfulness and her attraction to young men her own age. He was also, Votendahl submitted, worried because she had knowledge of some crimes he'd allegedly committed. Not only had he decided she should die, but he also intended to realize a tidy profit from her demise: $20,000 from double-indemnity life insurance.

The prosecution's position was that Dale Carrier had planned his wife's death very carefully so that it would look like the work of a sex maniac. To add credence to his murder scenario, he had intended to murder several more women in the Walla Walla area.

And then, Votendahl said, Carrier had schemed to blow up Chief Criminal Deputy Scotty Ray's house as payback for all the trouble Ray had caused him. Fortunately, he had been arrested before he could carry out that mission.

The star witness in the Carrier trial was a handsome bottling plant employee and community college student, Burt Long,★ one of Carrier's close buddies. Long verified the State's description of Carrier's conscienceless blueprint to destroy lives for revenge and profit. He was, of course, a prime target for the defense attorneys, who insisted that he was fingering the mailman to save his own skin.

But the story that Long told the jury was so incredible that no fiction editor would have bought it; it was so outlandish that it carried with it the ring of truth.

Carrier, with his Don Knotts physique and his heavy horn-rimmed glasses, had considered himself quite a lady's man. His hurry-up marriage to 14-year-old Pam had slowed him down only momentarily. It hardly made a dent in his pursuit of young females. He had attached himself to Burt Long because Burt's attractiveness drew women and Dale wanted to be around to pick up on the girls that Burt cast aside.

Long, who was also married but admittedly not working very hard at it, had found Carrier amusing at first. But later Carrier's plans got weirder and weirder. Long testified that a month before Pam Carrier was murdered, Dale had suggested to him that "if I could think of a way to get rid of his wife — to, ah, to go ahead and do it."

But Carrier had said that he didn't want to know any of the details of "Pam's murder," because then he wouldn't be able to pass a lie detector test.

In exchange for Long's murdering his wife, Dale had offered to murder Long's wife. He just couldn't bring himself to kill his *own* wife, and he wanted to be sure there was no physical evidence that might link him to her homicide. Quite possibly, Carrier had been inspired by a late-night TV showing of the old Hitchcock film *Strangers on a Train*, where Robert Walker offers a similar deal to Farley Granger, who considers their conversation only a macabre encounter — until his wife *is* killed and the plot thickens, as do all Alfred Hitchcock suspense dramas.

Wherever he got the idea, Long testified that Dale Carrier was very intense about his plans. "He offered to pay me $3,000 of the $20,000 policy on Pam's life."

Even so, Long hadn't really believed that Carrier was serious. However, he testified that after Pam's body was found, he got scared. "I told Dale, 'Man I didn't do that, so don't go through with the rest of the deal!' "

"What did you mean when you said that to Dale?" Votendahl asked.

"I was afraid for my own wife's safety."

Then Long said that Dale Carrier had attempted to enlist his help in his continuing plan to make Walla Walla County and vicinity look like the prowling ground of a sexual predator. Once, Long said, the two of them had picked up a young female hitchhiker near Milton-Freewater, Oregon, a town just across the Washington border.

Carrier had whispered to him, "Let's kill her and dump her somewhere to make it look like a sex maniac's loose."

Fortunately for the girl, Long said he had quickly vetoed the idea.

But Carrier had still another plan. He tried to convince Long and another friend to pick up a girl named Lindy Copperfield★ from a house in Walla Walla where she was babysitting. The plan was for the men to bring Lindy to Carrier where he waited on a lonely road. Then Lindy would be killed, stripped, and left to be discovered as the "perfect" victim of a sexual psychopath.

Burt Long testified that he and the other friend lied and said that they couldn't find Lindy, so she was saved from Carrier's scheme.

Lindy Copperfield herself was a witness for the prosecution. She was an attractive enough girl but not really a beauty. She admitted that she had been the hypotenuse of a peculiar triangle in the Carrier home almost until the day of Pam's murder. She testified that she had met Carrier in Wenatchee, Washington; she had evidently picked up the postman's signals loud and clear because they'd ended up in bed later.

Carrier wouldn't have been the first husband to fool around on an out-of-town trip — but he was one of the minority who had the nerve to bring the other woman home to live with his wife and children.

Evidently, the sexual connection between Dale and Lindy continued unabated under his own roof. Just to liven things up, Lindy told the bemused jurors that she'd informed Pam Carrier that she had been intimate with her husband.

Lindy also recalled a fight the Carriers had had in a restaurant on the night of August 6. According to the witness, Pam had told Dale that night that she wanted her freedom. To prove her point, she'd had Lindy give her phone number to a young man in a nearby booth.

That youth joined the motley parade to the witness stand. No, he hadn't met Pam that night, he testified. He had, however, known her for about a month and had sexual relations with her during that time.

Pam Carrier's teenage sister took the stand. To the prosecution's question, "Did the defendant ever make a pass at you?" she answered:

"Yes . . . practically every time I went over to their house."

She tearfully recounted one instance of alleged intimacy with Dale Carrier in a sleeping bag at his house. She also recalled that Dale had demonstrated to her once how it was possible to achieve a tremendous "high" with chloroform.

The mention of chloroform had interested Chief Criminal Deputy Scotty Ray the very first time the girl had brought it up during his interviews with her. A man adept at using the anesthetic, Dale Carrier could easily have sedated his wife into a helpless state and then press a pillow against her nose and mouth. The chloroform odor itself would have evaporated, and Pam would be left dead without a mark on her — or on her killer.

But it was just a theory. The chloroform, if there was any involved, was never found.

After Pam's death, the "grieving widower," according to Long, sought to forget his loss by finding a new bedmate as soon as possible. Long said he had been temporarily estranged from his wife, when he and "a lady friend" moved into the Carrier home a month after the murder.

Dale had asked Long's girlfriend if she knew of some woman who "wants to come up and live with me."

Another female witness testified that Carrier had come to her home in Portland, Oregon, with a gift of his dead wife's clothes. "He wanted me to leave my husband, come back here to Walla Walla, and live here with Burt and his girl and him."

Sandwiched in between the defendant's alleged efforts to simulate a sex-murder wave and to find a new sex partner himself, Long testified, the mailman was getting nervous about the steady pace of Scotty Ray's investigation. Maybe he'd really believed that his masterpiece of a letter in mid-September declaring his innocence would be enough to throw Ray off his trail. Instead, he had been concerned when it only served to make the detective regard him with an even more jaundiced eye.

So, Burt Long testified, Carrier was ready to eliminate Ray from the picture, if that proved necessary. Enlisting the reluctant Long's aid again, Carrier had turned his basement into a workshop where practice bombs were made.

Long said that Carrier had it all figured out. Black gunpowder, metal pipes. Simple and deadly.

If he had not been taken by surprise in his arrest on December 10, would he have used the bombs? It is an open question, luckily never to be answered, but one which still gives Ray a chill when he contemplates it.

An Air Force explosives expert testified in the trial that the items from Carrier's basement could have been used for a very effective bomb. The defense countered by asking if such items and ingredients could not have harmless uses, too, if they were employed separately. The expert witness agreed that they could.

The question of the elusive kittens, whose disappearance had allegedly lured Pam Carrier from her home, came up again and again. Several prosecution witnesses insisted that the Carriers hadn't had pets in their home for some time before Pam was murdered.

The lone defense witness in the matter of the cats was Burt Long's wife, who said she'd seen cats around the house shortly before Pam died.

Throughout the prosecution's case, the man who had come to be known around Walla Walla as the "Passionate Postman" sat quietly at the defense table, betraying little emotion. In his composure, he was the antithesis of the spectators who lined up early each morning to crowd into the courtroom. They were so deliciously shocked by the testimony that they often had to be hushed as they exclaimed, gasped, and commented in the presence of the tightly sequestered jury.

Dale Carrier's defense took only fifty minutes. In a rather unusual touch, one of his defense lawyers took the witness stand so that he could be questioned by his cocounsel about Pam and Dale Carrier's visit to his office on July 29, only nine days before Pam's murder.

He testified that Pam Carrier had first told him she wanted Dale to adopt the older of her two boys, the child conceived before the marriage. But when he'd explained that procedure to her, she had countered with the statement that she wanted a divorce.

"That threw me a little bit, and I asked her what's it all about," he told his cocounsel.

Apparently, Pamela had told him she'd married too young and "wanted time to play."

It had been agreed that Dale Carrier would sue for divorce because he had all the grounds, and she had none. Later, Carrier had told the attorney that he was not going to fight the divorce because he didn't want to antagonize his wife. He stated that he hoped his wife would reconsider and realize his home wasn't so bad after all.

The question of divorce, of course, soon

became moot; Pamela Carrier was found naked and dead in a ditch.

After a weeklong trial, the five-woman, seven-man jury was handed the Carrier case. Judge Albert Bradford informed them they had three choices: acquittal, guilty of first-degree murder, or guilty of second-degree murder. If they should rule for murder in the first degree, they would then have to decide for or against the death penalty.

After seven hours, the jury filed back in. In the first ballot, they had decided unanimously that Dale Carrier was guilty of murder in the first degree. They voted against the death penalty. That would soon have been overturned if they *had* voted for it. The Washington State Supreme Court soon voted against capital punishment, only to reinstate it some years later.

On December 19, Dale Carrier stood before Judge Bradford. He had a statement to make: "You may send me to prison but it does not alter the fact I am innocent. I would gladly volunteer to go to prison if it would guarantee this would not happen to someone else like it did to my wife, because whoever killed my wife is out there right now and may do this again. I am guilty of one thing and that is believing in my country."

The statement was a strange non sequitur. Immediately after Carrier finished, Judge Bradford sentenced him to life in prison. For what little comfort it gave him, Dale Carrier would not have to leave his hometown: the Washington State Penitentiary was right down the road in Walla Walla.

Carrier made news a week after his conviction when he and two fellow prisoners were caught attempting to tunnel their way out of the Walla Walla County Jail.

He tried a more socially acceptable escape route a few years later. His appeal to the Eastern District Appellate Court of Washington met with resounding failure. All three judges voted against granting the ex-postman a new trial based on his claims of irregularities in the original courtroom procedure.

What's Love
Got to Do with It?

This case was right out of the film noir movies of the fifties where B-list actors moved through smoky, dark sets in pale imitations of Veronica Lake and Robert Mitchum or Joan Blondell and Dick Powell. The blondes were always brittle on the outside and sentimental beneath their thick makeup, and the men they loved had wavy hair, glistening with Brylcreem. Nobody's love affair ever turned out well, and usually somebody died violently. Many of those screenplays are being revisited now, starring young actors who haven't the slightest idea what it takes to make an impossibly bad script into a pretty good movie.

The characters in this case were attractive enough to have been B-list stars and maybe even A-list, but their lives veered off course and they ended up far away from bright lights, big money, and public adulation.

Any veteran detective will tell you that there is really no such thing as an easy murder case. Even the homicides that look as if they will be a breeze to solve can take on unexpected twists. Solving a homicide is never simple; sometimes it seems impossible. On a humid Saturday afternoon in August 1969, King County, Washington, sheriff's detectives faced one of the toughest challenges they had ever come up against: an unidentified — and virtually unidentifiable — body.

When investigators have no idea who the victim is, they can't begin looking for his family, closest associates, *or* enemies. Where do you start?

Two 11-year-old girls found the body, a traumatic experience they would not forget even when they were middle-aged women. The girls had rented horses that day from the Gold Creek Riding Stable, which was located between the small towns of Redmond and Woodinville. In 1969, the towns were considered much too far out in the boonies to even be considered suburbs of Seattle. Today zealous builders have constructed subdivision after subdivision in that area and farther north and east as the new neighborhoods creep up toward Snoqualmie and Stevens passes. The forested acres and fields bristle with houses on small lots, and five-bedroom, three-bathroom homes sell for upwards of half a million dollars apiece. Displaced bears, deer, and even cougars sometimes prowl the newly poured streets, disoriented and looking for food in garbage cans.

But back then, this place was wide-open country, and there were many isolated trails near the stable. The preteens took turns leading the way, laughing and enjoying the last days of their summer vacation. Everything smelled like sunshine, pine and fir sap, and dried grasses bending in the wind.

As they neared a blacktopped road, however, the girls wrinkled their noses in distaste at a pervasive, nauseating odor that assailed their nostrils. Reining in their nervous horses, they looked toward what seemed to be the source of the smell, a pile of fir boughs and brush. They caught just a glimpse of white and assumed that a calf probably had become entangled in barbed wire or thick, vined foliage and died there.

They were aware that many local farmers gave rewards for information on livestock that had strayed, and the girls galloped back to the stable and told the owner they had found a dead animal, urging him to come and look for himself.

Worn down by their insistent pleadings, he finally agreed to ride back to the woods with them. Dismounting, he edged closer to the pile of boughs, and then gasped involuntarily as he saw not a calf, but a human arm beneath the branches.

He waved the girls away, telling them he would take care of it. "Don't look," he warned. "Go on back and turn in your horses. Just don't look."

He returned to his stables and phoned the King County Department of Public Safety, the official title for the sheriff's office at the time.

Deputy E. Cunnington responded immediately, followed shortly by Chief of Detectives Tom Nault, Sergeant Gordon Hartshorn, and Detectives Eugene Steinauer and Marley Anderson. They asked Dr. Charles Fontan, head of the King County Crime Lab, to accompany them.

Anderson photographed the site before any attempt was made to extricate the body. Then his camera shutter clicked again and again as the investigators began the grisly task of removing the tree limbs and brush that covered whoever was beneath them. When they finally got down to it, they could see that the body, lying prone and completely nude, was in advanced stages of decomposition.

"Frankly, at that point, we didn't even know if the victim was a man or a woman," Tom Nault recalled. "The hair was long, making us think that if it was a male, he might have been one of the hippies who attended the big rock festival held in Woodinville during the last week of July."

Hippies. The term sounds almost quaint now, but 1969 was the height of hippiedom, those "shocking" long-haired, drifting flower children with their peace signs and smelling of patchouli incense and probably marijuana too. Compared to the habitués of meth labs and the heroin smugglers of today, hippies seem benign.

The cause of death for the corpse was a long way from being determined, but the fact that someone had apparently taken pains to hide the body made the King County detectives lean toward foul play of some kind. It had to be either murder or illegal disposal of a dead body.

They searched for something that might help them identify the corpse, but there didn't seem to be anything at all. There was no clothing and no jewelry. After the body was removed to the King County medical examiner's office to await an autopsy, the detectives combed the area in a grid pattern, hoping to find some clue to who the victim might have been. They concluded that he — or she — had died somewhere else and that all links for identification had been scrupulously removed.

"The medical examiner's office may be able to tell us if this was a drug overdose, if the body hasn't been there too long," Sergeant Hartshorn speculated. "With all the hundreds of kids gathered for that rock thing, it's not a surprise that something like this could happen."

"Yeah," Nault agreed, "but I'm guessing that this body has been here for some time, maybe as long as three weeks. With the summer heat, decomposition was accelerated, of course."

Pathologist Paul Foster, deputy King County Medical Examiner, did the postmortem examination. He determined that the deceased was a male, about five feet eleven inches tall, and had weighed 185 to 190 pounds. He had been young, probably between 20 and 25, and muscular.

He hadn't died of a drug overdose; he had died because someone fired three bullets into the left side of his head. Foster recovered two .38-caliber slugs from the head. The entry wounds were in the eye, the temple, and the cheek. Decomposition made it impossible to tell if the neck or chest had suffered trauma. (Later, a question would come up: Could the deceased also have been stabbed or bludgeoned? But there was no way to tell, even during a very thorough autopsy.)

Foster attempted to take fingerprints, but the fingertips had degenerated to a state that made normal printing impossible. In the hope that the dead man's prints were on file in the FBI's national headquarters, Foster carefully peeled a layer of skin from each finger. They had at least a partial print left in the layer of skin below. It isn't easy to erase fingerprints completely, not without the deep plastic surgery some organized-crime figures resort to, because the ridges, loops, and whorls are etched deep down. Foster mounted the fragmented skin on slides with special chemical preservatives, and sent the tissue to the FBI.

There was little officers could do while

they waited for the FBI response, except go over the body site painstakingly again on the off chance that they had missed some particle of evidence. The area was isolated, so there were no nearby residents to question about the sounds of a shot or shots. The case had all the earmarks of a "loser," but Chief Nault and his men weren't ready to give up yet.

Gordon Hartshorn, a fifteen-year-veteran with the sheriff's office, assigned Detective Steinauer to the case. They both knew that if the victim was one of the thousands of young people who had attended the frenetic rock concert, he could have come from anywhere in the United States. Also, it was quite possible that he had never had his fingerprints recorded. At the time, the FBI had to have all ten prints to make a comparison; they maintained single-print files only on America's Ten Most Wanted criminals.

But the Washington State investigators got a lucky break: the FBI lab reported they had been able to make a match. It was the first faint ray of light in a very difficult case. The victim was foreign born and he'd been required to have his prints taken when he immigrated to the United States.

The dead man was Karsten Knutsen, 24,

who was a citizen of Norway. The Norwegian national had been in the United States for seven years, and he had a listed address in the Ballard area of Seattle.

Hartshorn and Steinauer studied the information. "That probably blows the hippie theory," Hartshorn mused. "But how on earth did Knutsen end up over east of Lake Washington?"

"Let's check his legal address and see what they know about him," Steinhauer suggested. "That's a tight community out there."

Ballard would be the natural place for a Norwegian to choose — Seattle's "Little Scandinavia." Built along the shores of Puget Sound in the northwestern section of the city, its residents are principally from the Nordic countries and have a strong sense of community spirit.

The two detectives visited the address given by the FBI and found that the resident there did know Knutsen; he had sponsored him when he first came to America at the age of 17. But he had not been in touch with him lately. The husky Norwegian had found work as a commercial fisherman shortly after he arrived in the Seattle area. And as far as his sponsor knew, Knutsen was still making regular fishing trips into northern Pacific waters in Alaska.

Hartshorn and Steinauer checked missing-persons reports in both their own department and the Seattle Police Department's files. They hit pay dirt in the Seattle records. Karsten Knutsen had been reported missing only a week before his body was discovered. The skipper of the fishing boat that Knutsen had been scheduled to sail on told detectives in the Missing Persons Unit that his crewman had not shown up as they were scheduled to depart for Alaska. It was unlike Knutsen, a very dependable guy, to miss a sailing date. His skipper had been concerned enough to officially report him missing.

Steinauer questioned the skipper, who explained that Knutsen had returned to Seattle from Alaska the first week in August. Knutsen had been working on an Alaska king crab boat in Dutch Harbor and Adak. His time was, of course, his own between trips. The skipper had assumed that the young bachelor probably would have enjoyed some bright lights and fun, including the female companionship that was missing on the icy and lonely fishing voyages to Alaska. The money was good but it was punishing work, and often dangerous on the crab boats. Over the years many boats that moored in Ballard between trips had been lost during violent storms off Alaska.

"He have any trouble with other men in the crew?" Steinauer inquired. "Any beef that might have carried over onshore?"

The captain shook his head; he was at a complete loss to explain how Knutsen could have met his death this way. "Everybody liked Karsten," he said.

Now Nault, Hartshorn, and Steinauer knew they had to trace Karsten Knutsen's life back for the weeks before his murder, and perhaps even longer. They hoped they could pick up threads of his world that would give them some clue to what had happened to him after he reached shore in early August.

"Gene," Hartshorn said to Steinauer, "you know the Ballard area. It looks like our only route is heel-and-toeing it. It means a lot of night work for you — canvassing every tavern and cocktail joint in Ballard. Somebody there saw Knutsen after he got back from the last trip. He's lived there long enough — between trips, at least — and he's bound to be a familiar face along Market Street and down on the wharfs. Maybe something happened. A fight, a scuffle, or even an argument that didn't seem important at the time."

Steinauer nodded. After eleven years in the department, he knew all too well the hours — probably days — of questioning it might take before something turned up that might hold the key to Knutsen's death.

"In the meantime," Nault said, "let's ask the Alaska state troopers to check on Knutsen's last trip up there. Maybe they can come up with something."

Steinauer spent the next four nights checking out a dozen taverns in Ballard, many of them down near the waterfront. The sunshine was suddenly gone as he plodded through an unseasonal rain that turned the late summertime evenings cold and gray. Steinauer showed Karsten Knutsen's passport picture to dozens of bartenders and patrons. The husky detective, his voice slipping unconsciously into the Norwegian dialect of his childhood, moved quietly among the patrons. If anyone asked, he identified himself as a sheriff's detective. Most didn't bother to inquire. They turned grudgingly from a foaming mug of beer, glanced at the picture in his hand, and shook their heads.

He checked each spot several times a night, hoping to catch all the regulars. After days and nights of footwork, it began to look like no one had seen Karsten Knutsen that first week in August — or even knew him.

And then, for perhaps the thousandth time, Steinauer showed the passport picture, this time to a couple sitting at the bar of a local tavern.

"You ever seen this man?" he asked, fully expecting the usual negative answer.

"Sure," the man answered. "Karsten Knutsen. Comes in here a lot — or he does when he's in town."

"When did you see him last?" Steinauer asked, trying to keep his voice casual when he felt such elation.

"Gee, honey, when was it?" the man asked the pretty woman with him.

"It must have been two or three weeks ago," she said after a moment's thought. "Wait, it was a Sunday night, because they closed at ten. I'm sure it was August tenth."

"Was he with anyone?" Steinauer asked.

"He sure was — a pretty little blonde," the husband responded.

His wife darted a glance at him, not that happy that he was getting involved.

He didn't notice, and went on talking to Gene Steinauer. "It was Dee Dee. Her name's Dee Dee Sogngaard.★ You know, the whole thing was really strange, anyway."

"Strange?" Steinauer asked. "In what way?"

"Well, Karsten and Dee Dee were sitting in that back booth, and they were very chummy. We thought that was odd, because Dee Dee was supposed to be going with Mick O'Rourke.★"

"O'Rourke?"

"Yes, Mick used to be the bartender at a place up the street. Dee Dee worked there for a while too, but they let her go. Then we heard they fired him because she kept coming in and hanging around the bar."

"She and O'Rourke were going together?" Steinauer asked.

"Going together? They were living together!" the wife said, jumping into the conversation. "Maybe even married, according to some —"

"Well, anyway," her husband continued in the way that some couples interrupt each other without meaning any disrespect. "While Dee Dee was in the back booth with Karsten, Mick came in and he was talking with us. After a while, Dee Dee got up and came over to O'Rourke. She acted like you would if you hadn't seen someone for a long time. Gave him a big smooch on the cheek and asked him what he'd been doing with himself lately."

"We just looked at each other," his wife said. "I guess we expected O'Rourke to go back and start something with Knutsen but he didn't say a word when she went back and sat down with Karsten. Mick kept right on talking to us as if his girl wasn't cuddling up to another man. Then he left."

Now the husband took up the story. "About ten or fifteen minutes after that, Dee Dee and Karsten left."

"Was he drunk?" Steinauer asked.

"Drinking, but not drunk — just having a good time," the man said.

"Do you know where Dee Dee and O'Rourke live?" Steinauer asked.

"Someplace over on Northwest 53rd, I think — in a duplex," the woman answered.

"Have you seen either O'Rourke or Dee Dee Sogngaard since?" Steinauer persisted.

"Come to think of it, no — not since that night," the man answered. "Haven't seen Knutsen, either, for that matter."

Gene Steinauer explained to the shocked couple that they wouldn't be seeing Knutsen again, gave them his card, and asked them to call him if they should see either Dee Dee Sogngaard or Mick O'Rourke.

The next morning, the Alaska State Patrol called to say that they had been unable to turn up information that Karsten Knutsen had had any difficulties in their state.

They did have some interesting information, however. The Alaska detectives found that, on the last day he'd spent there, Knutsen had received a tax rebate check on his Alaska state income tax. The check was for $40 and had been cashed and returned, with an endorsement allegedly with Knutsen's signature. But handwriting experts felt it wasn't his handwriting. The signature appeared very feminine when compared to Knutsen's own scrawling style.

The cooperative couple that Gene Steinauer interviewed supplied him with names of Knutsen's friends. And detectives spent the morning tracing down Mick O'Rourke and Dee Dee Sogngaard's address. They located a duplex at 821 N.W. 53rd and talked to the landlady, who verified that the couple had lived there.

"Until August eleventh," the disgruntled landlady recalled. "They lived here all right, and then they just left without giving me notice. Left the place dirty too."

"Was this a furnished apartment?"

"No, they had their own furniture, but they didn't take it with them. Some friends came around a few days later and moved everything out. Say," she said, "I've got something I saved. Probably isn't anything, but when I went to clean the bathroom, there was a piece of metal in the bowl. I tried to flush it down but it wouldn't go. I fished it out and it looked like a bullet. Well, I kept it for a while and then I threw it out with the trash."

The officers exchanged chagrined glances.

"And then," the woman said, "well, I felt kind of foolish but I went out and got it back before the garbage men came."

She handed the detective a battered slug. It looked as though it was a .38 caliber. The crime lab would check the weight and the lands and grooves (vertical ridges and depressions) carved there as it was fired through a particular gun barrel. If they found the suspected weapon, they might be able to prove that the gun had fired this bullet.

The investigators went over the apartment room by room. A screen door and the living room ceiling bore unmistakable damage from gunfire. The interior stairway leading to the basement of the duplex was stained with what appeared to be blood. The stained area was very small, but there was enough for criminalists to categorize for species and blood type.

Gene Steinauer talked with other fishermen who had known the victim. One of them came up with an interesting rumor. "I don't even know if this is true," the burly fisherman said. "Lots of stories have been flying around since Karsten was killed, but I heard that Karsten and another guy had a savings account together. We do that, you know, so if one partner is up in Alaska on a trip and needs money, the other one can draw it out in Seattle. Anyway, somebody said that after Karsten disappeared, the other guy checked the account — and most of the money was gone."

The informant gave Steinauer a hotel address in Ballard. Checking with Karsten's banking buddy, the detective found that someone had, indeed, taken $750 from the joint savings account on August 11.

Steinauer talked with officials of the Ballard branch of the victim's bank. Their records indicated that a man had presented a withdrawal slip, printed with Karsten Knutsen's name, at the Stoneway branch of the bank. The teller at the Stoneway branch had called them to be sure the money was on deposit in the Ballard branch and then paid the man $750. Bank officials released the original withdrawal slip.

Steinauer turned the slip over to ID Technician Jack Reid. On the surface, it didn't seem to be nearly as hopeful a clue as the .38 slug or the blood samples found in the duplex. And they had proved of little help: lab tests could not determine the blood type on the wall of O'Rourke's apartment. The sample was too small. And the bullet had been too battered and mutilated for the criminalist to say that it was absolutely identical to the .38 slugs taken from the victim's skull.

Many hands had undoubtedly touched the withdrawal slip since it left the fingers of the man who withdrew Karsten Knutsen's savings. Besides that, lifting prints from paper is often difficult, but there is a process using the chemical ninhydrin and heat that can bring up fingerprints left on paper even decades earlier.

Suspects who have done library research before committing their crimes have occasionally been shocked to learn that their prints or other minuscule crystals or fibers left on pages there helped to identify them.

Circumstantial evidence linking Dee Dee Sogngaard and Mick O'Rourke with Knutsen's death was building. But circumstantial evidence probably wasn't enough to get an arrest warrant for them. That small slip of paper could mean everything.

While the technicians worked with it, word came back from the Clark County Sheriff's Office in Las Vegas. Acquaintances of the missing couple said they had taken a trip to the gambling city in early August, and sheriff's detectives in Seattle had contacted the Nevada authorities for information about that trip.

Clark County, Nevada, officials now informed the Seattle investigators that Patrick Joseph O'Rourke had married Dee Dee Irma Sogngaard on August 1 in Las Vegas. Dee Dee had listed her age as 25 and O'Rourke said he was 37.

Mick O'Rourke might not be guilty of murder, but this information indicated he *was* guilty of bigamy. The detectives had located the third — and current — Mrs. O'Rourke, and she wasn't Dee Dee Sogngaard. The Seattle woman said she had married O'Rourke the previous March, only six months before, but she hadn't seen him since May. She had filed for divorce in June. Given Washington State's three-month waiting period for a final divorce decree, O'Rourke would not have been free to marry Dee Dee on August 1.

Jack Reid called Chief Tom Nault's office with some electrifying news. Using ninhydrin, he had been successful in lifting one perfect fingerprint from the bank withdrawal slip used to take the $750 from the account Karsten Knutsen shared with another fisherman. The print belonged to Dee Dee Sogngaard.

Now the sheriff's detectives had probable cause to connect Dee Dee to Knutsen's murder. With Teletype requests to law enforcement officials in the eleven western states, an arrest warrant was disseminated at once for Dee Dee Sogngaard's arrest on forgery charges.

There was nothing more the investigators could do, and they had to wait for the elusive couple to turn up. They wanted very much to talk with Dee Dee Sogngaard and Mick O'Rourke, but they knew the elusive couple had almost a month's head start to vanish.

Witnesses said that O'Rourke's 1967 Ford convertible had been loaded until it sagged on its springs when it pulled out of Seattle on August 11. The pair obviously meant to stay clear of the Queen City for a long, long time.

By monitoring mail and Western Union pickup addresses Dee Dee and Mick provided to friends, Steinauer was able to follow their progress across the United States, but it was little comfort to him to hear about where they had been. As September reached the halfway mark, the trail had meandered eastward across North Dakota, then to Kansas City and into New York State.

If the investigators had only had access to the Internet (which, of course, was still far in the future) they would have gotten a hit in a small-town newspaper in Crescent City, California. An item on the society page had appeared there in late August of 1969. A candid photo showed a handsome couple standing in front of their highly polished convertible. The part-time society reporter's headline gushed, "Crescent City Residents' Kin on Nationwide Tour."

Nault, Hartshorn, and Steinauer prepared a dossier on the missing couple for the National Crime Information Center in Washington, D.C., hoping that NCIC's gigantic clearinghouse for every law enforcement agency in the United States could aid in locating Dee Dee Sogngaard and Mick O'Rourke. On September 14, they also released nationwide Teletype information.

Three days later, Dave Wooster, resident deputy on exclusive Sanibel Island in Lee County, Florida, answered what appeared to be a routine call. Sanibel Island lies off the west coast of southern Florida along the Gulf of Mexico. The community could be reached only by boat or a bridge whose round-trip toll tab was then six dollars. The heavy toll had usually served to discourage troublemakers and undesirable transients, and the lush island's serenity was seldom disturbed. But on September 17, Wooster, who owned a motel himself, received a report of a "family fight" in a posh motel a few blocks from his own establishment.

The deputy entered the unit pointed out by the motel manager, and Wooster knocked on the door. It was flung open by the gorgeous blond female occupant of the room. She pointed at the man with her and began screaming hysterically: "He killed a man in Seattle. He *murdered* him!"

For a moment or two, the deputy assumed he had walked into the middle of a drunken fight, but this was surely not the usual domestic disturbance. Thinking quickly, Deputy Wooster advised the couple of their rights, obtained waiver-of-rights forms, and read them to the couple. He then had them sign the waivers.

When they were thoroughly apprised of those rights, he allowed them to talk, and an appalling story poured out.

Later, Wooster told the King County detectives what he heard. "First, *she* pointed to him and said he murdered a man in Washington State. And then *he* said he was glad it was all over because he'd been carrying an awful mental load the past few weeks. They said they had gone to Las Vegas to get married and he had lost all their money gambling."

Wooster got an earful. The "bride" wasn't very happy with her groom for leaving her alone so that he could spend the night in the casino, especially when he hadn't proved to be either adept or lucky at gambling. She had slept around the clock in Vegas, awakening only once when he came to their room to ask if she had any cash. She'd made the mistake of pointing out the $100 she'd won playing roulette.

Although their story burst out in almost hysterical dialogue, Wooster began to make sense out of it. After their wedding and the gambling disaster, the couple had apparently returned to Seattle flat broke. They were behind on their rent and on payments for O'Rourke's pricey Ford Fairlane convertible. And they had no prospects.

"So when they made it to Seattle," Wooster continued, "they hatched a plan to get some money. They decided to go to a tavern to pick up some guy, take him to their apartment, and roll him."

The male half of the couple told Wooster that he had been smoking marijuana that day, and somehow things got out of hand, and they ended up killing the man his wife had picked up.

"He said that he shot him, and then she stabbed him several times. They took a savings passbook from the guy's body and withdrew $700 from his bank account the next day."

The couple told Wooster that they had removed all their victim's clothing and then took the body to a remote area in Woodinville, Washington.

Both of them had been extremely eager

to talk to Wooster. They even told him who they were: Mick O'Rourke and Dee Dee Sogngaard. In fact, Dee Dee wrote down her name and drew a little map of the area in Woodinville where they'd left their victim's body, adding the date they killed the man on the back of one of the waiver forms.

When he realized he was dealing with two murder confessions instead of a simple domestic squabble, Wooster contacted his superior officers. Ed Jones, Investigator for the Lee County Sheriff's Office, and Captain Ted Smith, night supervisor of the Patrol Division, sped to Sanibel Island.

Although a "want" notice on the two hadn't been received yet in their southern Florida location, they tended to believe that the shapely blonde and her handsome traveling companion were telling the truth. If they'd started out in Seattle, they had literally run from one coast to the other. If they hadn't run out of cash, they might have driven south of Miami to the Florida Keys, but they would soon have run out of road there — just as they had on Sanibel Island.

They had trapped themselves in their frantic attempt to elude police. Sanibel was no place where someone could get lost; it was too small. And they clearly no longer enjoyed each other's company. Conscience, alcohol, too much togetherness, and recriminations made for an incendiary combination. Their nerves were frayed raw. Each of them pointed at the other as the guilty party.

Before the team of detectives removed the couple to the Lee County jail, Mick O'Rourke had voluntarily gone out to his Ford convertible and reached under the front seat of the car — while, of course, the Lee County detectives kept *their* guns pointed at him. He came up with his own weapon — .38 revolver — but he didn't point it at them. He gave to them quite meekly.

Dee Dee's purse held a partly opened switchblade knife.

At the sheriff's headquarters, the Lee County men learned that Mick O'Rourke had not picked the Sanibel Island retreat by accident: at one time he had lived in nearby Fort Myers and sold insurance there. That might explain his choice of destination, but he surely couldn't have expected to go back into the insurance business.

By the time they were booked into the Lee County jail, the couple had a scant

$200 left of the savings account nest egg that Karsten Knutsen had worked so hard to build up. That wouldn't have lasted them very long at the rate they were spending money.

The Lee County Sheriff's Office contacted the NCIC at once and asked that a message be relayed to the King County Department of Public Safety regarding a possible "want" on Mick O'Rourke and Dee Dee Sogngaard. The nerve center of all law enforcement communication in the country sent back the word: "King County wants them. Hold for further communication."

Tom Nault and Gordon Hartshorn left the next day for the long flight to Florida. There they expressed their appreciation to the Lee County officers for the apprehension of the much wanted suspects. Investigator Lee Jones handed over some very valuable items of evidence, the most important being the .38.

Mick O'Rourke gave a written statement admitting that he had killed Karsten Knutsen. Without fighting extradition, the prisoners boarded a plane for Seattle with Nault and Hartshorn. They smoked continually on the flight, and Dee Dee managed to cause panic on an otherwise uneventful flight by "accidentally" igniting a whole pack of matches as she sat next to Tom Nault. She blamed it on her nervousness, but after that either Nault or Hartshorn lit her cigarettes for her.

In her early statements, Dee Dee told detectives her first version of what had happened the night Karsten Knutsen died. She admitted that she was the bait to get Knutsen to leave the first bar with her. Mick joined them later in an apparently coincidental meeting, she said, and the trio hit a number of bars as the potential victim became more and more intoxicated.

At that point, she said Mick invited Knutsen to come to their apartment to smoke dope. After some time there, Mick left the room while Dee Dee allowed Knutsen to kiss her as they sat on the couch.

But then Mick came from the bedroom holding his gun and he crept up behind the victim and attempted to knock him out by smashing his head with the .38.

"I reached up to stop him," Dee Dee said, "and he broke my hand with the gun."

It was at that point, she said, that Mick O'Rourke announced that he intended to kill Knutsen and told her to get some clothesline they had in the bedroom to tie him up. She refused, and she said Mick then fired the gun twice at her. The slugs ended up in the wall of their apartment.

The King County detectives knew that. They'd found the fragments left in the wall.

Dee Dee said she had begged Mick not to kill the drunken fisherman, but she'd been terrified when he shot at her and she'd responded meekly to what he ordered her to do. She had left the apartment then to go to Karsten's apartment and get his bankbook. When she came back, she saw that he was unconscious.

She continued to plead with Mick not to go through with his plan. "I said, 'Please don't kill him, Mick!' "

But he carried Karsten to the trunk of his car and forced her to accompany him as he drove to Woodinville. "We were on this deserted road when he stopped. He got out and opened the trunk," she said, "and I heard three shots."

After that, O'Rourke drove directly to a car wash so he could rinse Karsten Knutsen's blood out of the trunk.

As they awaited trial for more than five months, Dee Dee Sogngaard and Mick O'Rourke each revised their memories of the events of August 10. They no longer wanted to be tried together. Their separate defense attorneys asked Superior Court Judge James W. Mifflin to detach their trials. By agreement with King County Chief Deputy Prosecutor C. N. "Nick" Marshall, and both the defense attorneys, Mifflin pronounced that Dee Dee and Mick could be tried separately. They would face two different juries in consecutive trials. Judge Mifflin would officiate at both trials.

Dee Dee was given a chance to plea bargain. Her attorneys urged her to accept it. If she would plead guilty to second-degree murder, she might be out of prison in ten years or maybe even less. At the time, most life sentences for first-degree murder in Washington State ended up being thirteen years and four months.

But Dee Dee was adamant. She insisted that she would not plead guilty to anything because she had nothing to do with Karsten Knutsen's murder.

Dee Dee Sogngaard's trial was first. It began on February 4, 1970.

Nick Marshall, who was a former FBI agent, was known for his devastating cross-examinations, and he had prepared a tight case against the defendants. Gene

Steinauer, who had devoted untold hours to successfully tracking down Karsten Knutsen's killers, sat at the prosecution table next to the red-haired prosecutor during all court sessions as a consultant.

Dee Dee Sogngaard looked very young and quite innocent, her blond hair grown out to its natural light brown, her eyes downcast. She wore a pastel short-sleeved sheath with white trim at the modest neckline. Dee Dee bore a striking resemblance to actress Lola Albright, who was familiar at that time to most television viewers as a frequent costar on *Peter Gunn.*

Dee Dee looked drawn and wan as she took the witness stand in her own defense to recount the events of the previous August. Speaking in a whispery voice, she told the jury about her life. She related that she had been sexually molested, and that her parents had abused her. The parental abuse had been too many slaps in the face or spankings with a strap that left red welts. She felt that she could never do anything to please them, particularly her father.

She'd begun to drink at the age of 15 and it softened the rough edges of her life. But it only accelerated Dee Dee's talent for picking the wrong men to love. She was soon pregnant, but there was no likelihood that she would be getting married: her boyfriend had impregnated three other girls within a two-month period and he didn't want to marry any of them.

When she revealed her pregnancy to him, Dee Dee's father threw her out of his house. She had no skills to earn a living for herself and her baby girl. She loved her baby, but she longed to regain the important years she'd lost and she realized she couldn't support the child, anyway. She put her daughter up for adoption.

Giving up her baby was much harder than she thought it would be. Dee Dee had the first of several "nervous breakdowns," and was hospitalized. She said she had been given shock treatments during that time. She may have; it was often used in mental hospitals in the forties and fifties.

When she was released, Dee Dee headed north to Seattle to start a new life in a city as different from her hometown as she could find. And it was. Rain instead of sunshine, and a great deal more nightlife. It wasn't long before she was hanging out in cocktail lounges and bars. She had no trouble meeting men; Dee Dee was soft and sexy-looking and they were drawn to her.

It seemed inevitable that Dee Dee would add drugs — mostly marijuana — to her penchant for alcohol, and by the time she was in her early twenties, she went from depending on boyfriends for money to prostitution.

Dee Dee, was, in reality, "right out of central casting," and so were the men she was attracted to when she sought real romance. She wasn't unintelligent, but she was a fatalist, and a pessimistic fatalist at that. She really didn't imagine a life for herself after 25 because she was sure she'd be dead by then. She lived life by the old adage "Live fast, die young, and make a good-looking corpse." She was drinking, smoking, and drugging too much.

To her surprise, she was still alive at 24, and that was when she met Mick O'Rourke. She was a little drunk, a little high from hashish, when she walked into the Ballard bar where O'Rourke was mixing drinks. He was a dozen years older than she was, which might have been part of the instant attraction she felt. He was very handsome, with his cleft chin and his sleek hair combed into waves ending in a "duck's tail." When he glanced at her as he poured drinks, smoke curling from the cigarette in his mouth, Dee Dee melted.

He helped her get a job as a cocktail waitress in the lounge where he worked. She soon found out he had been in prison in California for armed robbery and wasn't averse to anything it took to make some money. It didn't matter to her; she was besotted with him. Whether she knew he had just married his third wife a short time before is questionable.

Dee Dee was hooked, and she was willing to do whatever it took to stay with Mick. Everything about him was flashy and exciting and dangerous. When he asked her to move into his apartment, she knew it didn't matter that he had a wife somewhere in his life. She assumed he had divorced the woman or had it annulled — or something. She was definitely out of the picture, anyway.

They drove to California so Dee Dee could introduce him to her family. She had never gotten over trying to be what her father wanted her to be, and the more she tried, the more he disapproved of her. Her mother and her two sisters at least tried to keep the family together, and her mother kept track of where Dee Dee's daughter was and how she was doing.

But none of them was impressed with Mick O'Rourke. He struck them as a "hood" and a "lowlife," which was fairly accurate. Although he could be charming and glib, they saw through him.

This only motivated Dee Dee to get more deeply involved with O'Rourke: one way to get attention from her family was to do exactly what they disapproved of. She was more determined than ever to marry Mick.

Whether she approached Karsten Knutsen on the night he was killed with a frank offer of sex for money, or let him think she was inviting him home for a night of pleasure, only Mick and she knew. On the witness stand, she admitted that she and O'Rourke had planned that she would take the victim to their apartment. They were hungry and broke.

But Dee Dee said, as she had before, that she had never intended for Knutsen to die; she thought she was only going to get him so stoned or drunk that she and O'Rourke could take his money. Then they could take him out and leave him someplace in Ballard where he would wake up with a hangover and empty pockets.

"I never stabbed him," she said fervently, although one of O'Rourke's earlier statements said that she had. "There is no way that I had anything to do with that murder. . . .

"I begged Mick not to shoot Karsten," Dee Dee told the jury. "I was afraid he would shoot me too."

In her trial, she denied that the fisherman had been shot in their apartment. Instead, she now said that O'Rourke had forced him into the trunk of his convertible before they drove to the spot in Woodinville where Knutsen was found. "Mick shot him while he was in the trunk of the car after we got to Woodinville. I waited in the car while Mick hid his body."

With every retelling, Dee Dee was distancing herself from the murder of Karsten Knutsen.

Dee Dee discussed her "wedding" in Las Vegas, saying that she knew it wasn't legal but they had gotten married just to spite her father for criticizing her judgment.

The cross-country "honeymoon" financed by the victim had, in Dee Dee's current view, been a terror trail for her. She testified that she stayed with Mick O'Rourke only because she feared for her life.

Dee Dee sat with eyes averted as Deputy Dave Wooster related to the court the statements given him on the previous September 17. They did not jibe with what she had just testified to.

After only three days of testimony, the case against Dee Dee Sogngaard was given to the jury. They adjourned to the jury room to deliberate at four p.m. and returned at eleven. The verdict: guilty of murder in the first degree.

Dee Dee appeared stunned as she was handcuffed and led back to jail.

The next day, another jury was selected. Now Mick O'Rourke sat at the defense table, and faced the new jurors. O'Rourke's story about Karsten Knutsen's murder had undergone massive changes. Although his memory of the murder had been precise and detailed in September, he couldn't remember the killing at all when he came to trial.

O'Rourke testified that he remembered nothing between the time he began to smoke a marijuana cigarette on the night of August 10 and the next morning when he woke up in the apartment he shared with Dee Dee. All he knew was that he felt vaguely "guilty" the next morning.

He said that he had been concerned when he found a bloodstained revolver and a switchblade knife in the bedroom, but it hadn't triggered his memory. He said that he had consumed vodka, beer, and narcotics on the day of the murder, and thought that might explain his blackout.

Mick's attorney submitted that O'Rourke's knowledge of the murder of Karsten Knutsen had come almost entirely from what Dee Dee Sogngaard told him about what had happened.

Asked about his alleged plan to rob Knutsen after the victim was lured to Mick and Dee Dee's apartment, the defendant said he didn't remember that, either.

Any number of defendants have tried the "complete loss of memory" approach in trials, but it seldom works. Prosecutor Nick Marshall reminded the jury that voluntary intoxication is not a valid defense. Even if someone has a blackout after he *chooses* to drink or take drugs, that does not release him from culpability.

Marshall pointed out the beneficial aspects of O'Rourke's "amnesia." The timing was convenient, since the defendant's memory was perfect right up until the so-called murder plot began, and it had returned as clear as ever — *after* the body had been disposed of. Marshall suggested that O'Rourke's gambling losses in Las Vegas made robbery the most likely motive for murder. He reminded the jurors that Dee Dee Sogngaard and Mick O'Rourke had known where to find Knutsen's bankbook, and that they had each practiced forging his signature before they cleaned out his savings account.

The fisherman's brutal death was only part of a well-thought-out, premeditated plan.

Mick O'Rourke's jury deliberated for seven hours. They had listened to his passionate plea from the witness stand — "I am very sorry for what happened: nobody's life is worth a few dollars" — but in light of the State's case, they were not impressed. They found O'Rourke guilty of first-degree murder.

On February 25, 1970, Dee Dee Sogngaard and Mick O'Rourke appeared before Judge Mifflin for sentencing. They were both sentenced to up to life in prison. Judge Mifflin recommended a twenty-year minimum term for O'Rourke, but no minimum recommendation was made for Dee Dee.

Although they had fought bitterly at the end of their long journey to Florida, and betrayed each other in their testimony, they now looked at each other tenderly, as if none of that had happened.

As they left the courtroom after sentencing, Dee Dee spotted a news photographer and called, "Are you going to take pictures?"

The lensman nodded.

"Wait," she said, "take us together!"

Smiling, like the bride she never quite got to be, she leaned close to a worried-looking O'Rourke. Despite their handcuffs and the uniformed deputies behind them, they still made a great-looking couple.

Apparently, Dee Dee had forgotten her fear-filled "honeymoon" and realized suddenly that she and Mick were about to be separated for a very long time.

Then their smiles faded. Mick O'Rourke still looked dapper in his dark suit, pristine white shirt, and striped tie, his wavy hair gleaming. But his face had already taken on the yellow white of prison pallor and he did not appear cheerful as he contemplated two decades of prison.

One bizarre psychological aspect of the crime that came out as I discussed the Karsten Knutsen case with detectives was the possible reason behind O'Rourke's choice of a dump site for the too-trusting fisherman.

They showed me a photograph of a fir tree growing next to the country road O'Rourke had taken to the Woodinville field. It stood only a few yards from the body site, and its trunk was marred with old, partially healed-over scars where a car had crashed into it, gouging it deeply.

Exactly one year and ten days before Karsten Knutsen's murder, Mick O'Rourke had had an accident on that spot. He could easily have been killed as he left the road and hit the tree head-on. Why, of all the hundreds of thousands of areas O'Rourke could have chosen to hide a body, did he return to the scene of that accident that might have taken his own life?

Maybe he felt the area was lucky for him, and that it would hide the evidence of his crime forever. He could never give a good reason for it.

Tom Nault, in recalling the investigation, smiled as he mentioned the many "doubters" among the Major Crimes detectives who felt that they would never identify the body, much less find the killer or killers. He praised Gene Steinauer highly for his meticulous investigation and exhaustive legwork in tracing Karsten Knutsen's life.

Detective Steinauer said only, "My bosses insist on answers. I knew I had to come up with some."

Dee Dee's minimum sentence had never been set, so there was a fairly good possibility she would be out of prison long before Mick O'Rourke was. She must have wished, though, that she had taken the offer of a plea bargain for admitting to second-degree murder.

She had always believed her life would be over before she was 25, and in a way it was. She was transported in the "chain," a line of prisoners going to the Washington State Penitentiary in Walla Walla.

Dee Dee was a free spirit and a woman whose emotions were sometimes erratic. Prison was exceptionally difficult for her. Things got slightly better when the new women's facility in Purdy, Washington, was opened. The first ninety-four women prisoners to be housed at Purdy were loaded onto a bus in 1971. If you have to be locked up, Purdy was a lot better facility than Walla Walla was.

But Dee Dee didn't want to be locked up. After being behind bars for three years, her delicate mind broke in 1972 and she was taken to Western Washington State Hospital in Steilacoom for treatment. Two weeks into her stay, Dee Dee escaped. She managed to stay free for five days, but one

of her sisters called Washington authorities to say that Dee Dee was at their parents' house in California, and she was arrested and returned to prison.

Dee Dee paid a high price for five days of freedom. All of her three years of "good time" were erased and she had to start serving her sentence from scratch again.

She tried to fit within the parameters set for prisoners who got time off for good behavior, although it went against her sometimes stormy temperament. Prisoners got twenty-five cents an hour for doing work around Purdy — gardening, filing, painting. Dee Dee took classes until she had enough credits to earn *two* associate in arts degrees. But it was the superintendents who determined which prisoners received good-behavior merits, and Dee Dee called one a "drunken bitch." And not behind her back, giggling with other prisoners, but to her face.

That didn't bode well for her good-behavior points.

At first, Dee Dee was in a tight group of fellow inmates, women who bonded and looked out for one another. They laughed at the same things, traded what few clothes they had, got to know one another's families on visitors' days.

But the other women were all paroled. One by one, they walked out of Purdy, and Dee Dee was left behind. They wrote to her for a while, but she had learned not to get too close to anyone after that because, in the end, she was left alone.

Her two sisters had visited her a few times when she was first in prison, but they gradually stopped coming. Mick O'Rourke was in prison in Walla Walla. Both her parents died, so Dee Dee had no more news about her daughter. She really didn't have anyone.

Dee Dee felt tremendous guilt over Karsten Knutsen's murder, although she never admitted to participating in killing him. She called him by his first name — as if he'd been a friend — and grieved that *he* had never lived to see 25.

For the first sixteen years of her daughter's life, Dee Dee had sent little presents of toys and clothes she sewed herself, unaware that the child never saw any of them; her adoptive parents stored them in a trunk. At 16, the girl found out who her real mother was and wrote to Dee Dee, complaining that her religious parents were too strict with her. Dee Dee wrote back in her usual combative way, telling the girl that she was "a brat," that she

should be grateful that someone loved her enough to take care of her and worry about her.

She never heard from her daughter again.

She wrote letters to Mick and sometimes he answered. They were three hundred miles apart, but even if they had been free and together, the ghost of Karsten Knutsen would have haunted them.

The photographs Dee Dee kept in her cell of people who had meant something to her began to look dated to anyone who had been in the outside world; the clothes and hairdos were old-fashioned.

Mick's slicked-down look in the one picture she had of him was right out of the fifties. Sometimes it was difficult to believe they had ever been together.

She hadn't heard from him in a long time when she sent him a letter in late 1979. It came back to her stamped DECEASED. He had been dead since Christmas Day 1978, and no one had told her. He'd succumbed to diabetes and cancer at the age of 46.

She wasn't really his wife, but it seemed as though someone should have let her know.

Dee Dee Sogngaard passed through her

thirties, and then she was rapidly heading for 50. She finally got her own cell, a huge luxury in prison. She made pets of the tiny tree frogs that were all over the grounds at Purdy and kept dozens of them in her cement-block cell.

Of all the ninety-four women who came to Purdy in that first bus in 1971, Dee Dee would be the last one left, imprisoned for twenty-two years, longer than any woman in the Washington State corrections system. She saw the world outside on rare occasions — during visits to a dentist or doctor.

She was trained to work outside the walls, if she should ever be free, but it seemed that she might die in prison as Mick had when she got breast cancer, especially when she refused chemo treatments.

But Dee Dee survived. In September 1991 she was paroled to a halfway house, where she had guidance as she encountered a world that must have seemed as if she had stepped onto another planet. She took her most precious possessions — her photos and her tree frogs — with her.

Dee Dee Sogngaard spent less than six months with Mick O'Rourke. Together — in greater or lesser degree — they led a

man to his violent death. In the end, all three of them saw their pursuit of pleasure end in ashes and blood.

If she is alive, Dee Dee turned sixty years old in 2004. She has been absorbed into the world outside prison walls. Records show she has not reoffended, and that is all I could learn about her. It's just as well. Both prisoners and guards cried as she walked out of prison, pulling for her to make it in the free world.

What she did was wrong, but she served almost double the time that most *male* inmates convicted of first-degree murder in the sixties did. She was an elderly woman when she was paroled.

When she walked out of Purdy, she was still slim, but the years had etched her face prematurely. She was a long way from the gorgeous blonde who turned every male head in a cocktail lounge when she walked in.

I have changed Dee Dee's name; she has paid her debt to society, and any other debts she might still owe are not up to me or to anyone. She sometimes said that prison saved her life, and perhaps it did. I hope she is alive.

Sandy Bowman (*in front*) with a friend when they were both about eleven. Within just a few years, Sandy would be a teenage bride and, sadly, become a victim of an unsolved homicide.

Sandy Bowman, just turned 16, was a new bride and expecting a baby at Christmas, 1968, when a murderous stranger got into her apartment. Her murder would not be solved for more than thirty-five years! But DNA made the difference.

When Sandy's husband came home from the night shift, he found her purse, its contents dumped out, her shoes scattered, and half-wrapped Christmas packages on the coffee table.

Mary Annabelle Bjornson lived on the second floor of the apartment house on the right, in Seattle's University District. Although she was expecting her date any moment, she vanished completely, leaving dinner cooking on her stove.

Lynne Tuski disappeared from the snowy parking lot of the Sears store where she worked, in the north end of Seattle. She became the second "Saturday night victim" of an unlikely killer.

When the snow began to melt on scenic Stevens Pass in the shadow of the Cascade Mountains, some horrifying discoveries were unveiled.

A local resident of Gold Bar kneels where the body of Lynne Tuski was discovered, frozen in the deep snowbanks of Stevens Pass.

Charged with two murders, a rape, and an abduction, the high school athletic hero had even more secrets he did not reveal. It would take DNA evidence evaluated in a crime lab decades later to find the answers.

Eighteen months after Sandy Bowman, Mary Annabelle Bjornson, and Lynne Tuski were murdered in Seattle, flight attendant Eileen Condit was also stabbed to death.

Hallie Seaman was a brilliant postgraduate student in architecture, hoping to design housing for low-income families, when she met her killer.

For almost thirty years, Katherine Merry Devine, 14, was believed to be a Ted Bundy victim. Thurston County detectives used DNA to arrest a surprise suspect instead.

Thirteen-year-old Kristen Sumstad. DNA on the back of an ordinary postage stamp identified her killer decades after her murder.

WHAT'S LOVE GOT TO DO WITH IT?

Karsten Knutsen, 24, an Alaskan crab fisherman, who trusted a beautiful blonde. She would become his final date.

King County Sheriff's Office Chief of Detectives T. T. Nault (*at left*) along with Detective Gene Steinauer. Steinauer spent many nights questioning bar patrons before he met a couple who were the last to see fisherman Karsten Knutsen. The investigation that began near Seattle ended on Sanibel Island, Florida.

Lovers Mick O'Rourke and Dee Dee Sogngaard leave court after being sentenced. Dee Dee pleaded with a photographer to "take our picture together, please?" After this photo, they never saw each other again.

OLD FLAMES CAN BURN

The beer bottle sitting upright below a blood-spattered wall was only one of dozens of empties in the victims' apartment. Even though the suspect was drunk, there was no explanation for his maniacal fury. One young woman survived against all odds; the other did not.

Mallory Gilbert fought hard against the man with the knife as the couch where she slept and the items knocked to the floor show. She lost half the blood in her body in the struggle.

Seattle Homicide Detective Owen McKenna managed to calmly talk a violent killer into giving himself up to state police investigators in another state.

Stephen Meyer, 20 (*at right*), on his way to court with Deputy C. L. Duncan. Meyer said he loved one girl, but he went berserk when an old flame turned him down.

LONELY HEARTS KILLER

A trio of photos taken by Harvey Glatman of Judy Ann Dull, 19, a fledgling model who thought she was posing for the cover of *True Detective* magazine. She soon realized to her horror that the ropes and gag were real, and that she had become the captive of a maniac. Glatman kept her in his apartment for a day, and then disposed of her in the California desert. In the left picture, she is posing. The other two were taken after she realized Glatman had tied her up for real. (*Pierce Brooks Family Collection*)

Shirley Bridgeford, 30, signed up at a Hollywood Lonely Hearts Club to meet men. The divorced mother of two was disappointed in her date's appearance and personal hygiene, but she went out with him to avoid hurting his feelings. She never came back from their first date. (*Pierce Brooks Family Collection*)

On October 30, 1958, Harvey Glatman led Sergeant Pierce Brooks (*at right*) of the Los Angeles Police Department to Shirley Bridgeford's remains in the Anza-Borrego State Park desert. (*Pierce Brooks Family Collection*)

Homicide detectives from San Diego County, Orange County, and the Los Angeles Police Department searching for the remains of Shirley Bridgeford and Ruth Mercado on October 30, 1958.

Sergeant Pierce Brooks, LAPD, points a flashlight at the last remains of model Ruth Mercado, who was abducted and murdered by Harvey Glatman. The investigators searched the lonely San Diego County desert near the Mexican border and finally located Mercado.

303

(*Left*) Captain Pierce Brooks, Commander of the Homicide Unit of the Los Angeles Police Department in 1968. He solved the Harvey Glatman serial murder cases in 1958 and went on to become one of the most admired lawmen in the United States.

(*Right*) The late Pierce Brooks near the end of his forty-year career contributing to law enforcement. He helped establish VICAP (Violent Criminal Apprehension Program), wrote *Officer Down, Code Three,* a book which is credited with saving many cops' lives, and became an expert adviser to many serial killer task forces, including the Green River Killer cases. The Glatman case was Brooks's prototype to develop the theory of Serial Murder. (*Pierce Brooks Family Collection*)

THE CAPTIVE BRIDE

Bob Keppel, now renowned for his expertise in serial murder and author of *The Riverman*, was one of the King County Police detectives who approached the isolated cabin where they expected to be met with gunfire from Wayne Merriam — who would rather have his ex-wife dead than divorced.

BAD BLIND DATE

Homicide Sergeant Elmer Wittman, who led a crew of detectives into the deep wooded ravine of Cowan Park, where Victoria Legg's body lay. None of them had ever encountered such a terrible crime scene.

THE HIGHWAY ACCIDENT

When Marion County detectives developed film found in a camera in the victim's home, they found photographs of a happy couple. Within a few weeks, they would be separated forever. (*Police file photo*)

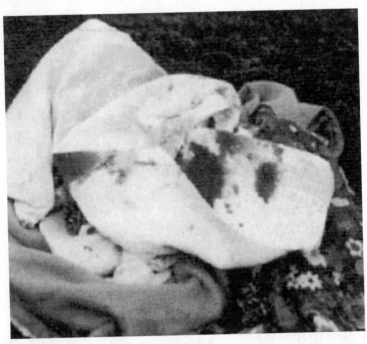

Bloodstained bedding found many miles from the duplex on Cedar Court matched sheets found in Lori and Walt Buckley's home. (*Police file photo*)

When Detectives Jim Byrnes and David Kominek arrived at the fatal accident site along the Van Duzer Corridor between Salem, Oregon, and the Pacific coast, they were surprised to find there were no hesitation marks where the Buckleys' Vega left the road and crashed over a bank and into the forest. (*Police file photo*)

YOU KILL ME — OR I'LL KILL YOU

Fran Steffen had no idea that the older man who was giving her too much attention was very, very dangerous and obsessed with a bizarre sexual fantasy.

307

Silverton Police Officers Frank Wilson (*above*) and George Holland (*below*) were the first investigators to arrive at the crime scene in Fran Steffen's apartment. They were stunned by what they found there.

Lieutenant Jim Byrnes of the Marion County, Oregon, Sheriff's Office led the investigators in the search of Kent Whiteside's house. The detectives found a number of bizarre items that hinted at what was really going on behind Whiteside's calm facade.

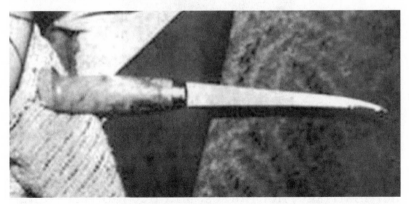

The weapon used by the out-of-control masochist was a Finnish filleting knife, razor sharp.

Julie Weflen was an outdoors girl who loved to camp and ride horses. She disappeared in September 1987.

Julie Weflen as a bride. She loved her husband, her marriage, her horses, and her job. Yet something — or someone — took her away from all of them.

Search and rescue teams, sheriff's deputies, friends, family, and strangers volunteered thousands of hours to look for Julie Weflen. She was lost somewhere in the vast rugged wilderness outside Spokane, Washington.

Sheriff's detectives and deputies from Spokane County, Washington, set up roadblocks on every road leading to the Spring Hill power substation where Julie Weflen's rig was found. She was a skilled worker for the Bonneville Power Administration, even though she looked more like a beauty queen. Someone followed her there and forced her into another vehicle.

For the first two months after Julie vanished, her husband, Mike Weflen, was never far from the Bonneville power substation where she was last seen. He organized a huge effort to find her.

Old Flames Can Burn

Television talk shows can always rely on a solid Nielsen rating when the topic concerns the reunion of onetime lovers who have lost touch with one another. The moment of revelation is fascinating to watch: the homecoming queen who has put on forty pounds confronted by the man she dumped when they were teenagers; the couple who have been separated by disapproving families; the man who went off to war and came home to find his girlfriend had married someone else.

Will they reignite the cold ashes of their relationships over a romantic dinner paid for by the talk show host? Have they longed for one another for years? Will the now-successful man be grateful that the onetime beauty queen didn't want him twenty years earlier?

Even though the viewers may hope for instant romance or just deserts, most of the couples lured in front of the cameras return to their current lives with hardly a ripple. Life goes on and we all mature. High school heroes fade and love cannot be rekindled so easily. The most we can hope is that we still have anything at all in common with the people we knew in our teenage years, especially if we've moved away to a different city, where careers make school days seem only a distant memory.

But disappointment, new perceptions of reality, and the dashing of rosy hopes that dating after many years is going to end like the lyrics of a love song usually aren't fatal.

In the following case, it was.

Fourteen-year-old Debbie Marvin★ was visiting her older sister, Mrs. Diane Russell,★ on the Friday night of November 8, 1968. She always looked forward to visiting her sister and brother-in-law in their cute little duplex apartment near Alki Beach in West Seattle. She didn't mind at all that she had to sleep on a couch in the living room. Teenagers can sleep anywhere, and Debbie was no exception.

She, her sister, and her brother-in-law had been out that evening, returning to their apartment shortly before eleven p.m. Her sister gave Debbie bedding and a pillow for her couch-bed, and the three retired. The couch was located about three feet from the front door, and against the wall that divided the two units of the duplex. She stayed awake awhile, watching the headlights of approaching cars sweep across the ceiling and listening to the faint sound of records and muffled conversation from the adjacent apartment, although she couldn't really make out what people were saying. She finally drifted off to sleep.

Debbie had planned to sleep in on Saturday morning, but something woke her early, around 6:30 a.m. The sun wasn't up yet and, sleep-dazed, she thought that it was still night and that she was hearing records again from next door.

But then she heard sounds of bumping and banging against the wall, as if some heavy object was being slammed against it. The force was enough to shake the couch she lay on.

Suddenly, she froze as she heard a woman's voice scream — just once. Hardly breathing as she strained to listen, Debbie heard a male voice say, "I'm sorry."

And then she relaxed. She was just overhearing a family fight. She didn't know who lived next door, and nobody else in her sister's house even woke up. Things were quiet next door now, so she turned over and went back to sleep, not anxious to get up in the dark before dawn.

Sometime later, Debbie heard the door to the neighboring apartment open and shut. By this time her sister was up and working in the kitchen. She had finished fixing breakfast for her husband, Dan, who had to work that weekend. She glanced at the clock to see if she was on schedule. It was 7:10 a.m.

Diane heard the front door of the next apartment slam closed too. Staring out through the window in the rain-washed morning light, she saw a young man leave her next-door neighbor's apartment and walk down the street toward Admiral Way. He didn't seem to be in any hurry and there was nothing unusual about him.

Diane knew Ruth Coster,* the woman who lived next door, but not very well. They were both in their early twenties, and they chatted once in a while as they picked up their mail or worked in the yard. But she hadn't even seen Ruth for about two weeks. That wasn't unusual, especially in the winter, because they both had jobs.

Absently, she noticed that the man leaving was young, white, and had light hair. He looked to be about six feet tall and in good condition. But she wouldn't be able to pick him out from other men who matched the same general description. Her neighbor had apparently had a male visitor stay overnight — and that was unusual.

While Dan finished eating, Diane Russell continued to work in her kitchen, stacking dishes to drain, sweeping the floor, and putting out milk and cereal for her little sister.

In the living room, Debbie was wide awake now. The voices and then the door's slamming had made more sleep impossible, and she was at the point of deciding to get up and eat breakfast with her brother-in-law when she heard more sounds coming from next door. The wall between the two units wasn't particularly thin, but noises carried easily through the heat registers. This time the sounds were kind of scary. She strained to hear what seemed to be moans. She started to call her sister to come and listen when she heard a voice at the front door and a feeble knock.

Dan Russell went to the door. "I answered the knock on the door — it must have been 7:15 a.m. or so," he recalled. "I found a female there. I didn't know who she was, but she was sitting down on the front steps. I could see blood in the front room next door, too, through the open door."

Russell was shocked at the condition of the woman on his porch. He could barely see her face because she was "dripping blood." Her nose might have been broken, but he got the impression that her whole face had been "bashed in."

"I couldn't tell for sure where the blood

was coming from," he recalled, "but some was from her nose.

"I called to my wife to stay inside and I stepped out and shut the door and locked it. I saw a sleeping bag in the living room next door so I got that and covered the girl with it. We didn't have a phone and I ran next door to Mr. McNeill's house to call for help, then came back to the girl. When an ambulance and police didn't come right away, I got worried. I told the girl I was going for help and I got in my car and drove to meet the police. I met them a block away. I guess the girl didn't understand me because she got up and somehow made it across the yard to Mr. McNeill's house."

Ralph McNeill,* whose home was next door to the duplex, wouldn't ordinarily have been home at 7:30 in the morning as his railroad job required him to be away most weekends. But November 9 was his day off. He was as shocked as Dan Russell had been by his first glimpse of the stricken girl.

He saw that a young woman was half-crawling, half-staggering toward his house with hands holding her throat. He noticed that she wore slacks and a blouse, and that they were completely saturated with blood, both in the front and the back.

"She was a pretty bloody mess," McNeill said. "Her face was covered with blood too. It was hard to tell where she was wounded. For some reason, I got the impression that her throat was wounded but I couldn't tell how bad because her hair hung down over her neck. She was still actively bleeding, but not too heavily, it seemed. I sat her down on the porch, and then the police car arrived."

Officer Charles E. Larsen was working without a partner on First Watch, and he was the initial officer to respond to the call for aid. He spotted the wounded woman sitting on the McNeill porch and wheeled his squad car to the curb, jumping out of his car and running toward her without shutting the door. He could see already that she had multiple wounds and that her clothing was soaked with scarlet blood. Knowing it would be like a finger in a dike, Larsen turned back to grab his first aid kit.

"I saw she was wounded — slash wounds around the neck that seemed to be knife wounds. I put gauze compresses on her neck but I couldn't completely stop the bleeding. I asked her who hurt her, and she said, 'My friend. He cut me and hurt me.' Then she said, 'I think he hurt my girlfriend too. I couldn't wake up my girl-friend.' "

Larsen knew an ambulance was right behind him, and he left the wounded woman with Ralph McNeill and raced to the duplex apartment with its door standing open. He saw the large pool of blood on the porch and the bloodied sleeping bag Dan Russell had used to cover the woman.

Larsen, of course, had no idea what had happened or how many people were still inside the apartment. He drew his service revolver and entered the apartment. There was a couch against the west wall with a bloody quilt, and large pools of coagulating blood on the floor. It was difficult to believe that one woman could have bled so much and still be alive.

The white Formica coffee table in front of the couch was knocked over and he saw two women's purses, their contents spilling out, open on the floor.

Cautiously, Larsen walked toward the duplex's single bedroom. "I saw a figure on the bed with the blankets pulled up over the head," Larsen said. "About three-quarters of the head and the right arm showed."

He had no idea if it was a male or female in the bed, but he couldn't stop to check until he scoped out the rest of the apartment to be sure that there was no one hiding there. The tiny kitchen was empty. Absently, Larsen noted a number of beer bottles on the counter. He found the back door was locked, the bolt slid into place from the inside. There was a little bathroom that opened off the bedroom. That was empty too.

Now Larsen turned back toward the bed. As he pulled the blanket down, he saw another young woman who was lying facedown on the bed. There was no blood here at all, but the woman lay so quietly. The officer saw that she had a piece of pink lingerie twisted tightly around her neck. Carefully, he loosened it with his finger, but he felt no reassuring pulse in the carotid artery in her neck.

"Her right arm was hanging down," Larsen said, "and her fingers were cold. There was no pulse in the wrist."

She looked so young that he wasn't ready to give up. "I put my ear to her back and listened for a heartbeat," he said quietly. "There was none."

There was nothing more he could do for the dead woman. Larsen then checked the apartment more thoroughly. "There was a stained pink towel soaking in the bathroom sink and a T-shirt and dress shirt — both of them bloody and sopping wet — on the floor along the bathroom wall."

He looked at the old-fashioned patchwork quilt on the couch and saw the blade of a knife, about eight inches long, its handle broken. It was heavily stained with blood.

Larsen felt as if he were walking through a nightmare. Even though only three or four minutes had passed, it seemed to him that he'd been in the apartment with the dead woman for hours.

"My main concern was for the wounded woman," he said. "I shut the door of the murder apartment and ran back to her. The front door was directly in my line of sight all the time I was with her, and I could observe it to see if anyone went in or out. No one did."

Once more, time dragged as Larsen comforted the critically injured woman and tried to assure her that she was going to be okay when he wasn't so convinced himself that she would be. He estimated that it was about ten minutes before the ambulance arrived.

He asked her what had happened to her, and she gasped, "Steve cut me."

But she had no answer when Larsen

asked her, *"Why?"* She didn't know why.

While the wounded woman was being rushed to West Seattle General Hospital, more patrol cars and detectives from the Seattle Police Department's Homicide Unit sped to the crime scene. John Nichols, Larsen's partner, arrived first and he moved to guard the door of the apartment where the women had been attacked. He strung yellow tape around the area to protect whatever clues that might be present.

Homicide detectives Richard Schoener and Elmer Wittman reached the apartment a few minutes later, followed by Owen McKenna and George Berger.

They talked with the Russells and other neighbors who were able to identify the tenant who lived there. It was Ruth Coster, a young divorced woman who was only 20 years old. None of them recognized the wounded woman; they had never seen her before.

From information in the two rifled purses, the investigators were quite sure that the bleeding woman was her former sister-in-law, Mallory Gilbert,[*] 22. They learned from other relatives that Mallory had been staying with Ruth for only a week. That would explain why Dan Russell didn't know her when she came to his door for help.

Grimacing, Owen McKenna glanced around the gore-stained living room. The leafy pattern on the wallpaper was sprayed with blood droplets that could only have come from medium velocity arterial spray, coupled with larger drops with "tails" that indicated the stabber had lifted the knife again and again as he inflicted more wounds. It looked as if a terrible struggle had taken place there. It seemed eerier, somehow, to see the *normal* things there too: the phonograph with a 45 rpm Patsy Cline record on the turntable, a small white sneaker, an ashtray, an alarm clock. But the record player's needle had worn a groove into the record and scratched it deeply, and the other items were scattered on the worn carpet.

Oddly, just as in the bedroom, there was a single empty beer bottle sitting upright on the floor next to a chair. It looked almost as if the assailant or assailants had taken time to drink two beers after the attacks, but before he left Ruth's apartment. Debbie Marvin estimated that she had heard a man's voice say "I'm sorry" more than a half hour before she heard the door slam next door.

McKenna had the same thought that Charles Larsen had had: "It's hard to believe that girl's still alive when you look at this room."

"I know," Berger answered from the bedroom. "But look in here: There's absolutely no sign of struggle." He gestured toward the bedside table. The telephone, some trinkets, and even a glass of water rested in place, all of them undisturbed. The covers of the bed were only slightly rumpled. "It looks like she didn't — or maybe couldn't — fight back at all."

Ruth Coster's body lay facedown as if she were sleeping. The only indication that she might have suffered as she died was her right hand, which was clenched tightly around the edge of the blankets.

The four detectives busied themselves gathering evidence, which they found in abundance. The blood-soaked T-shirt, dress shirt, towel, quilt, and the victim's sleeping garments were labeled and slipped into plastic evidence bags, while all likely surfaces were dusted for fingerprints.

"You know," McKenna remarked, "this whole place looks like a normally cluttered apartment after a party — except the living room. That's a bloody shambles. I don't see how this victim could have slept through what went on there — unless she was already dead."

"Yeah," Berger mused, "and if both women fought him off in the living room, the dead woman would certainly have some bloodstains or cuts on her body. We'll have to wait for the medical report, but it looks like she's been strangled and that was all."

Larsen had told them about what might have been Mallory Gilbert's deathbed statement. She had managed to tell him that "Steve did it." And she had referred to him as a friend.

Larsen had also asked her if there had been some kind of a fight in the duplex, but Mallory had said no. She had absolutely no idea what had made their "friend" attack them.

She didn't know yet that her sister-in-law was dead, and no one was going to tell her in her extremely critical condition. Nor could they question her further; they could only hope that she would live.

She might have been out of her head from loss of blood and shock, but it seemed unlikely that a stranger had broken into the apartment where two young women slept. The back door was bolted from the inside, and the front door locked automatically when it was closed. In November, in a storm, it wasn't likely that they had left any windows open.

Alcohol had probably played some part in what had happened. Berger counted eighteen empty beer bottles placed next to the small gas range in the kitchen, and there were more around the apartment. There was also a large can of tomato juice on the kitchen floor next to the six-pack containers of drained bottles.

The homicide investigators' best witness so far was Patrol Officer Charles Larsen. "As close as Larsen could get it," Wittman said, "the injured woman knew the man who did this. She had been out with him last night. I gathered that she'd known him before — he wasn't a pickup. I think his name was Steve, and the last name sounded like Maier or Meyer."

The investigators spent over five hours in the death apartment, taking scores of pictures, gathering evidence. By the time they had finished collecting evidence, there was one man they wanted to talk to, and that was 20-year-old Steven Meyer. But Meyer was gone. Diane Russell had seen a man who matched his description walking away from the duplex next door, but hadn't thought much of it at the time.

While Mallory Gilbert fought gallantly for her life in the hospital's intensive care unit, deputy medical examiners removed the body of Ruth Coster.

ER physicians worked frantically to save Mallory. She had lost so much blood, and they guessed that she was stretching the limits of the "golden hour" beyond which critically injured patients often go into irreversible shock. The ambulance EMTs had already started a line to keep her veins from collapsing, and now the doctors cross-matched her blood as quickly as they could and started transfusing whole blood. Her skin was chalky white, and it took two quarts — a quarter of the volume of blood in a normal adult woman's system — before she began to pink up even a little.

Replacement blood, however, does not have the oxygen-carrying properties that a person's own blood has, and she was in danger of a brain hemorrhage or a stroke.

Life gradually began to take a firmer hold on the brave girl, and though she was still in shock, physicians permitted the detectives to talk with Mallory Gilbert — as long as they promised to keep their questions short.

It was around noon when she was finally able to tell them her chilling story. The lovely gray-eyed brunette, her throat full of stitches and tubes and heavily bandaged, could barely speak above a whisper.

She explained that she and Ruth were both from Yakima, Washington, a medium-sized fruit-growing city about 150 miles southeast of Seattle. They had both known Steve Meyer there, and believed they knew him well. In fact, Mallory said she and Steve had dated for quite a while. Their breakup had been amicable as far as she knew, and Steve was dating someone else back in Yakima.

On Thursday, November 7, Steve and his apartment mate, Dave Romano,★ had asked the two girls for a date the following evening. Although Mallory and Steve were no longer dating seriously, she assumed there were no hard feelings: Mallory paired off with Dave Romano while Ruth and Steve were a duo. Since Ruth had a practically new Camaro, she and Mallory drove to the men's Queen Anne Hill apartment. Then the four of them walked to the nearby Brownie's Tavern, where they drank beer and reminisced about their school days in Yakima.

After an hour or so, Ruth offered to cook a late supper for all of them at her apartment. Steve said he'd like that, but Mallory and Dave decided to go back to the men's apartment to talk and listen to records. Mallory shook her head when George Berger asked her if this was a romantic date for either couple.

"We were all just old friends," she whispered.

Dave Romano wasn't used to drinking much beer, and he fell asleep while he and Mallory were listening to records. Mallory watched television by herself, but it wasn't long before Ruth and Steve returned to the Queen Anne Hill apartment. At that point it was getting late, and the two women just wanted to go home and get to bed, but Steve insisted on accompanying them.

"We didn't want him to come," Mallory said, "but he was insistent about it, even though we promised him we'd be back for our date the next day. We finally gave up arguing with him, and he ended up coming back home with us."

The girls were tired and went to bed while Steve Meyer sat up drinking beer by himself. Ruth slept in the bedroom while Mallory bedded down on the couch, under the patchwork quilt.

They had given Steve a sleeping bag and told him he could sleep on the living-room floor when he got tired enough. They had no fear of him; he was an old buddy. He'd never given Mallory any indication that he had any tendency toward violence.

She fell asleep with the sound of Patsy Cline singing "I go out walkin' after midnight" in her ears.

Her next recollection was one of shock and disbelief. "I was sleeping facing the back of the couch. I became aware of Steve trying to wake me up, but I was tired and I just wanted to sleep. Then I felt something grab me by the hair and pull my head back. Something sliced across my throat and I felt something warm dripping down on my chest.

"I screamed, 'Steve!' and he said, 'I'm sorry,' and then he cut my throat again. I don't know how many times he cut me. I remember that I crawled to the front door and somehow I got it unlocked, but I couldn't get out because he dragged me back.

"The coffee table tipped over. Once, he had my head pinned between his knees and he was still stabbing me. He pushed me down on the couch and strangled me. Then I must have passed out."

Mallory recalled that she thought she was dying as she lost consciousness. After an interval that she couldn't begin to estimate, she regained consciousness. She had the impression that Steve wasn't in the apartment any longer, and she managed to stagger to the bedroom to find Ruth. When she couldn't rouse Ruth, she crawled next door to the Russells' for help.

It was the morning of November 9 now, and the detectives listening to Mallory's story were determined to find Steve Meyer. They visited Dave Romano's and Meyer's Queen Anne Hill apartment and roused the still-sleeping Romano. When he heard what had happened to Ruth and Mallory, he looked stunned. He said that as far as he knew, Steve hadn't come home at all on Saturday, and he had no idea where he might be. It was possible that Meyer had come back to the place they shared while Romano was sleeping, but Romano had no recollection of seeing him.

"This doesn't sound like Steve," he muttered over and over. "I've known him for a long time and I've never even seen him lose his temper. I just can't believe it."

"Were there any arguments Friday night?" Berger asked him.

"No — nothing like that. Nobody disagreed with anyone. We just had a good time."

Through discussions with Mallory

Gilbert and Dave Romano, the detectives learned that Steve Meyer was currently dating a Yakima woman named Linda Crousseau.* And that relationship seemed to be going smoothly.

"He's running — that's for sure," Dick Schoener said. "Probably in Ruth Coster's car. Maybe he'll head to this woman in Yakima. It sounds like she means quite a bit to him.

"Notify the Yakima police and have them contact Linda Crousseau. If she hears from Meyer, ask them to have her call us right away."

In the meantime, a bulletin on Ruth Coster's car was issued to the eleven western states. It was missing from its usual parking place near her apartment, and her keys were gone from her purse. The car was only two years old, a sporty Camaro with a dark top, a beige bottom, and a Washington license plate reading EUW-753. While Ruth's apartment was tiny and furnished with odds and ends, her car had been her extravagance.

Mallory Gilbert's doctors were cautiously optimistic that she was going to live, but it would take a long time before she could hope to leave the hospital.

King County Medical Examiner Dr.

Gale Wilson conducted the postmortem examination of 20-year-old Ruth Coster. He found that she had died as the result of manual strangulation. Although Officer Charles Larsen had loosened the pink lingerie where it had been cinched tightly around her neck, the finger-shaped bruises on her neck indicated that the actual death weapons had been human hands. Blood vessels had burst in her eyes — tiny petechial hemorrhages which confirmed strangulation.

There were no other marks on her body, and certainly no defense wounds or bruises that would indicate she had tried to fight for her life. Dr. Wilson found no evidence that Ruth had engaged in sexual intercourse before her death, but noted that an act of sodomy had been attempted on her body.

Steve Meyer had many directions in which to run: east to Yakima, which was home; north to the Canadian border, or south to Oregon and California. He had a good car and a few hours' head start. It would be easier for him to cross state lines than to try to go through customs into British Columbia, where every car was automatically stopped for quick questioning. Seattle authorities had alerted every agency possible, but until the victim's car was spotted, there was nothing for the detectives to do but keep checking on Meyer's background and label the evidence they had found.

Later that Saturday afternoon, an Oregon State Police trooper was answering a routine "car in ditch" call 215 miles south of Seattle. Phil Starbuck, assigned to patrol the I-5 freeway south of Salem, Oregon, pulled up behind a fairly new Camaro that was balanced sideways across a shallow ditch beside the freeway. He noted that the car had probably spun several times; there was damage to all four fenders and the front grille was severely crunched. He could discern no obvious damage to the undercarriage, and the car was probably drivable.

But when Trooper Starbuck looked in and around the wrecked car for signs of the driver or passengers, he didn't find anyone. There was no indication, such as bloodstains, that anyone had sustained injuries in the accident, nor could he find any identification documents in the car.

Starbuck looked up to see an elderly man approaching him. The man said he lived nearby and he had seen the driver of the car crawl out of the wreck and hitch a ride toward Salem. "He shouted at me that he was going for help and he'd be back with a tow truck."

"Anybody with him?" Starbuck asked.

"No — just the driver. Young guy."

While Starbuck jotted down pertinent information on the abandoned car, and checked the VIN (Vehicle Identification Number) so he could trace the ownership, the driver was already in a Salem phone booth, making a long-distance collect call to Yakima, Washington. The recipient of the call was Linda Crousseau, the slender blond woman Steve Meyer had been dating before he moved to Seattle.

Linda had already been alerted by Yakima Police. She knew Ruth Coster was dead, but she hadn't been informed that Mallory Gilbert had been critically wounded.

Linda Crousseau was as shocked as Meyer's other friends — perhaps more so. Her role was not unlike that of Amber Frey's in the Laci and Scott Peterson case three decades later. She was in love with Steve Meyer and she believed what he told her, but now something terrible had gone wrong. She was at her father's sometime after two that Saturday afternoon.

When Steve called her, he told her he

was in Salem. She didn't know where that was, and he told her it was in Oregon.

"Then I asked him, 'Why did you do it?' — meaning why would he have hurt Ruth — and he just said, *'I don't know.'* I didn't know that Mallory had been stabbed until he told me, and then I asked him if he knew Ruth was dead and he said, 'Yes.'"

The Seattle detectives later asked Linda if Meyer had told her what happened during the fatal night he spent at Ruth's apartment. "Yes," she told them. "He said the girls had been teasing him and saying he was no good because he didn't have a job."

Linda urged Steve to contact the detectives or at least call the police in Salem, and he told her that he was going to do that as soon as he hung up the phone: "He said he had already planned to do that."

Steve Meyer sounded frightened and he cried sporadically during the ten or fifteen minutes she talked with him. Then he suddenly hung up, leaving only a dial tone on the line.

When the telephone rang in the Homicide Unit of the Seattle Police Department shortly before three, Owen McKenna almost didn't answer it, because their procedure dictated that a current homicide takes precedence over everything else, and detectives weren't supposed to interrupt their work to answer phones. But McKenna and Schoener were trying to check in the loaded evidence cart from the Coster murder site, and the ringing phone was an annoyance. There weren't any secretaries working on Saturday afternoon, and there was no one else to pick up the phone.

McKenna sighed and reached for it.

The voice that came over the line electrified him; seeing McKenna's expression, Dick Schoener paused, too, and raised his eyebrows questioningly. McKenna signaled to him to pick up the line that was lit up, but held his finger to his lips.

"This is Steve Meyer," the caller began. "Do you know about that thing in West Seattle?"

Cautiously, McKenna answered, "It so happens that I do."

"I just wrecked the car —"

"Whose car?" McKenna asked.

"Ruth's car." There was no question now that this was Meyer.

"Well, what do you want to do?" McKenna asked easily, fearful that Meyer would panic and hang up.

"I want to give myself up."

McKenna questioned Meyer gently, never pressing but gleaning as much information as possible. He learned that Meyer was calling from Salem, Oregon, and that he was in a phone booth near a gas station.

"What I'd like you to do, Steve," McKenna said, "is stay on the line, but stretch the cord so you can just step outside the phone booth there and see if you can give me the address of the gas station next door. I'll wait while you do that."

He held his breath, but within thirty seconds Meyer was back on the line and telling him the address. He had to trust that it was really the address where the fugitive was.

Without altering the soft, almost casual tone of his voice, McKenna gestured to Schoener and scribbled on a message pad: "Call Salem State Police office. Have them go to the Texaco station at 1390 Broadway North. *Meyer!!!*"

Schoener nodded. He quietly placed the call and quickly reached Lieutenant B. L. Kezar of the Oregon State Police and gave him the information. In the meantime, Detective McKenna kept Meyer on the line.

"If I arrange for someone to pick you up, will you wait there?" McKenna asked, as calmly as if he were inviting Meyer to join him for a beer. "I can have them give you a lift."

Meyer hesitated. "Well, if it doesn't take too long, I might wait."

Meyer was waffling, and he sounded as if he was about to "rabbit" on McKenna and run. But the patient detective kept Meyer talking, heaving a silent sigh of relief as Schoener signaled to him that the Oregon officers were on the way.

And then suddenly Meyer muttered, "I have to hang up now."

McKenna's heart sank as he heard Meyer go off the line. He could picture him running away before the Oregon troopers got there. He didn't know that Lieutenant Kezar, along with fellow troopers John Newell, Phil Starbuck, and Kenneth Lamkin, had pulled up to the Texaco station phone booth within five to ten minutes after Dick Schoener's call.

"This fellow was sitting on the curb," Kezar said. "I went over to him and he walked to meet me. I said, 'Are you Steve?' and he said, 'Yes.' John Newell, who's one of our investigators, was with me and we informed Meyer of his rights. We leaned him up against the car and checked him for weapons, and then we took him to our Salem Patrol Headquarters. We informed him again of his rights as we traveled in the car."

In Seattle, Owen McKenna and Dick Schoener waited anxiously by the phone, willing it to ring. Finally, Lieutenant Kezar's voice came over the line: "We've got him!"

Kezar questioned Meyer, who appeared to him to be rational. "To the best of my knowledge, the suspect behaved in a normal manner," Kezar said, "but I hadn't known him before, so I couldn't positively state what *was* normal for him."

Neither Newell nor Kezar thought Steve Meyer was intoxicated or even hungover. He didn't smell of alcohol at all.

When they had Meyer take his shirt off, John Newell saw that he had scratches and nicks on his hands and a three-inch scratch on his shoulder, but it wasn't possible for the Oregon State Police investigator to say for sure how fresh they were. However, one of the cuts on his hand was severe enough that Newell gave him a small bandage for it.

As soon as they knew Steve Meyer was in custody, Owen McKenna put in a requisition for a car, and by evening he and George Berger were on the way to Salem to bring Steven Meyer back to Seattle for arraignment. He had waived extradition, agreeing to return to Washington State.

The two Seattle detectives arrived in Salem late that night. Ruth Coster had been dead only twenty-four hours before her killer was in custody. But it had seemed like a week, especially when McKenna was convinced that when Meyer hung up the phone he had disappeared in Oregon.

On Sunday morning, they looked at the wreck of the car that Ruth Coster had treasured. That afternoon, McKenna and Berger were on their way back to Seattle with Meyer.

On Monday morning, November 11, Steven Meyer gave a written statement to Seattle homicide detectives. It answered many questions, yet cloudy areas remained. Perhaps nothing could ever really explain his maniacal attacks on November 9.

"I, Steven Terry Meyer, born June 30, 1948, have been advised of my constitutional rights and choose to make this statement of my own free will, knowing that it may be used against me in a court of law.

"On November 8 about 8:30 p.m., Mallory Gilbert and Ruth Coster came to Dave Romano's and my apartment. Dave was not home. We met Dave at Brownie's Tavern and drank beer. Dave and Mallory then went to our apartment, and Ruth and I went to her apartment. We drank and ate stew she made. Then Ruth and I went back to our apartment. Dave was passed out on the couch. I drove back to the girls' apartment with them. Ruth drove and Mallory sat beside her and I sat by the door. I was drunk. We all sat around and talked at the apartment. I had two or three beers."

Meyer described where he had put the empty bottles when he finished and said most of it was Rainier beer. His statement verified what the detectives knew: the bottles *were* on the floor of the kitchen, next to Ruth's bed, and on the living-room floor, just as Meyer described.

"The girls were tired and went to bed. Mallory slept on the couch and Ruth in the bedroom.

"Ruth had on a pink negligee and black bikini panties when she brought out a sleeping bag and gave it to me to sleep on the living-room floor. The girls went to sleep. I wanted to go to bed with Mallory and I tried to wake her up. She said, 'No.' I went back to sleep and later I heard Ruth crying. I went in to see what was the matter and she said she'd had a nightmare. She told me her mother had died in a fire when she was away from home and she'd dreamed about it. She said, 'I should have been there . . .'

"I got her a glass of water," Meyer continued. "Then she asked me to lie down beside her because she wouldn't be so scared with someone beside her. We started to 'make out.' I got completely undressed. We had intercourse — it was the first time we ever had. I dreamed about Linda and I wanted to be with her. I knew she'd leave me if she found out."

He had not been a faithful lover to Linda Crousseau. He had first attempted to have sex with his former girlfriend as she lay sleeping on the couch, and he admitted to having intercourse with Ruth Coster, despite the fact that the detectives knew that wasn't true. Her autopsy report refuted that.

"After laying on my side for an hour," Meyer said, "I went berserk. I choked Ruth with my hands. She struggled for a short time and then went limp. I kept on, and then snapped to and realized what I was doing.

"I tried to wake Mallory, but she wouldn't wake up and talk to me. I got scared and I went to the kitchen and got a knife from the top right-hand drawer. I tried again to talk to Mallory but she wouldn't wake up.

"I grabbed her by the hair and I cut her throat from left to right. I cut her again. I hit her twice. We knocked over the coffee table and I hit her again. She headed for the door and I dragged her back. She grabbed my legs and held on. I think she scratched me. She was sitting leaning against the couch. I squatted down and took the broken knife blade and cut her throat twice more. I used my T-shirt to wipe the blood off my arms and hands. I went to the closet and grabbed a patterned shirt."

The defendant went on to say that he'd spotted Ruth's car keys and took them. Then he said that as he was leaving, he glanced at Mallory where she half-leaned, half-sat on the floor and saw that she was still breathing. "I was sorry then, and I wanted to help her, but I was afraid."

Meyer said that the next several hours were a blur of headlights coming toward him, endless freeways and service stations where he'd stopped to ask directions. He thought that he must have fallen asleep at the wheel as he headed south from Salem. "When I woke up, the car was spinning. Then I had no car and only fifty-six cents in my pocket."

Steve Meyer spent the upcoming holidays in jail, and it was almost spring — March 10, 1969 — when he went on trial for murder and attempted murder. Outside the windows of Superior Court Judge George H. Revelle's courtroom, the sky was blue and cloudless, and spring was making a false start with temperatures hovering close to 60 degrees.

Inside the courtroom, however, everyone's thoughts were on the grim predawn horror of the previous November 9, where one lovely young woman had died and another had been permanently scarred. The death and the disfigurement were known facts that had been emblazoned in headlines in Seattle papers. Still, there were questions to be answered that might shed some light on how a pleasant evening for four young people had degenerated into a fatal bloodbath.

If court watchers had expected the defendant to look like a glowering killer, they were surprised as Steve Meyer walked in and waited for court deputies to remove the handcuffs from his wrists. He was very handsome, with dark blond hair and brown eyes. He looked more like a California surfer or a heartthrob actor than he did a cold-blooded killer. The sports shirt he wore added to that impression, and there was a murmur that rippled through the courtroom at the sight of him.

He sat down, flanked by his attorneys, Steven A. Mack and Walter T. Greenaway. King County Chief Deputy Prosecutor C. N. "Nick" Marshall would represent the State.

It took a while to pick a jury. Finally, both sides were satisfied with a jury made up of seven women and five men.

Mallory Gilbert could not be in the courtroom before she testified, standard procedure so that prospective witnesses won't be influenced by what others who take the stand say. Mallory sat nervously on a long oak bench just outside the courtroom. If the media cameras hoped to get a look at her scars, they were disappointed: she wore a blouse with a high collar.

Meyer's other alleged victim could no longer testify — not in person, anyway. Marshall would have to get as much of the gruesome physical evidence as possible and the dozens of graphic photographs entered into the record so that the jurors would have some concept of the abattoir Ruth Coster's apartment was when detectives arrived. That would have to speak for Ruth.

There was, of course, Steve Meyer's own confession, but his attorneys would try to keep the jury from hearing that. The jury's decision could mean death for the defendant, who was now pleading innocent to charges of murder in the first degree and first-degree assault.

Despite the defense's objections, the confession *was* accepted into evidence. The courtroom was hushed as Detective George Berger read the shocking statement. Steven Meyer sat, head bowed, eyes closed, as his words of confession filled the room. How much of his statement was realistic was a matter of conjecture. Ruth Coster could not defend her reputation. Had she really tempted Meyer by wearing a filmy pink negligee and black panties? Marshall quickly erased that impression. He showed the jurors the gown that was tightened around her neck like a garotte to render her unconscious before she was manually strangled.

It was pink all right; however, it wasn't a diaphanous sheer pink gown but rather what is commonly known as a "granny gown." It was made of opaque flannel and it had a high neck and long sleeves.

The defense argued that consideration should be given to another pink gown found on the floor near the foot of the bed, allegedly of the type described by the defendant in his statement.

Marshall reminded the jurors that there was absolutely no evidence that Ruth Coster had engaged in intercourse, either on Friday, November 9 or for several days before her murder. If she had, Dr. Wilson would have found evidence of it during her autopsy. It was more likely that the sex — consensual or forced — was only one of Steve Meyer's fantasies.

The prosecution thought so. The passions or bizarre mental processes that had triggered the homicidal rage were known only to the defendant — and possibly not even to him, for he had told his girlfriend, "I don't know — I just don't know why I did it."

Mallory Gilbert gave her testimony in a determinedly firm voice. The blouse she wore was high-necked, with a ruffled jabot at the throat, but it didn't completely hide the numerous angry red scars that crisscrossed her neck. As she spoke, spectators realized that they were seeing and hearing a girl who had undoubtedly been as close to death by murder as anyone ever had and still survived. It was a sobering experience to hear testimony about acts that usually were reconstructed only by evidence found at a crime scene.

Nick Marshall led Mallory gently through the events of the fatal night and morning. As she left the witness stand, she avoided Steve Meyer's eyes. There was little doubt that she would never completely recover from either the physical or the emotional ordeal she had been through.

Testimony in the Meyer trial continued for five days. The jury heard statements from members of the Seattle Police Department: George Berger, Owen McKenna, Charles Larsen, and John Nichols; from Oregon officials John Newell, B. L. Kezar, Phil Starbuck, and Kenneth Lamkin; from witnesses Linda Crousseau, Dave Romano, and Mallory Gilbert; and from the Russell family and Ralph McNeill.

Dr. Wilson's testimony was vital in helping the jurors understand why death by strangulation can, indeed, be premeditated under the law — just as much as a death resulting after a killer spends months plotting his crime.

Wilson explained that there is no way to know how quickly a human being will die when his or her breath is cut off, when blood flow to the brain is blocked. For some people, it takes only seconds; for others, it may take several minutes. During those seconds and those minutes, the strangler has time to form intent, aware that if he does not release his grip, the person will die.

As always, Nick Marshall had prepared a watertight case, and he gave his summation address to the jury with assurance. As Meyer was charged with first-degree murder and first-degree assault in the cases of Ruth Coster and Mallory Gilbert, respectively, Marshall stressed that the premeditated action necessary for conviction of murder in the first degree *was* present in Ruth Coster's death.

"There need only be sufficient time to formulate the intent to kill, no matter how short — even seconds. Steve Meyer stated that he felt Ruth Coster go limp and he could have stopped then, but he did not: he choked her until she was dead.

"This man is an animal, devoid of any human feeling. He is capable of killing at the snap of a finger, cold-blooded and heartless. He is not fit to walk the streets of Seattle."

Defense attorneys, in their summation,

urged the jury to remain unemotional — to view only the facts in the case — and, particularly, to judge each charge separately. "You will be shown pictures when you enter that jury room which will shock you, but you must struggle to avoid an emotional decision. This man, if convicted of less than first-degree murder, will still undoubtedly spend the rest of his life in prison. He will not be walking the streets of Seattle. He is not like you; his thinking processes are not like yours. Try to project yourselves into the events of that night — to the shock and fear he felt. He had no sleep for days, drank twenty-five or more beers, and was not responsible for his actions."

For an hour the two defense attorneys pleaded eloquently, but it was, perhaps, one of their own phrases that provided Nick Marshall with his strongest rebuttal argument:

"If you will project yourselves, project yourselves instead into the minds of those two girls. Feel the helpless terror they felt. Feel Ruth Coster's agony as the life was squeezed from her. Steven Meyer said he felt 'sorry' for Mallory Gilbert when he saw she was still breathing. Yet, he went calmly about washing her blood from himself and changing clothes as she lay there gurgling, choking on her own blood."

The sun was gone from the courtroom windows and stormy gray clouds lowered outside by the time the final arguments were over.

On Friday, March 14, 1969, at 3:30 p.m., the jury retired to make their decision. The bailiff followed them with the physical evidence: a score of photographs, the victim's nightgown, the defendant's knife that had broken in half by the force of the attack and was still stained scarlet, carrying with it the memory of Mallory Gilbert's testimony that Steve Meyer had taken half of that blade to slash her several more times as she sat on the floor, already grievously wounded.

Most of us in that courtroom expected a quick verdict and were loath to leave the courthouse, so we sat on the benches that lined the marble hallways outside Judge Revelle's courtroom. I watched Steven Meyer as he was led, hands manacled behind him, toward the jail elevator. He would wait to hear his fate in his cell, and would be brought back into the courtroom only when the jurors were finished adjudicating. As he walked the long courthouse hallway, he passed Mallory Gilbert and slowed his step to stare curiously at her.

What did he want? Was he going to apologize? Was he, perhaps, reliving whatever rush he'd experienced as he plunged the knife into the soft flesh of her neck again and again?

The pretty brunette drew her coat more closely around her and looked straight ahead, although she had to know that the man who had tried to kill her was only three or four feet away. The regular elevator, used by court personnel and visitors, stopped, the doors slid open, and she stepped in, mercifully through at last with her unbelievable ordeal. She did not intend to wait around for the final chapter.

The jurors took longer than most of us had wagered. At ten p.m. on Friday night, after seven hours of deliberation — minus a dinner break — they announced that they had reached a verdict. Steven Terry Meyer was found guilty of murder in the first degree and guilty of first-degree assault. However, they did not recommend the death penalty. With recommendations by the prosecuting and defense attorneys, the Washington State's Board of Prison Terms and Paroles eventually set Meyer's sentence as life in prison. That didn't mean much: life was really thirteen years and four months. Meyer also had the right to appeal.

Just as the death sentence doesn't always mean death, a life sentence can't be taken literally, either — unless it is mandatory.

In 2004, Steven Terry Meyer turned 56 years old. He had been paroled sometime during the eighties, but he violated his parole when he was convicted of sodomy and on illegal drug charges. By 1996, Meyer was back in prison. He now resides in the Airway Heights prison in Spokane, Washington, one of Washington State's newest prisons.

His earliest possible release date is January 22, 2007.

He will be almost 60.

Mallory Gilbert returned to life outside media headlines. She, too, would be in her mid-fifties now.

The Lonely Hearts Killer

Although the phenomenon of serial murder was not widely recognized until the early 1980s — when it was embraced enthusiastically by the media — the first significant modern-day killer of this genre was largely ignored, at least outside the boundaries of Los Angeles, California.

Jack the Ripper was a serial killer. So were Albert Fish, who killed children, and the Boston Strangler, Albert DeSalvo — who some believe was not as prolific a murderer as he is usually portrayed as being — convicted of killing mostly elderly women in the nursing or music professions. There have been many other murderers whose victim tolls were high but who failed to garner sweeping headlines. Even so, all multiple killers were referred to as *mass murderers.*

That was the term used by even the most sophisticated criminologists — until Pierce R. Brooks, a Los Angeles detective doing research on his off-duty hours, focused on the kind of murderer who picks a specific victim type and literally becomes *addicted* to murder, taking one or two victims at a time, over a long time, until he is either caught or dead.

The Harvey Glatman case is a classic, made more so because it predated the Boston Strangler — considered by most experts to be the first serial killer in modern culture. Glatman's murders made headlines in Los Angeles and Southern California, but they were largely eclipsed nationally by coverage of Charles Starkweather, the spree killer who traveled west in the late fifties with his teenage girlfriend, Caril Ann Fugate, killing anyone who blocked his path or had something he wanted. Starkweather was not a true serial killer: he fell into the category of a "spree killer." Neither was William Heirens of Chicago, the young premed student who killed two adult women and 5-year-old Suzanne Degnan in 1943, scrawling on the wall of one victim in her own lipstick "Catch me before I kill more!" Heirens's victims had no particular profile that singled them out as fitting within certain descriptive parameters.

Pierce Brooks, who may be better known as the prime investigator in the "Onion Field murder" of a fellow law enforcement officer, was never a man to toot his own horn, but I believe he did more to help both police officers and laymen understand the threat of serial murder than anyone I ever knew.

I consider Pierce Brooks my mentor, an outstanding detective whom his subordinates admired, a quiet man whose mind was always working. It was Brooks who called me out of the blue in 1983 and said, "This is Pierce Brooks — you may have heard of me."

I had, but I certainly never expected that a man as revered as he was in law enforcement circles would be calling me. Brooks invited me to participate in the task force that was being formed to set up a tracking system to catch serial killers. It would be called VICAP (Violent Criminal Apprehension Program), and representatives from the U.S. Justice Department, the FBI, and law enforcement agencies in every state in America were prepared to meet at Sam Houston State University in Huntsville, Texas, and see that it succeeded.

One of the biggest problems lawmen faced was the growing mobility of roving killers. There had to be a better way to keep track of murderers who were clever enough to kill their victims in one police jurisdiction, leave the bodies in a second jurisdiction, and then move on to a new killing ground.

In the eighties, most police departments didn't routinely use computers as a large part of their investigations, and identification based on DNA was on a distant horizon, but Pierce Brooks believed the only way to catch the most elusive slayers was to recognize the patterns of serial murder, and to make it easier for far-flung law enforcement agencies to communicate.

I became part of that VICAP task force at Brooks's invitation after I presented a four-hour seminar on the fatal travels of Ted Bundy, who had taken victims in Washington, Oregon, Idaho, Utah, Colorado, and Florida, and probably in other states.

Bundy may have been the "poster boy" for serial murder in the eighties as the concept became known, but it was a sadistic sociopath named Harvey Glatman who raised Pierce Brooks's antennae and his curiosity back in the late fifties.

Glatman was Brooks's prototype as the detective read scores of books, journals, and periodicals, looking for other murderers who operated in a serial manner.

No matter how many criminologists and detectives claim that *they* were the first to recognize the dark phenomenon of serial murder and coin the term *serial killer*, the truth is that it was Pierce Brooks.

When the FBI's Behavioral Science Unit was formed, many of the astute special agents had also detected the similar patterns of an especially deadly kind of killer. Howard Teten, Roy Hazelwood, John Douglas, Gregg McCrary, and Bob Ressler were seeing commonalities in the multiple murderers they profiled and interviewed — people like Edmund Kemper, Coral Eugene Watts, and David Berkowitz. Good fortune and shared ideas brought them together with Brooks and Bob Heck of the U.S. Justice Department in working to establish VICAP.

My assignment in the VICAP task force was to work with a New York detective who had been instrumental in capturing Berkowitz, the "Son of Sam" serial killer. We did the first mock-up of a questionnaire that would be sent to any police agency requesting help in closing unsolved murder cases that fit within the parameters of those committed by sadistic sociopaths.

There were so many aspects to consider: victim description, method of murder, posture of the corpse, day of the week, time of the month and year, season, weather, topography, occupation of victim, sex of victim, age, "souvenirs" probably taken from the body site by the killer . . . Each aspect we thought of seemed to bring three more that needed to be added to the questionnaire. Long after I left the task force, the final form consisted of scores of pages.

VICAP was Pierce Brooks's vision of how to track and trap a serial killer come true.

And Harvey Glatman was the macabre inspiration who began it all thirty years earlier.

A Los Angeles detective in 1957 had to get his satisfaction from a job well done; an honest policeman wasn't going to get rich. In December of that year, the Chief of Police made $18,500. A detective sergeant grossed $575 a month. That was less than the one "City Mother" who cared for abandoned children and made $641.

Los Angeles was a different world in the late 1950s. There were still orchards full of blooming orange trees in between the buildings, there was no graffiti, no gangbangers — no *gangs* as we know them now for that matter — and most citizens respected their police department. In 1958 — in the *entire year* of 1958 — Los Angeles policemen seized only 4,523 barbiturate tablets, 37 capsules of cocaine, and 148 pounds of marijuana.

In 1957, Pierce Brooks was a handsome detective in his mid-thirties who wore a fedora and chain-smoked. He was the epitome of what television viewers expected an LAPD detective to be. He even served as a technical adviser to Jack Webb and the immensely popular *Dragnet* series. Brooks made sure that Webb's fictional depictions, based on actual cases, rang true. He was also a certified blimp pilot and had his picture taken once as he piloted a blimp high above Los Angeles: his passenger that day was Howard Hughes's discovery, Jane Russell. One day, he would be featured as the detective sergeant whose interrogations tripped up the cop-killers in Joe Wambaugh's *The Onion Field*.

Pierce Brooks worked scores of homicide cases; it was in 1958 that he found himself working concurrent unsolved cases — one that involved multiple murders and one with a series of violent rapes. It seemed to him that there had to be some way to find out if there were other jurisdictions working similar cases.

Somewhat naively — because he was so far ahead of technology — Brooks went in to talk to the Chief of Police. He asked if the Los Angeles Police Department might be able to buy a computer. The chief checked it out and called Brooks in. "For one thing, Pierce," he began, "a computer would cost our entire budget for a whole year. For another, it would be so huge that it would fill up the police building and there wouldn't be room for anything else."

Chastened but determined, Pierce Brooks began his own primitive "human computer" project. Every day after his shift was over, he went to the Los Angeles public library's media room, where he perused out-of-town newspapers for an hour.

"It wasn't a bad deal," he recalled. "I avoided the traffic and I found out what crimes were happening outside Los Angeles. I found my rapist that way. But I didn't find Shirley Bridgeford's killer — not then."

Shirley Ann Bridgeford haunted Brooks. She was a 30-year-old divorcée with two little boys. She had virtually nothing going for her beyond her extended family who loved her. Shirley was plain — even a little homely. She'd given herself a home permanent and it left her with curls that were too tight, making her bad haircut even worse. She was thin and flat-chested and her elbows and knees were knobby. Her nose was a little too large for her face, and her complexion was flawed. Shirley just wasn't the sort of woman that men would approach for a date. Any money she made went to support her two little boys, so she did the best she could without spending it at a beauty parlor.

Shirley Bridgeford was very shy and she was poor enough that she couldn't even think about affording an apartment for herself and her sons. For the moment, she had to live with her sister's family, but she still had romantic dreams of remarrying someone who would be kind and caring and provide a nice home for all of them.

She had answered personal ads, but nothing came of it. Then she signed up with a lonely hearts club on S. Vermont Street. It was called "Patti Sullivan's Lonely Hearts Club." "Patti" — whose real name was Irby Lameroux — would give out the names, addresses, and phone numbers of three women to any man with ten dollars and a driver's license, ostensibly to verify that he was who he said he was.

Shirley wasn't expecting Prince Charming; she hoped instead for a Nice Guy. Early in March 1958, she received a phone call from a man who said his name was George Williams. Patti Sullivan had given him Shirley's name and phone number. He sounded kind of shy and stammered a little when he said he was a plumber.

Well, that was okay. Plumbers weren't exactly exciting, but they made a good, solid living. Shirley agreed to go dancing with Williams on Saturday night, March 8. She hoped that he was a little more interesting in person than he had sounded on the phone.

Shirley dressed carefully for her date, playing up her good features, like her slender waist. First the undergarments: a lacy slip and a panty girdle — which all women wore in the fifties — along with a garter belt that held up her nylons. She chose a pastel dress with a bertha collar, draped at the neckline. The extra flounces of material made her look bustier. Her belt was black with a huge gold buckle, and she wore black high heels.

George Williams showed up about half an hour early, while Shirley was still getting dressed. That made her nervous. She couldn't see him, but she could hear him in the living room talking to her family as she threw on her clothes more hurriedly than she'd planned.

When she walked out, her heart sank. She met her sister's eyes and both women silently agreed with their raised eyebrows that Williams was not the kind of man they'd been hoping for. They excused themselves for a moment and went into the kitchen to talk.

Later, Shirley's sister told Pierce Brooks

that Shirley didn't want to go on the date at all. "But she didn't want to hurt his feelings," Shirley's sister said. "She's like that. He didn't look very attractive, and he certainly didn't smell very good, but she couldn't think of an excuse not to go. She decided she would go for an hour or so, and then make an excuse so she could come home early."

George Williams hadn't seemed very taken with Shirley, either, but his conversational abilities were so lacking that it was hard to tell what he was thinking. Shirley Bridgeford shot her sister a last despairing look as she slipped into her coat.

An hour passed, and then two. As midnight came and went, Shirley's family began to worry. What had seemed only a disappointing blind date was turning into something far worse. In fact, the last time anyone ever saw Shirley Bridgeford alive was on that Saturday night, just as spring came to Los Angeles in 1958.

It was to be a spring full of portents and shocking news, rife with headlines, many of them centering around Los Angeles. Show business entrepreneur Mike Todd's plane crashed in a violent storm and Elizabeth Taylor mourned; Lana Turner's teenage daughter, Cheryl, confessed to having fatally stabbed Johnny Stompanato, her mother's gangster lover; and Elvis Presley was inducted into the Army — all within the space of two and a half weeks.

Pierce Brooks scarcely noticed. He was working around the clock trying to find Shirley Bridgeford. All her family knew for sure was that she had left on a blind date with a man referred by Patti Sullivan's Lonely Hearts Club. They described him as being about 30, Caucasian, with dark hair. He was about five feet ten but couldn't have weighed more than 145 pounds. "He had a large nose," Shirley's brother-in-law said, "and it was kind of bulbous on the end."

"He's a plumber named George Williams," Shirley's sister said. They had no idea where he lived, and they weren't sure what kind of car he drove. "He's got big ears, though," a family member said. "*Really* big ears, but it wasn't just the way he looked. Shirley just didn't want to go out with him."

As Pierce Brooks feared, Patti Sullivan knew nothing about "George Williams." She'd barely glanced at his driver's license. She had no address on file for him, and she couldn't even remember what he looked like, or the names of the two other women on her list that she might have given him. For Patti, he'd been only a quick ten bucks. She promised to contact Brooks at once if "Williams" should return for more women's names.

Of course, he didn't.

Brooks found a lot of George Williamses in the Los Angeles area, and some were plumbers as Shirley's blind date had said he was. But none of them looked like the description given for Shirley Bridgeford's blind date. And they all had alibis for the night of March 8. The detective sergeant figured from the beginning that "Williams" had given both Patti Sullivan and Shirley Bridgeford a fake name.

Shirley was just *gone,* and as days and then weeks went by with no word from her, it seemed likely that she was dead. Still, none of the unidentified bodies of young women in the Los Angeles County Morgue resembled her.

In the end, Brooks would find her body, and he would chart a pattern as clear as a flight plan. But only in retrospect. And that would fill him with a fire to identify patterns of serial murder early on so that he could stalk the killers even as they stalked their victims.

For the thousandth time, he wished that there could be some central clearinghouse — like the computer that was still out of the question — where he could look for similar victims, suspects, and M.O.'s under investigation in other police agencies. Instead, he read through all the LAPD's missing-persons reports involving women and then he went back to the library to pore through newspapers. He'd solved three cases through his library research already, so he kept spending at least an hour a day there.

One missing Los Angeles woman had virtually nothing in common with Shirley Bridgeford. Like thousands of other young women, she had come to Hollywood believing that her looks could propel her into the heady life of a movie star. If that had happened, the first thing powerful studio executives would have changed would have been her name: Judy Dull.

At 19, Judy Ann Dull was very pretty and she had a figure that would rival Marilyn Monroe's. She was a blue-eyed blonde too. She found an apartment at 1304 N. Sweetzer in West Hollywood, sharing the rent with a roommate. In the glory days decades before, many big stars owned homes on Sweetzer: Charlie Chaplin, for example. The brick houses were comfortable and cottagelike, with stucco interiors, dark oak beams and flower-filled courtyards. Later, they were divided into apartments that were far more utilitarian.

The fact that Sweetzer was close to Hollywood Boulevard was thrilling to Judy. She was as beautiful as Shirley Bridgeford was plain. Given other circumstances — a little luck and, hopefully, a new name — Judy Dull could have gone far in Hollywood, but so much of stardom is a matter of timing and luck, and Judy missed out on both. Marilyn Monroe and Jayne Mansfield already had a lock on the voluptuous-blonde image, and Sandra Dee was the leading sweet-faced blonde. So Judy took whatever jobs she could, and she was grateful for the chance to make $50 modeling for "Johnny Glenn," a Hollywood freelance photographer. Johnny had met her roommate first, but he had quickly noticed some pictures of Judy and asked if he might meet and photograph her.

It was late July 1957 when Judy Dull heard from Glenn. She was divorced with a child who was living with her ex-husband. She wanted desperately to get custody, but she needed money for an attorney to do that. On August 1, Glenn picked her up at her apartment, although the arrangement had originally been that he would photograph her there. He explained quickly that the lighting in her apartment wasn't suitable, and that his studio caught the light perfectly.

His "studio" was really his apartment. He lived at 5924 Melrose. Today, Melrose, which runs parallel to and a block away from Santa Monica Boulevard, is where the stars shop for trendy clothes, furniture, and antiques. It wasn't quite as fashionable in 1957. Still, everything seemed all right to Judy Dull; there were lights and other camera gear set up. Johnny Glenn's apartment was small, but it was neat enough. Some of his furniture was rather nice: classic mahogany veneer — a round end table, a coffee table. But the chair he wanted Judy to pose in was a cheap-looking easy chair with the kind of stretchy cover sold at Sears, Roebuck to hide worn upholstery.

He explained to Judy that he had been commissioned to take pictures for a fact-detective magazine. All the covers featured women in jeopardy. So he would have to tie her hands and ankles and put a gag in her mouth, and she would be required to act a little and look frightened. She agreed to the first poses. It wasn't as if she was half-nude; she wore a long tailored skirt, a sweater that buttoned up the front with two dozen tiny buttons, open-toed pumps with four-inch heels, and nylons with the usual seam in the back.

The first pictures of Judy weren't disturbing. The gag in her mouth looked loose, and so did the white rope binding her ankles. At Glenn's direction, she opened her eyes wide and looked up to her left as if she were watching someone warily.

It would be a long time before anyone saw Judy's photos, and they would never appear on the cover of *True Detective* magazine, although some pictures of her would be printed *inside* the fact-detective monthly. . . .

The pictures "Johnny Glenn" took still exist. Initially, Judy Dull's expression of horror is plainly bad acting. In later frames, the gag in her mouth has been cinched tight, her knees are bound together, her sweater is unbuttoned to show her bra, and her skirt is gone: she wears only a half-slip. Even so, she showed far less skin than most starlets do in 2004. But, later, there is no question that Judy has realized she has made a terrible mistake.

At the end of the roll of film, she is naked except for her nylons, which fall below her knees, her nose is bloodied, and her expression is all too real. She is clearly a captive, caught in a bondage scene that wouldn't be publishable in the kinkiest magazine. Judy Dull's expression is one of dread resignation, as if she has been raped and she knows she is going to die.

When Pierce Brooks read the file on Judy Dull's disappearance, she was still missing. And he had no way of knowing then that the ghastly photographs of her even existed. All her roommate had been able to tell detectives who worked the West Hollywood district was that Judy hadn't come back from an appointment with a magazine photographer named Johnny Glenn.

The roommate described Glenn and co-operated with a police artist who came up with a sketch of the man Judy was supposed to meet on August 1. He looked like an accountant with his short hair and horn-rimmed glasses. And he had large ears that stood out from his head like the open doors of a car.

Nobody seemed to know who he was. He'd shown up at a few low-budget studios where photographers could pay by the session to take pictures of the models that were available to pose there, many of them nude or nearly nude.

There was a seven-month time span between the disappearances of Judy Dull and Shirley Bridgeford. The victim type was completely dissimilar, of course. The artist's sketch, however, matched the description witnesses had given in each case. One man had gotten a name from a lonely hearts dating service, and the other from a modeling agency. They were both stranger-to-stranger encounters.

It was only four months after Shirley Bridgeford disappeared that another woman agreed to model for a stranger. Ruth Mercado, 24, who sometimes went by the name of Angie or Angela Rojas, didn't look like either of the first two missing women. She had olive skin and long black hair that she usually wore pulled back, leaving tendrils curling around her face. She had classic features and an opulent figure. Ruth Mercado had come to Los Angeles from New York, and she was a bit more worldly-wise than Judy Dull, and nowhere near as naive as Shirley Bridgeford.

In the middle of July 1958, Ruth Mercado, using the name Angela Rojas, advertised in the *Los Angeles Times* seeking modeling jobs. A man named Harvey called and arranged to meet her at her apartment at 3714 W. Pico Boulevard. They settled on a price and she agreed to pose for him as long as their photo session took place in *her* apartment.

When he showed up, he wasn't very professional looking, although you couldn't really tell with photographers: some of them weren't at all concerned with *how* they looked. It was the models they were fussy about. And this guy had a state-of-the-art Rolleiflex camera around his neck.

Ruth let him in, and bought his story about shooting covers for the detective magazines. Only after he had bound her hands behind her, tied clothesline around her ankles, and had a gag in place in her mouth, did she realize why he had really answered her ad.

He would spend the night and the next day and night alone with her. And then the apartment on Pico was left unoccupied, and Ruth Mercado was never seen there again.

Now there were more similarities. Two of the missing women had been models who had agreed to photo sessions with photographers they didn't really know.

There were no witnesses to Ruth Mercado's meeting with the photographer, and she had made her own arrangements with him when he phoned in response to her ad. So no one knew who she had left with, or even if she had met the man at her apartment or someplace else.

They were the most difficult kind of case to solve: the women didn't know each other, the cameraman hadn't seen any of them before he met them, and there were no bodies to discover and, consequently, no evidence to be gleaned from them. No one could be sure that Shirley, Judy, and Ruth/Angela were dead. In Hollywood, women moved on every day, disillusioned by unfulfilled expectations, broke, and ready to try their luck in another city.

But Pierce Brooks doubted that Shirley Bridgeford would have deliberately left her two little boys behind. And Judy Dull, for all her dreams of stardom, had been trying so hard to regain custody of her child. Only Ruth Mercado was a free agent.

The man with the big ears and glasses who stared back at Brooks from the sketch drawn by the police artist looked like thousands of other guys in Los Angeles. *Who was he?* And *where was he?*

Or was he, perhaps, *three different men,* all

of them nondescript?

As Brooks checked out every report on sexual attacks and missing women that came into the Los Angeles Police Department, a man named "Frank Johnson" started showing up at a modeling agency on Sunset Boulevard. The women who posed were neither starlets nor prostitutes; they were looking for legitimate assignments to pose for ads or magazine still shots.

Frank Johnson's hair was greasy and dirty, and he smelled rank, as if he wore the same clothes day after day and perspired a lot in the hot southern California sun. But he became a familiar figure at the studio and he had the thirty to fifty dollars it cost to hire a model for an hour or two. The studio had their own rooms and studios where photo sessions could be held in relative privacy.

Lorraine Vigil hadn't been with the studio long, and she was anxious to build a regular clientele of photographers who would ask for her. She was an attractive woman, with Hispanic coloring and features. Sonya,★ the proprietress of "Sonya's Still Shots," sometimes worked as a model herself, but she didn't like the hinky feeling she got from Frank Johnson, and she gave him an excuse when he sought to hire her to pose for him. Instead, she suggested Lorraine Vigil.

Lorraine was initially pleased to get the assignment and gave Johnson her address. They agreed that he would pick her up on the evening of October 27, 1958. He said he would drive her to Sonya's studio and would probably need her for a two-hour session.

Sonya felt slightly guilty about pushing Johnson onto Lorraine Vigil, so she warned her new model that Johnson was a little weird, although she was hard put to say what it was about him that bothered her — except the way he smelled. The minute Lorraine was in Frank Johnson's car, her nose told her that Sonya had been right. It was a junker of a car, too, the cheapest Dodge model of several years earlier.

Lorraine had already accepted $10 in advance and so she didn't argue with him as he turned in the opposite direction from where Sonya's studio was located on the Sunset Strip. Instead, he headed down Santa Monica Boulevard toward the freeway that led south into Orange County, explaining that there'd been a change in plans. He told her that Sonya's studio was already booked, but he had another location that would work even better.

Lorraine got more and more suspicious as they left Los Angeles far behind. They were at least forty miles south, and whizzing past exits that led to Anaheim and Santa Ana. She saw a sign that said Tustin, which wasn't far from Santa Ana. Any farther and they would be in the desert, a lonely place where nothing much survived beyond yuccas and rattlesnakes.

He had told her that he lived past Anaheim. But the skin on the back of her neck prickled when he took an off-ramp that seemed to lead to nothing but orange groves.

Serial killers then — and now — are invariably caught by accident. Either something goes wrong with their carefully executed plans or they are tripped up by a minor traffic violation, defective equipment, or, rarely, a victim who does not react as the killer expects. Unlike the other women, Lorraine Vigil shouted at the man behind the wheel, demanding to know where he was going. Rattled, he wrenched the wheel and skidded into a narrow turnout beside the road. Frank Johnson reached beneath his seat and pulled out a gun, instructing her not to fight him. "Don't cause any trouble," he said. "I probably would shoot you if you do."

"Do you want to rape me?" Lorraine Vigil asked.

"Maybe I will. Maybe not." He hadn't expected such a direct question.

"Well, you can rape me," she said with a hardness in her voice. "But don't shoot me."

In his previous three encounters with his chosen victims, he had felt entirely in control, but Lorraine Vigil threw him off balance. "I had a piece of rope in my pocket and I wanted to get more assured of my control over her," he said later. "I wasn't too sure of her at this point. She seemed kind of edgy, so I told her to put her hands behind her back and I started to make a little loop and I put it over one wrist. I had laid the gun down on the seat because I needed both hands for this, and she seemed to be very balky . . ."

She fought him, kicking and clawing, desperate to get out of the car. She was not going to go quietly. There beside the Santa Ana Freeway, she screamed and tried to shatter the windshield with her heel. Yes, he had a gun in his hand, but that didn't stop her from struggling to get away from him. In their fight over the gun, it went off, leaving a grazing wound on Lorraine's thigh as it narrowly missed doing internal damage.

But it must have scared Frank Johnson, too, because he lost his grip on his handgun and she grabbed it away from him. She ran into the road, preferring to be run over than face whatever he had planned for her. He chased after her blindly and then realized that the tables were turned: she was pointing his own gun at him.

California highway patrolman Tom Mulligan had already slowed his patrol car when he saw the car parked diagonally beside the busy road, and then he saw the woman in her torn clothing and the man who still threatened her. Lorraine Vigil had uncommonly good luck that warm night just before Halloween when Mulligan rescued her and arrested the man who had kidnapped her.

His name wasn't George Williams or Johnny Glenn or Frank Johnson — or any of the other common names he had given to people he didn't want to remember him. His name was Harvey Glatman.

He was taken to the Orange County Sheriff's Office in Santa Ana, and it wasn't long before L.A. detectives Pierce Brooks and Elmer Jackson heard about his arrest. Lorraine Vigil's description of what had happened to her answered a lot of their questions. She had almost become the *third* model to disappear after making an appointment to pose for a stranger. Her captor was clearly heading for the desert with her, and Brooks doubted that she would have been with Glatman on the trip back.

He and Jackson set out immediately to talk with the prisoner.

With skilled interrogation by Brooks and Jackson and San Diego County detectives Lieutenant Tom Isbell and Sergeant R. B. Majors, the most detailed confession they had ever elicited emerged.

They knew where Judy Dull was. Her scattered remains had been found more than a hundred miles from Los Angeles, in the desert between Palm Springs and Indio in the autumn of 1957. Still, it had taken months to identify her through dental records. There was a commonality here. Brooks figured that if Judy had been left in the desert, and Lorraine Vigil and Harvey Glatman were headed into another desolate section more than an hour away from Los Angeles, there was a good chance that

that was where they would find Shirley Bridgeford and Ruth Mercado.

Still, there were so many square miles of desert stretching south and east of Los Angeles County, Brooks doubted that they would ever find the missing women unless Harvey Glatman chose to tell them exactly where he had left them.

In custody, Harvey Glatman lost any power he might have had. He had shown himself to be an extremely dangerous sexual predator — but that was only when he faced helpless women. Now he was up against investigators who had been frustrated at the ease with which he spirited women away, and Harvey wasn't so tough.

When Pierce Brooks checked Glatman's background, he realized that the man in custody had been a walking nightmare since before he entered puberty. He was *exactly* the kind of killer Brooks had been tracking: a sadistic sociopath who had managed to avoid the attention of police many times because he left one jurisdiction for another — and before 1985, there was no central clearinghouse for detectives across the United States to follow the bloody trail of killers like Glatman.

Thirty years old at the time of his arrest

in 1958, Harvey Glatman would become the archetype for every serial killer who came after. Although it was to take him three decades, Brooks was determined to see that killers who were addicted to murder would be stopped before they ran up horrendous tolls.

Harvey Glatman was the only child of a Jewish couple who had emigrated from Europe to the Bronx. When he was born in December 1927, his parents were eking out a spare living from the small stationery store they owned. Harvey's mother, Ophelia, would recall later that she and her husband worked twelve-hour days, seven days a week.

Harvey Glatman was an absolutely brilliant — but strange — child. Totally indulged by his mother, he would always be something of a loner and inadequate when it came to relating to females. Other children, male and female, sensed that he wasn't like them; he seemed to have no interest in joining in their activities in school or on the playground. He was the skinny boy in corduroy knickers who stood at the edge of any group.

Harvey was fascinated with ropes from the time he was three — and with masochistic masturbation. On one occasion, Ophelia Glatman was horrified to discover that her toddler son had tied a string to his penis, placed the other end in a drawer, and was leaning back to enjoy the sensation. Unable to deal with such "nastiness," she put it out of her mind.

Harvey's father, Albert, never a success at business, finally gave it up in 1930 and moved his family from New York to Denver, where they had relatives. The best job he ever had was as a cabdriver in Denver.

While they lived in Colorado, Harvey's parents had to face the fact that he had severe problems. At 12, he returned home one day with rope burns on his neck. They were fearful that he was suicidal, but it wasn't that: he had discovered a new way to reach a sexual high. He described to detectives later how he had hanged himself, deriving sexual pleasure at the moment he began to pass out. He was, of course, engaging in autoeroticism by strangulation, although psychiatrists who did early studies on his personality did not use the term.

Autoeroticism is more dangerous to those who practice it than it is to anyone else. Experts like retired FBI Special Agent

Russ Vorpagel, who presents seminars on this particular form of sexual aberration, have gathered scores of photographs of deceased subjects. They are usually dressed in either black leather or frilly feminine underwear, but they are all restrained by ropes, scarves, chains, and locks. Their addiction to an orgasm accentuated by being choked escalates to a point where being bound adds to the thrill. Some of them challenge themselves in a dark game where they have to get out of the locks and chains before it is too late.

And, from the awful photographs taken by crime scene investigators, many of them obviously lost the race. Ordinarily, as they pass out from near-strangulation, it's only for the moment. But some don't come back at all: they die because they actually hang themselves when they are unable to undo their bonds or when they kick over the stool they stand on. Some come to after choking dozens of times, but then, one day, they don't.

Finding the body of someone who has died during an autoerotic episode is, of course, a horrible way for wives and families to discover a sexual secret they never knew about.

The tragic victims who met Harvey

Glatman some years later might still be alive if Harvey had suffered such a fate — but, despite his risky practices, he survived.

Harvey Glatman's parents had at least a partial idea of their son's sexual preoccupation. Harvey and his father had bitter disagreements over masturbation. Harvey grew up totally obsessed with sex and females, and yet he was terrified of actually approaching girls to ask for a date. If ever a young male's psychopathology predicted tragedy, it was Harvey Glatman's.

Harvey had a genius I.Q. and he was a talented musician and skilled in science. His constant dream was to become famous; he longed to be a celebrity, someone who would appear in the headlines of the newspapers and on radio — and, after it was invented, on television. He was so obsessed with the need for celebrity that it didn't seem to matter to him if he was famous or infamous.

Pierce Brooks found more and more indications that Harvey Glatman had apparently never been normal. His autoerotic asphyxiation obsession changed to something more dangerous by the time the Glatmans moved to Denver. He began — as William Heirens had in Chicago —

breaking into houses, where the act of crossing a forbidden threshold or window sill gave him a sexual thrill. He stole things only as an afterthought, probably to take souvenirs.

Next, like Gary Ridgway, the "Green River Killer," and Jerome Brudos, the "Lust Killer" — both of whom came much later — Glatman looked for pretty girls on the street, watched them, and followed them, enjoying the sense of power that came with their ignorance that he had them in his "sights."

Like almost all sexual predation, Glatman's voyeurism progressed to a point where he actually confronted women in their bedrooms at night. Harvey didn't rape them, but he now tied *them* up, rather than himself. He used a gag to quiet them — a new twist that would become a part of his scenarios that gave him orgasms. Once the women he chose were helpless to fight back, he put his hands on the most private places of their bodies.

Harvey was still in high school.

He touched some young women in the darkness of their bedrooms, but he actually abducted a woman when he was 17, took her to a desolate spot, tied her up, and felt her body. He was still too timid to commit rape, and he took her back to her house before the sun came up.

This time he was caught, charged with some of his burglaries and with molestation, and sent to the Colorado State Prison for a year.

A detective at that time didn't take Harvey's sexual fumblings very seriously; he characterized the crimes as "girl trouble."

When the teenage Glatman was paroled in Colorado, his mother quickly spirited him off to Yonkers, New York, and found him a nice little apartment. She enrolled him in a course in television repair. Then she went back to Denver, sure that Harvey's troubles were over. Actually, they were only beginning. His need for bondage and sexual attacks grew, and he was never without a length of rope and a small handgun in case he spotted a woman who attracted him. He still was too fainthearted to actually *rape* the women he tied up until they were completely helpless. But each incident made him bolder, and it took more and more invasion of their privacy to turn him on. On occasion, he even confronted couples — but he only tied up the man so he could have pleasure from the woman.

He was caught again, and this time he

was sentenced to five to ten years in the New York prison facilities of Elmira and Sing Sing. Psychiatrists who examined Harvey concurred that he wasn't out-and-out crazy at all, but suggested that his sociopathy be treated — something that has yet to succeed with any antisocial subject. It was a naive and misguided suggestion. It just doesn't work.

Sociopaths have no conscience, no guilt, no empathy, and no remorse. Harvey Glatman had never been able to identify with the emotions of other human beings. He'd always taken what he wanted and what gave him pleasure. Still, like most sociopaths, he was an easy prisoner and earned a lot of "good time" — so much good time that he was out of prison in less than three years. According to his parole restrictions, he had to live with his parents.

The elder Glatman continued to drive a cab in Denver, and he died in the driver's seat in October 1952, when Harvey was 24.

But by the fall of 1956, Harvey Glatman, 28, was finally off parole and on his own. He headed to California to seek his fortune and find the fame that had always eluded him.

Although he had never dated, his

thoughts were still completely consumed with women — with controlling women, touching them, and maybe even having sex with them in a situation where he was the powerful one. Not surprisingly, Glatman's demeanor turned women off, and the suspicious ones who simply turned away from him survived, never knowing how lucky they were.

Harvey supported himself with his TV repair business. It could be quite lucrative in the late fifties. Most families had only one television set and they were lost when something went wrong, which happened often.

For his entertainment and pleasure, he used his camera and his visits to the studios in West Hollywood, where he was pleased to find there were women who would take their clothing off and let him "shoot" them for $30 an hour. For a while, that was enough.

Clearly, he had gone over the edge. While some masochists are satisfied with mutilating and scarring only themselves, it is not unusual for them to transfer their aberration to hurting other people. The line between masochism and sadism is very thin. Harvey crossed that when he moved to Los Angeles. Pierce Brooks realized that if Lorraine Vigil hadn't been able to get away from Glatman, he would undoubtedly have continued to abduct and murder hapless women.

Captive now, and once he was cleaned up and shaved, Glatman looked just like the artist's sketch done from witness descriptions. But, more than that, Harvey resembled Eddie Fisher, who was at the height of his popularity in the fifties. The resemblance was almost uncanny. Even so, the features that made teenage girls fall in love with Fisher didn't quite match up in Glatman. His cheeks were a little fuller, his hair not as wavy. And he certainly didn't have the expansive self-esteem that Eddie did. What's more, his personal hygiene left a lot to be desired.

Pierce Brooks was never the tough, confrontational interrogator. He was far more interested in finding the remains of Shirley Bridgeford and Ruth Mercado — and who knew how many other victims — than he was in frightening his suspect. They had Glatman — he wasn't going anywhere — and Brooks had a lot of questions to ask the killer who had eluded him for sixteen months. He also wanted to know what made Harvey Glatman tick.

Because Harvey Glatman/George Williams/Johnny Glenn/Frank Johnson, et al. had planned his meetings with his victims and the scenarios that followed with infinite care, no one had had any idea that he was a man acting out his darkest fantasies. And, because no one knew, he'd continued. He took care of every detail from the food they would eat, the name he would use, and the murder weapons, to the route to the desert, the cameras, and the film.

Glatman slipped when he assumed that Pierce Brooks and his fellow detectives knew about the stash of photos he kept hidden in a toolbox in his apartment. Once he mentioned that, his confessions bubbled up like geysers.

And the photo souvenirs he had kept to remind him of the power he'd had over his victims were probably the most shocking any of the California investigators had ever — or *would* ever — see.

Looking at the awful pictures, they noted that Glatman had kept a visual timeline from the moment his unsuspecting model victims had begun to pose for him. Ruth Mercado and Judy Dull didn't look afraid in the beginning, but gradually fear dawned in their eyes as they realized they were actually tied up and could not get free.

Judy Dull in her long skirt and neatly buttoned sweater, and then with her skirt pulled up and her slip showing, her sweater opened and her bra visible. The next sequence showed Judy lying on Glatman's floor on her face, literally hog-tied. And the worst photos of all were when she sat almost naked, her face bloodied, her eyes betraying shock and hopelessness.

Harvey Glatman's long confession explained the sequence of events of that afternoon and night. He bragged that he had untied her to rape her, tied her up again, and repeated the process several times. He had even promised that he was going to let her go if she would behave and do as he said.

But, of course, he hadn't meant it. He had taken Judy Ann Dull to the desert close by Indio and strangled her with the ropes that had bound her, leaving her to the animals who would scatter her bones.

As for poor Shirley Bridgeford, there were no "modeling" photos. He had been somewhat disappointed in her appearance. He had expected more for his $10. Harvey said he had simply driven her farther and farther from home, making excuses about why they weren't going to the dance after all, until she realized they were in the desert. He said he had considered just taking her home, but they had driven so far that he decided to kill her too. He saved pictures of Shirley, taken after the sun rose. She sat on her tan coat, in various stages of undress, her hands bound behind her, her ankles lashed together too, and a tight gag in her mouth. Her eyes showed her fear.

"Where is she?" Pierce Brooks asked.

"I can show you," Glatman said. "She's out in the desert, just east of Banner."

And Ruth Mercado. Her photos showed that she was tied up in the same manner as the other women, hands behind her back, knees and ankles bound tightly. She wore a pretty white slip with lace at the bottom. With the desert vegetation behind her, Ruth Mercado had a defiant look on her face, although she clearly didn't look hopeful. It was as if she would not let this creepy little man know that she was afraid.

Glatman said that he had left her in Anza-Borrego Desert State Park too. She was, by his estimation, south of Agua Caliente Hot Springs — but before you got to Coyote Wells or Plaster City.

Looking at a map, Pierce Brooks saw

that Mercado's body had been cruelly thrown away very close to the Mexican border. He wondered if they would find anything left of the mortal remains of Harvey Glatman's victims.

It was a solemn procession of investigators who headed east of Riverside on October 30, 1958, having no idea what they would find. They had seen the terror in the eyes of the women who knew they had no hope. Usually, homicide detectives could only imagine what the moments before victims' deaths had been like for them. This was far worse than looking at the decomposed bodies they routinely saw.

It was hard for them all: they wished so much they could somehow go back and stop the action that came next. But it was much too late.

Pierce Brooks's map of San Diego County as it was in 1958 is markedly different from those found in current atlases. Many communities have sprung up since then. The old map still has Brooks's arrows indicating where the women's bodies were found, written in red pencil, and the distances they were placed from narrow little roads, labeled in blue pen and in his familiar sprawling printing.

After leaving Indio, heading south on

Highway 99 past the Salton Sea, they turned east on the road to Ocotillo and then south again to a spot near the Vallecito Mountains. There, Glatman led them to where he had left Shirley Bridgeford. Her pastel dress was still there, torn and faded in the sun now.

His hands cuffed in front of him, Glatman stood beside Pierce Brooks and pointed to Shirley's decomposed remains. His face was nearly expressionless; it was the lack of affect so common with sadistic sociopaths. Brooks, who had seen it all, looked sickened.

Glatman seemed almost pleased with himself as he led detectives out into the California desert and to the bleak landscape where he had left Judy Ann Dull, Shirley Bridgeford, and Ruth Mercado, and where he had been heading with Lorraine Vigil.

"He was as interested as we were," Pierce Brooks recalled as he pointed to police photographs of the search crew in the desert. "That's Harvey kneeling beside me as I'm looking at what was left of Shirley Bridgeford."

Except for Judy Dull, whose skull had been found earlier, the victims were still out there in the desert. The clothing they wore in the pictures in Harvey Glatman's "collection" was rotted by the sun and scattered by animals, and the victims themselves were reduced to skeletons.

There was very little left of the bodies, but Shirley's coat was there, and the California investigators gathered most of her bones. They would be arranged on a medical examiner's table, making almost a complete skeleton.

The burning sun was descending over the desert when the detectives continued their search south on the ever-narrowing road in Anza-Borrego Desert State Park to the Carrizo Mountain area.

By the time they had spent hours of tedious labor at the Bridgeford body site, they had to finish the search for Ruth Mercado by flashlight. It was an eerie sensation to realize that Glatman's victims had spent hours of torture out here in the darkened desert too.

They found what was left of Ruth Mercado beneath a shaggy yucca tree.

Harvey Glatman was formally arraigned in Case #255504 on November 3, 1958.

Justice came far more swiftly in California almost fifty years ago. Glatman pleaded guilty to first-degree murder, and the only decision left was his punishment. In the punishment phase of the proceedings, Judge William T. Low sentenced him to die in the gas chamber.

Anyone who had listened to the tapes of his detailed confessions might have done so. The years-long delays and postponements of carrying out the death penalty that are familiar today didn't happen often in the late fifties.

On September 18, 1959, Harvey Glatman entered the glass-walled cubicle and was strapped into the death chair. As cyanide capsules were dropped into an acid vat beneath that chair, he inhaled the fatal fumes. He was dead in less than ten minutes, and was probably unconscious long before that.

How many victims did Glatman take? No one knows for certain. There was at least one woman who listened to her gut instinct and backed away from him in time. There were probably others who were afraid to come forward. From what we know about serial killers today, they approach dozens of women for every one who falls for their ruses and devices.

In a sense, Harvey got his wish to become a celebrity; he was never famous but he became infamous, and he made headlines.

Pierce Brooks was present in 1959 when

Harvey Murray Glatman died in California's gas chamber. From that point on, he worked to set up a tracking system to allow police agencies to share information on *serial murder*, the term he chose to describe killers like Glatman. Pierce Brooks went on to be captain of the Los Angeles Police Department's homicide division for a dozen years, and chief of police in Lakewood, Colorado, and Springfield, Oregon. More than twenty years later, Brooks saw his dream come true when the first task force meetings on VICAP took place at Sam Houston State University in 1981. The Violent Criminal Apprehension Program became operative in June 1985 after Brooks testified before the U.S. Senate Judiciary Committee, and he spent a year in Quantico at FBI Headquarters as head of the program.

Brooks, whose book *Officer Down, Code Three* had already saved countless lives of law enforcement officers by forewarning them of situations where cops can get killed — and giving them instructions that would become ingrained reactions to save themselves and others — left several vitally important legacies. VICAP was only one of them.

He was a gentle man, a brilliant man, and "a cop's cop."

The Captive Bride

Certainly, there are women who die — either at a lover's hand or by their own — because the men they're involved with don't love them enough. When most of us cry over love, it's because we can't be with the person we think we must have to be happy. It seems sometimes that all the love songs ever written are about unrequited passion. There are few people who don't remember at least one broken heart. But there is something far worse. Any woman who has ever been entrapped in a relationship where she has become a possession and the focus of obsessive jealousy would agree that being alone — and free — means more than any romantic affair.

There may be a basic difference in the way in which males and females react to rejection. When love has gone, women tend to cry and beg a lover to come back. Rarely do they react with violence. A man who has been cuckolded — or thinks he has — is much more likely to seek to destroy the very woman he has claimed to love.

Throughout history, men have cried, "If I can't have her, then no one can!" A woman who is "loved" by such a man is caught like a butterfly, beating her wings helplessly against an invisible web of ownership. At some point she has stopped loving the man who trapped her and she can't talk herself into loving him again. Neither can she get away.

A young woman named Kaitlyn Merriam*
lived in fear for her life because a man loved
her too much. Although hers was the very
first story I ever wrote about such a phenomenon, I would encounter hundreds of
all-too-similar cases over the years. Kaitlyn's
fate plays over and over in my mind every
time I do. Her life is a classic example for me
every time I think of domestic violence. To
this day, I wish I could go back and change
the ending of her story.

In spring 1978, Kaitlyn Merriam found
herself a virtual prisoner of love. She was a
beautiful young woman, just past her twentieth birthday; she had a loving family, a
good job, and the future that seemed to
promise a long life of happiness. Instead,
she would come to live in utter terror,
afraid of the man who had been everything
to her since she was barely 15 years old.

She made only one mistake: she fell out
of love.

She was Kaitlyn Welles* when she met a
tall, handsome fellow sophomore in Sep-

tember at a Seattle high school. She soon had a crush on Wayne Merriam.* By December, they were going steady. She scribbled his name on her book covers and talked about him continually to her girlfriends. She believed she was in love, but later she would come to realize what she felt was only a crush. Looking back, Kaitlyn would define what she felt as "only puppy love."

The vast majority of couples who begin dating at 15 soon break up, and they date dozens of others before finally deciding on a mate for life. But Kaitlyn and Wayne stayed together. Nobody ever thought of one without the other. Kaitlyn-and-Wayne were a couple, always referred to in one breath as if they were joined at the hip. At first, that seemed wonderful. Kaitlyn never had to worry about having a date for a prom. Her friends actually envied her because Wayne was so crazy about her. They all thought he was "cute" and told her she was lucky.

Even she couldn't remember when she began to feel a little bit smothered. There were times she would have liked to go to a slumber party or to the movies with her friends, but Wayne disapproved of that. Why would she want to do that when she had *him?* She couldn't come up with a really good reason, because she *did* want to be with him, at least most of the time. The only time they ever argued was when she suggested they should have interests of their own. He, however, saw no need for that.

If Kaitlyn ever felt misgivings — and she did — she was dissuaded by Wayne's arguments. He was afraid that they would drift apart like some of their friends if they started "going in different directions." That wasn't what she meant at all, but he saw her need to expand her horizons a little as a threat. Wayne told Kaitlyn how much he loved her, and that he would never love anyone else. He said he couldn't bear it if they broke up.

Kaitlyn wanted to experience a little more of life before she married and settled down for good. Now, she sometimes thought it might be fun if they dated other people, but her suggestion upset him more than she imagined it would. Wayne wouldn't even discuss her dating other boys. She belonged to him; he didn't want anyone else and he couldn't see why she should. Time after time, she gave in to his wishes.

Kaitlyn and Wayne turned 16 and then

17. She wasn't in awe of him any longer, and she suspected she wasn't in love with him, either. She was fond of him, she liked his family, and her family liked him. Sometimes it seemed as though he was more like a brother than a boyfriend. About the only freedom she ever had to be herself was when she worked at the Safeway store near her home. She was able to joke with the other teenagers who worked there without looking over her shoulder to see if Wayne was watching. And it was natural that boys working there would ask her for dates.

But Kaitlyn had to refuse. It would upset Wayne too much. Secretly, she envied her girlfriends, who were caught up in a round of dating, while her life was set on a straight course without any surprises or possibilities. She would graduate, marry Wayne, and live happily ever after.

Their wedding date was set for June, right after they graduated. She had become so used to accepting Wayne's plans that she didn't know how to ask him to slow down. But at this point Kaitlyn had doubts — real doubts. She had never had an adult love, and although she felt true affection for Wayne, she kept thinking that there should be something more. Instinctively, she knew that what she felt was not the overpowering love that a woman should have for the man she married. Propelled by everybody else's enthusiasm, Kaitlyn went through the frantic preparations for her wedding. There were bridal showers, wedding gown fittings, invitations to send. She tried to fight down her feelings of panic. Things were moving too fast. Her friends were excited about going to college but that was out for her. A career was out too. She wanted to shout "Slow down!" but she didn't.

She wasn't ready to get married. Not just get married to Wayne Merriam; she didn't want to marry anyone. Maybe, if she had had a chance to date others, she would have found that it was Wayne she cared about the most after all. But she never had the chance. She didn't even tell her parents, or her sister — who was her best friend — about her reservations. There never seemed to be time, and whenever she tried to discuss slowing down with Wayne, he would begin to cry and tell her that he just couldn't live without her because she meant everything to him.

Wayne idolized her. He told her that all the time. He promised Kaitlyn that once they were married she would see how happy they would be. But if she pulled out of their wedding, he hinted that he might kill himself. Although that was emotional blackmail, she bought it. She couldn't bear the thought of that.

Kaitlyn went through with the wedding ceremony. She had no illusions at that point about the future. It wasn't as if they could separate if it didn't work out. She had been raised in a very strict Protestant church in which divorce was not an option. Once you were married, you were married. Even though she felt as though she'd been dragged through a tunnel with no exits until she reached the altar, she was determined that her marriage would be for keeps.

No one who saw her blinding smile as she threw her bridal bouquet had any idea that Kaitlyn had just married a man she didn't really love — married him out of guilt and pressure. Had she confided in her family or her pastor, they would have supported her and advised that she wait, but she hadn't felt she could do that.

Perhaps Kaitlyn Merriam had really believed that marriage would set Wayne's mind at ease, putting an end to his petty jealousies.

She was wrong. Wayne hovered over her like a watchdog. He was a poster boy for

410

the overly possessive husband. Now that they were married, he forbade Kaitlyn to wear makeup. He went through her wardrobe with her and told her which clothes she had to either give away or throw away because they were too provocative. He wanted her to dress like a prim middle-aged woman, not a 19-year-old girl. He didn't want to take any chance that other men might be attracted to his bride.

Kaitlyn had gone into this marriage with a positive attitude, convinced that Wayne meant it when he described how happy they were going to be. It didn't take long for her to realize that she was in a cage. When love is held loosely and allowed to breathe, it can grow, and she had hoped she would learn to love her new husband. But even though she had promised their families, their friends, and her church to love Wayne forever, he obviously didn't believe it. He was so jealous of her, imagining things that never happened. Kaitlyn was afraid she could not survive in a marriage in which she had no freedom whatsoever.

Wayne was devoted, yes, and he acceded to all her wishes — as long as she behaved like a cult bride, kept her eyes downcast when other men were around, and dressed like a frump. He had a job as a loading clerk for a department store, and he let her keep her job as a grocery checker at Safeway, although he met her right after work and followed her home. They didn't have money problems, and they seldom argued, but it just wasn't the way Kaitlyn had pictured marriage.

It was probably inevitable that Kaitlyn — who had always been sweet-natured — would become irritable, chafing at her restrictions. Wayne couldn't understand. He had given her everything and he was loyal and accommodating. When he pointed that out to her, she just seemed more unhappy.

"What is it you want from me?" he asked uncomprehendingly. "You have everything any woman could want."

She just shook her head. He had never understood that all she wanted was to be a person — her own person — with some freedom to decide things for herself.

Although, Wayne discouraged socializing with Kaitlyn's friends, they sometimes double-dated with a couple Wayne knew from work. Sometimes, in the safety provided by being with another couple, Kaitlyn picked at her husband, daring to disagree with him. Wayne's friends, unaware of how cloistered her existence was, thought that she was unkind. She wasn't; she was fighting back against the man who wouldn't let her breathe.

With her own family, Kaitlyn tried to keep up their portrait of her as a happy bride. Her sister had a good marriage, and although she noticed that Wayne and Kaitlyn seemed strangely formal with one another, she assumed that their marriage was working out all right for them.

The strain of pretense and the frustration at being a captive bride became almost more than Kaitlyn Merriam could bear. After only eight months with Wayne, she knew she had to get away. He had insisted that they buy a house, a move that made her feel even more trapped, but the papers had been signed. She was caught again, but Kaitlyn told Wayne she couldn't make love to him any longer. She slept on the couch and he slept in the bedroom. Of course, he was more suspicious than ever, asking her whom she *was* sleeping with.

"When would I have the chance?" she snapped. "Even if I wanted to — which I don't. You're always watching me."

In early February, she and Wayne moved out of their Seattle apartment and in with Kaitlyn's sister and her husband for the two weeks they would have to wait to take possession of their new home.

Everything started to sour that February. Wayne had lost his job; he was under investigation for the theft of several guns from the loading dock at the store where he worked. They couldn't afford to buy a house; they would have been lucky to pay their apartment rent. Their marriage was foundering, but Kaitlyn still didn't tell her sister of her problems.

It was Wayne who first broached the subject. He told his brother-in-law that Kaitlyn wanted to leave him and get a divorce. He seemed totally bewildered and couldn't understand that she didn't love him and didn't want any kind of relationship with him. His brother-in-law was astounded too. Kaitlyn's determination not to disappoint her family had made her a flawless actress, but even her loyalty was crumbling under the strain of living a lie.

When her sister questioned her, Kaitlyn finally admitted that it was true. "I can't stand being with Wayne any longer," she confessed. "I didn't want to get married in the first place, but everything snowballed and I felt like I had to go through with it."

"Oh, Kaitlyn," her sister sighed. "I had no idea. Why didn't you tell me?"

Kaitlyn only shrugged helplessly.

Once their split was announced openly, Kaitlyn moved to the living-room couch at her sister's house. Wayne slept in their guest room.

Kaitlyn's sister urged her to seek counseling, telling her that she just couldn't end a marriage so easily. Kaitlyn agreed to talk with their family pastor. The minister talked to Kaitlyn for two hours, and then he talked to Wayne, explaining to him how his wife felt. It was a tearful confrontation, and the minister suggested that they try a trial separation for a month.

"See if your feelings don't fall into place when you spend some time apart," he counseled. "You might be surprised to see what you really feel for one another."

Kaitlyn leapt at the chance. After five years of being bound to Wayne by promises, threats, and guilt, it was a way out for her. She knew in her own heart that she was finished with the marriage, and it wasn't fair to Wayne to continue to stay with him feeling the way she did. He would come to see that too. But, given the chance to separate for even a month, she believed that she could stay free.

She was hopelessly naive.

When their house was ready for occupancy, Wayne Merriam moved in without Kaitlyn. But he couldn't bear to live in it alone, so he fashioned a bedroom for himself in the garage, avoiding the rest of the house. He tacked pictures of Kaitlyn up so that he would always have her face before him.

There is no question that Wayne Merriam felt a deep sense of loss. As strong as his feeling of possession had been about Kaitlyn, the gradual realization of his loss was cataclysmic. He was a young man with single-minded goals. He did not ever consider that he might one day find another woman. He was only 20 years old and, for him, life seemed to hold no purpose without his wife. He seemed to have blinders on, blocking him from seeing where he had failed in the relationship. As far as he was concerned, Kaitlyn belonged to him and she always would.

He had always been doggedly determined. Now he was unhinged.

Kaitlyn, on the other hand, felt as if she had been let out of jail. She rented an apartment close to her job, and began to think that she might be able to start a life on her own. She worried about Wayne, but she felt he would be all right once he accepted the fact that their marriage wasn't meant to be.

She could wear makeup now, she could wear the clothes she wanted, and she could consider dating other men. But that was a long way off. She certainly hadn't left Wayne because she wanted another man. She had wanted only to be herself. Alone.

Kaitlyn told her parents, of course, that she and Wayne were separated. Wayne didn't tell his family. He continued to carry on a fantasy marriage, acting as if everything were fine. Kaitlyn's parents and family were understanding when Wayne visited them frequently. They tried to help him adjust to his loss, and let him know that they still considered him a good friend and that they were there for him.

At six feet two inches, Wayne had always been tall and thin. Now he began to lose weight, which he could ill afford to spare. He didn't comb his hair, and his clothes were wrinkled and dirty. He spent a good deal of time with the couple he knew from work. They listened patiently as he went over and over his confusion about Kaitlyn's defection. "How could she *leave* me?" he asked. "I don't see any reason for it. Do you?"

Even when Wayne was questioned by federal agents from the Bureau of Alcohol, Tobacco and Firearms concerning the gun theft from his employer, he seemed more concerned with his broken marriage than any possible charges against him.

He called Kaitlyn repeatedly at her apartment and bombarded her with presents and flowers. But none of it convinced her that he had changed. If she went back to him, she knew he would start tightening his invisible bonds around her.

Wayne had several friends who tried to cheer him up, and he attended church regularly. His pastor counseled him. He actually seemed to be getting a little more cheerful, and those who knew him relaxed a little bit. They didn't know his attitude was only a facade.

Early in April, with the "month long" separation extending for more than sixty days, drivers crossing Seattle's soaring Aurora Avenue Bridge noticed a tall, dark-haired man standing at the edge of the pedestrian walkway. The ship canal was hundreds of feet down. The bridge, for good reason, is known as a suicide spot. Pedestrians loitering on the bridge always alarm observers. Too many of them have gone over to land in the water or the docks below, and most of them die.

Someone called the police, and a patrol unit arrived to find Wayne Merriam leaning against the rail, gazing down. The officers approached him quietly, careful not to startle him. But he caught the movement behind him out of the corner of his eye. As he spotted them, he lurched forward. It took both officers to grab him and wrestle him to safety.

Wayne was admitted to the mental ward of the Harborview Medical Center for observation, There he phoned, not his own parents, but Kaitlyn's. Because they didn't know the truth about what their daughter had gone through, they had always supported him. But, for the first time, his in-laws felt compelled to let his family know that Wayne and Kaitlyn had separated. It wasn't breaking a confidence — something had to be done.

Kaitlyn felt terrible; she could see no future for herself if anything happened to Wayne because she had deserted him. She decided to talk to him and let him know that she wanted him to be happy. If she could convince him that their marriage held no happiness for either of them, maybe he could deal with it. She wasn't afraid of him — she'd never been afraid of him, except in the sense that he might harm himself. It was this fear that had kept her bound to Wayne ever since they were in high school. Early on, he'd learned that he could push that button.

On April 14, Wayne accepted Kaitlyn's invitation to visit her at her new apartment. Things appeared to be going really well, and she was relieved to see how calm he was.

"Wayne," she said, "I really do care about you and I'm worried about you. I'm glad that we can get together and talk because I think we can work this out. Don't you?"

He nodded, waiting for her to go on. She spoke about some of the good times they'd had when they were a lot younger. "We'll always be friends, Wayne," she stressed. "We have so much history we've shared."

As he got up to leave, he was actually smiling and joking. He seemed to agree that their marriage was over, and that it was best for both of them.

She had no warning of what came next. Suddenly, Wayne turned toward her and grabbed her around the neck with both hands. He was a foot taller and outweighed her by a hundred pounds. He was choking her, and she could do nothing to stop him. She saw flashes of light and then nothing but blackness. She was unconscious when she landed on her couch.

Kaitlyn wasn't dead. When she came to, she could hear Wayne frantically pounding on other apartment doors. He was shouting for someone to help her. She screamed, and Wayne ran back to her.

"I hate you!" she gasped. "Just get away from me."

Kaitlyn stumbled to the manager's apartment and waited, nearly hysterical, while he called police.

Kaitlyn might well have died then; strangulation can result in death in a matter of seconds. It all depends on the person who is being choked. But she was lucky: she survived with only a wrenched neck and two huge black bruises on her throat where Wayne's thumbs had pressed against her arteries.

She had never suspected that Wayne was capable of physically harming her. He never had; he had only threatened to hurt himself. But Kaitlyn Merriam now lived with fear. She was afraid to go back to her apartment, and afraid to go to her parents' home: they had given Wayne a key to their front door. Her family decided to move her into one of her aunts' houses. They figured that would be a safe hiding place because Wayne had never been there and had no idea of the address.

The police were keeping an eye on him too. He hadn't just walked away from Kaitlyn's apartment. When he tried to run after he choked her, he was arrested. Charges were now pending against him for assault, and he was still being questioned about the gun theft.

Kaitlyn moved ahead and filed for divorce, despite all of Wayne's attempts to make up for what he had done to her. She was too frightened of him to ever live with him again. Now he didn't know where she lived, but she often saw his car circling the Safeway parking lot when she was working.

Once or twice, she accepted dinner invitations from men at work, but it wasn't worth the hassle. Wayne followed them and caused scenes. They didn't ask her out again and she couldn't blame them.

Never before had Kaitlyn even considered that Wayne might try to kill her. Now she did. If he could strangle her until she was unconscious, he was probably capable of anything. She was convinced he would try again, and she feared that they might both die in some kind of compulsive act on his part.

It was a heavy burden for a 19-year-old girl to carry. Living with her aunt wasn't safe enough. All Wayne had to do was follow her home. Then he could find out where she was living, and he could break in if he decided to. Finally, after a family conference, they all decided that the safest thing would be for Kaitlyn to share an apartment with a cousin in a building known for its top security. The young women would have an unlisted phone, and they wouldn't put their names on the apartment house mailboxes. Even if Wayne should somehow get into the lobby, he wouldn't be able to determine which apartment they were in — not among the dozens in the building.

Kaitlyn had considered moving far away, but she didn't want to leave her job, her family, and the city where she had always lived. Somehow, she would manage to get lost among the half million people living in Seattle.

But Wayne was a man on fire. He called Kaitlyn's family to apologize for choking her. "I just woke up and found myself doing that. You know I wouldn't have done that on purpose, and I'll never do it again."

He didn't come close to convincing them, and they were adamant that they could not tell him where Kaitlyn lived.

Still, he knew where she worked, and he

checked often for her car in the store parking lot so he would know what shift she was working. Although Kaitlyn and Wayne had no contact after the strangulation attempt, she always knew he was around, watching her.

He made sure she did. When she got to her car, she froze as she found things he'd placed inside. He still had a key. He left her flowers and candy. He even put a television set in the backseat. And there were always his notes in which he begged her to come back to him. Together, they had once collected fifty-cent pieces. Now she saw that he had balanced a row of the coins on her dashboard.

When the coins appeared on her car while it was parked in the lot of her new apartment, she was filled with dread. That meant Wayne knew where she lived. It was eerie: even though he had stopped trying to approach her directly, *he knew where she lived.*

Kaitlyn talked to the apartment house managers, a couple in their fifties, and asked if she could have a parking space in sight of their windows. They agreed at once, and gave her a spot close to their apartment and also to the front door. They promised to watch her car and to keep an eye out for anyone prowling around.

On her twentieth birthday, Kaitlyn had the locks changed on her car, an expense she could ill afford. But at least Wayne couldn't get into it and leave notes and gifts. Although she didn't tell anyone else because they might think she was paranoid, she was actually afraid he might hide inside to surprise her. He might even put a bomb in her car.

Thwarted when his key didn't open her car's doors, he started to leave presents in her sister's car or on her family's doorstep. There was a huge mirror and a pair of earrings for her birthday. On what would have been their first anniversary, he left a large carton on her parents' porch. She was afraid to open it.

Wayne had huge arrangements of flowers delivered to the store where she worked. She gave them away to other employees. The very sight of them frightened her.

Kaitlyn felt almost as trapped as she had been when she was living with Wayne. He simply would not let her go; everywhere she went, there were reminders that he was following her, watching her, waiting for her. He didn't call because he hadn't been able to get her number. She wasn't sure why he no longer confronted her, but she feared he would when she least expected him.

Kaitlyn had asked her manager at Safeway to assign her to continually changing shifts, so that her comings and goings were difficult to chart. When she left work, she always arranged to be accompanied to her car by a fellow employee. Before they even left the store, she checked the parking lot to see if one of the three cars Wayne had access to was parked there. In some ways, Wayne was like a ghost. She never actually *saw* him, although she sensed that he was often around. She realized that people were going to think *she* was crazy, but she could feel his presence, and the little hairs on her arms and the back of her neck stood up and she shivered as if a rabbit had run over her grave.

Kaitlyn did her grocery shopping at the store, and then she drove directly home. She parked in front of the managers' apartment, glanced around, and then sprinted for the front door of the building. The front doors of the apartment house could be opened only with a key, and then the dead-bolt lock slid into place immediately when the heavy glass doors closed behind her. She felt safe only when she was inside the lobby. There were no apartments opening off the lobby — just the stairs leading down to the basement floor and to the upper levels.

Kaitlyn didn't dare get in the elevator for fear Wayne might be waiting inside. Instead, she ran up the stairs to her third-floor apartment and double-bolted that door behind her. Only then could she take in a deep breath and try to relax.

It wasn't any way to live, but she had no choice. Short of moving away from Seattle completely to a strange state where she knew no one, the "secret" apartment seemed the safest plan.

Kaitlyn had dinner with her sister's family on Sunday, June 18. The question of Wayne came up, as it always did now. She was adamant when she told her sister and brother-in-law that she hadn't changed her feelings about Wayne at all. She was going ahead with the assault suit against him, and planned to give an affidavit on June 26.

On June 21, a Wednesday night and the first day of summer, Kaitlyn worked at the store until 11:15. There was a light rain falling as she walked out to the parking lot with another clerk, who would recall that

Kaitlyn seemed to be feeling secure in her belief that Wayne was nowhere around. She got into her car, clicked the locks, and tooted her horn lightly to let her friend know she was okay as she drove off into the rainy June night, her car disappearing into the mist.

Her neighbors at the apartment house on Bothell Way and N.E. 148th were snug inside. Some had gone to bed, some were watching the Johnny Carson show, and one man was switching the channels back and forth between watching the extra innings of the Seattle Mariners' baseball game and *The Odd Couple.*

Kaitlyn's cousin was getting ready for bed. She expected Kaitlyn to be home just before midnight as she always was when she worked the late shift. At 11:45, her cousin was washing her face when she heard several "banging" sounds. She turned off the water, listened, and heard only silence. Given their circumstances, she was frightened and she checked the apartment door to see if it was locked. It was, and she went to bed, although she would soon waken to loud pounding on her door.

At the same time that she heard the loud sounds, the man who'd been watching the

Mariners game was especially watchful of the parking lot. Someone had looted his truck recently, taking his work tools and his stereo. He noticed a green Mustang with a black vinyl top make a U-turn in the center driveway in the west end of the lot. It was going too fast for a parking lot. He watched as it exited at the south end and zipped across Bothell Way.

Some minutes later, he looked out the window again when he heard a car door slam. He saw a girl wearing a yellow smock and dark slacks walking briskly toward the apartment entrance. He recognized her as one of the occupants of a third-floor apartment.

As the girl left his line of vision, he heard what he took to be firecrackers exploding in rapid succession. He mused to himself that the girl in the yellow smock must have been frightened at the noise, as she would have been just inside the entrance at that point.

He looked outside again and saw the same green Mustang drive onto Bothell Way with its lights out.

Other residents had heard the loud pops reverberating in the night, and they, too, had seen the Mustang with its lights out accelerate and disappear onto the main street. The night was quiet again, and they had returned to their dreams or TV sets when they were distracted by the wail of sirens in the distance, growing louder and louder as they approached.

The apartment building's managers had heard the popping sounds too. Together, they had run to the top of the stairs that led down into the small lobby. The husband reached the stairs first, looked down, and signaled to his wife that she must not come any closer.

"Go back! Don't look," he cried. "Call an aid car — quick!"

Then he ran to the girl who lay facedown just at the top of the stairs. He recognized her at once as the young woman who lived on the third floor with her cousin. He knelt beside her, saw the blood welling up from several holes in her yellow smock. In shock, he wondered how she could have torn it in so many places.

She was alive, moving feebly and making sounds.

"We'll get help," he promised. "Help's on the way."

She didn't seem to hear him. He looked beyond her down the stairs to the double glass doors and saw that the glass was shattered in several places and the frame was bent and twisted. Still, his mind could not comprehend what had happened.

He bent over the young woman, helpless to do anything for her but mutter words of comfort.

She didn't hear him. She would never hear anything again, and none of the expertise of the aid crew that arrived within minutes could do anything to save her. She had been shot in vital organs and she had rapidly bled out.

Kaitlyn Merriam was dead, cut down with a barrage of bullets even though she'd reached the "safety" of the apartment house lobby. Indeed, she had almost made it to the top of the stairs and with two more steps could have rounded the corner, putting a wall between herself and the gunman.

The first deputies who responded to the murder scene cordoned off the parking lot and the apartment's lobby and steps. Now it was up to the King County Sheriff's Major Crimes Unit to sort out what had happened. Detective Sergeant Harlan Bollinger, and Detectives Donna Nolan, Frank Atchley, Ben Colwell, and Bob Keppel arrived at the apartment house.

Colwell and Atchley photographed the scene, capturing the slender body that rested at the top of the stairs on film. Then they drew an outline in chalk around it on the bloodstained carpet. The other investigators fanned out in the complex to try to find witnesses while Keppel surveyed the scene.

Bob Keppel — who would one day be known as Dr. Robert Keppel, co-lead investigator into the Ted Bundy murders, consultant to the Green River Murder Task Force, and a university instructor in the investigation of homicides — was a young detective on the night Kaitlyn Merriam died.

Keppel counted ten bullet holes in the glass front doors and in the frame of the doors. The shooter had been an expert marksman. Seven of the holes were in the entry door, piercing the word *Push*. The highest hole was five feet five and a half inches from the sidewalk — the lowest three feet three and a half inches.

The gunman had aimed well.

Detective Donna Nolan assisted Keppel as he measured the site from triangulation points. Long after Kaitlyn's body was removed, they would be able to tell *exactly* where she had fallen, how far she was from the shooter, and where he — or she — had stood.

The two investigators collected the copper jackets and slugs that lay scattered around the lobby and on the stairs and bagged them into evidence. The small area looked like a shooting gallery.

The dead girl lay on her back now, with her head tilted to the side. Her beige purse lay against a wall. It wouldn't be difficult to determine who she was. Her Safeway smock had a name tag pinned to it: *Kaitlyn*.

Keppel gently took the keys from her hand and tested them on the front door. He found that one did open the front doors, and saw that they were designed to immediately swing shut and lock after someone passed through, so that no one could slip in afterward.

He checked the bullet holes in the glass door. By looking at the wavy pattern along the broken edges, he could establish the direction of fire. All of the bullets had been fired from the outside in.

The dead girl had clearly made it into the building and was climbing the stairs as her killer stood just outside the doors, firing methodically as she'd tried to outrun the gunfire. She had had nowhere to run but downstairs or upstairs, and she probably had chosen not to be trapped in the basement if the shooter followed her through the shattered door.

It would have been like shooting fish in a barrel.

At this point, the detectives could detect four wounds — three in her back and one in her arm. An autopsy would give a more definite answer on the number of times she had been hit.

Dr. Robert Eisele, King County deputy medical examiner, arrived to check the victim and to oversee the removal of her body. Bob Keppel made arrangements to secure the doors for evidence. Apartment dwellers would have to leave by the rear exit until they were thoroughly processed. He retrieved the remaining evidence — Kaitlyn's purse and her keys.

The bullets appeared to have come from a .30-caliber M1 rifle, a most accurate weapon commonly used by the military.

Kaitlyn Merriam's family had received word that she had been shot, and they rushed to her apartment building, only to be told that they could not enter while the detectives were processing the scene. Her sister waited there. Detectives had broken the news that Kaitlyn was dead, and she fought back hysteria as the investigators questioned her gently.

"Do you know anyone who drives a green Mustang, or anyone who might have wanted to kill Kaitlyn?"

"You'd better believe I do," she said quickly. "Wayne — Wayne Merriam . . . her husband. That's one of his cars, and he was hounding my sister, stalking her."

It was 5:15 a.m. when the probers met to coordinate their information on the case. The victim's full name was Michelle Kaitlyn Merriam, born in May of 1958; she had been barely 20 when she died. The suspect was Wayne A. Merriam, who was seven months older.

The detectives quickly found the last three addresses for Merriam. His driver's license picture showed a thin man with a short beard. They had his car descriptions and his license numbers.

"Seattle Police have checked with Merriam's parents," Sergeant Bollinger said. "They haven't seen him all day. They have a cabin on Stampede Pass and think he might have headed there. He had a good friend who lived right across the street from the victim's apartment house, and another friend over in Bellevue who's been taking him to church for counseling."

In the early-morning hours, detectives drove to the new house that Wayne

Merriam had insisted on buying, the one where he moved in without Kaitlyn. There was no one there, but they saw that the house itself obviously hadn't been lived in. The garage had a bed, dresser, and some men's clothing on hangers.

"This is where he's been living," one of the investigators commented. "Odd — when he has a whole new house to live in."

Ben Colwell and Bob Keppel headed out to talk with the suspect's parents to get a more accurate location on their mountain cabin. Frank Atchley would watch the new house Merriam had bought, and Donna Nolan would talk to Safeway employees to get more background on the case. Possibly they had seen him around the store just before Kaitlyn was shot.

Merriam's parents said they hadn't seen or heard from him for the past day and a half.

"That's unusual," his father said. "He usually checks in every day. As for the cabin, it's up on Stampede Pass. It's green with a metal roof and there's a flagpole out in front. It's not that far from the weather station."

Merriam's family and friends were concerned that he might do harm to himself, but they all agreed that he would probably head for the cabin if he was attempting to leave the area.

The King County detectives checked all of Merriam's friends in Seattle and on the east side of the Floating Bridge on I-90, but none of them had seen him.

Merriam was not known to have owned a gun — at least, not by his intimate acquaintances. None of those close to him even knew about his being investigated by the ATF about the missing guns from the store where he worked, so the King County detectives didn't have that information in the first twenty-four hours of their murder investigation.

Bob Keppel contacted the Kittitas County Sheriff's Office 120 miles east of Seattle and asked that officers from that department locate the family's cabin and put a stakeout on it to watch for the missing suspect and the green Mustang.

A Bellevue police officer called in to say that Wayne Merriam had once told him that he might kill a man Kaitlyn had dated. The man lived in southern King County. "He wanted to know the guy's address," the Bellevue cop said, "but I wouldn't give it to him. He was jealous and he was mad, but I figured he'd cool down."

As each department's new shifts came

on duty, command officers announced the urgency of finding Wayne Merriam to all King County patrol deputies and Seattle police officers. Every cop in the Greater Seattle area was looking for him.

An ATF agent who was very familiar with Wayne Merriam contacted Bob Keppel and let him know about his possible involvement in the gun theft from the Fred Meyer department store. "When I interviewed him," the ATF investigator recalled, "he told me that his wife had left him and that he'd lost his head a while back and almost strangled her."

That answered more questions.

Wayne Merriam had slipped through the fingers of the detectives who were so anxious to find him before more tragedies unfolded. To their frustration, they learned that he had been stopped about 1:30 a.m., less than two hours after Kaitlyn was killed — even as the King County investigators were still at the crime scene. A patrolman had noticed his car weaving as he drove along Bothell Way. When he was pulled over, he had seemed quite rational and had no odor of alcohol on his breath. He explained that he was very tired, and he was allowed to go with a warning ticket. At this point, the information on the murder of his wife hadn't been put out on the air.

Now Wayne Merriam could be anywhere, and might well be in possession of guns and ammunition. There was no way of knowing how many other people he blamed for Kaitlyn's leaving him. Her family, her coworkers, her friends, even her minister, had advised the couple to live apart until they could work things out. To someone like Wayne Merriam, that would have been likely to inspire a need for revenge.

While investigators and patrolmen fanned out over the western part of the state searching for Merriam, Detective Frank Atchley attended Kaitlyn Merriam's postmortem examination.

Her killer had been deadly accurate. Bob Keppel had counted ten bullet holes in the doors of the apartment house. Dr. Eisele said that nine of those bullets had found their mark. It was almost as if she had had a target painted on her back. Kaitlyn would have been knocked down almost at once by a bullet in the back, but her killer had fired repeatedly into her prone body; the angle of many of the bullets showed that she had been facedown — helpless —

as he continued to shoot. The EMTs had turned her over to treat her before she died.

Some of her wounds were comparatively minor, piercing only the soft tissue and muscles of her arms, thighs, and legs. But at least two bullets had been fatal shots. One slug had entered the lumbar region in her back, perforating her kidney and literally shredding it, and then continued on through the pancreas, the large intestine, the stomach, and the left pleural cavity, until it penetrated her heart. No medical aid could have saved Kaitlyn, even if she had been taken into an operating room at once.

It has been said that each man kills the thing he loves; Wayne Merriam had killed his Kaitlyn many times over.

The general consensus was that Merriam would be found dead. He had tried suicide at least once; now that he had made sure that Kaitlyn was dead and would never date another man, he must have come to the realization that she was forever lost to him too. Since he had told her he couldn't live without her since she was 15, what reason would he have to go on now?

Word came from the Kittitas County

Sheriff's Office. Deputies there had located the cabin on Stampede Pass and said that the green Mustang was parked outside. They noted that the cabin was tightly padlocked, and there was no sign of the suspect around the car. They were hesitant to approach the Mustang until they got a go-ahead from King County, so they didn't know if it was locked.

"We're on our way," Bob Keppel told them. "If you'll sit on the car until we get there, we'd appreciate it. He may be inside it — dead — or in the cabin itself. Or he may be armed and waiting."

The cabin was located a half mile from a tiny lake high up in the Cascade Mountains. Bob Keppel and Detective John Tolton picked up Deputy Glenn McKinney along the way. McKinney was the only King County deputy working the thinly populated mountainous area to the eastern border of King County and he knew every road and stream. They arrived at the isolated spot shortly after 5:00 p.m. on June 22.

The Mustang was indeed parked alongside the cabin. It was photographed before they made any attempt to approach it and look inside. It appeared to be empty, and it was locked, but McKinney found a spare key in the windshield wiper reservoir.

Keppel and Tolton searched the car and found one cartridge casing next to the driver's seat and another under the rear seat. A Bible lay between the front seats, and, wedged in the transmission covering, there was an ace of hearts and photographs of Wayne and Kaitlyn Merriam in happier times.

There was no weapon in the car. They approached the cabin with extreme caution, half-expecting bullets to fly toward them. But there was only the serene quiet of the mountain. The padlocks were dusty. It was clear that no one had entered the cabin for some time. Wayne Merriam was either escaping on foot, or his body was somewhere nearby, hidden by evergreen branches, sword ferns, salal, and huckleberry growth.

If he was there, he made no sound. The detectives called for a tow truck, and the suspect's car was impounded and transported into North Bend at the western slope of the pass for safekeeping.

In the morning light, they could bring more deputies in to search the wilderness for his body.

But Wayne Merriam was not dead. It

was 10:00 a.m. the next morning when Lieutenant Frank Chase, commander of the Major Crimes Unit, received word from the Spokane County Sheriff's Office that they had a suspect in custody who fit the Wants and Warrants bulletin from King County. Spokane was near the Idaho border, more than three hundred miles east of Seattle.

It was a clerk in a 7-Eleven store at Argonne and Indiana Streets in Spokane who called the Spokane sheriff. She had become alarmed by the actions of a tall man who'd come into the store earlier that morning. He had seemed agitated when he asked for the latest editions of both Seattle papers, saying, "Haven't you heard about the shoot-out there?"

The clerk hadn't. The Seattle papers hadn't yet been delivered, but she attempted to help him find the news item he was looking for in the Spokane *Spokesman-Review.*

The man had been very intense as he leafed through the paper — so intense that she was frightened after spending about half an hour with him. "I told him that he should go to another store. I said the Seattle papers might have come in on a bus and they usually got them earlier than we did."

As soon as he walked outside the 7-Eleven, she had called the Spokane County Sheriff's Office: "There's a man here who's been asking about a murder — or a shooting or something in Seattle. He seems to know a lot about it."

When the Spokane officers arrived, they found Wayne Merriam wandering in the 7-Eleven's parking lot. He asked them if they knew where to get Seattle papers, and accepted their invitation to get into their patrol car without hesitation.

When they asked him why he was so anxious to see a paper, he only shrugged. Almost absently, he said, "Why did you come to pick me up?"

"Because we've been told you might be involved in a homicide in Seattle," they said truthfully. "We don't know if you're a witness or a suspect or *what* at this point."

Moreover, the Spokane deputies didn't even know who the murder victim was.

"What's a homicide?" Merriam asked curiously, as if he had never heard the term before.

"Basically, it's the killing of another human being."

"You mean someone's dead?" Merriam demanded.

At the word *killing*, the young man in

their car became very emotional, and tears filled his eyes. Finally, he said, "Then I guess I'm a suspect."

The deputies exchanged glances. One of them said, "I'm going to advise you of your rights. I don't have any questions right now, but it's obvious you are upset because you think someone has died."

". . . I think I did it," he said slowly.

Transported to the Spokane County Sheriff's Office, Merriam was turned over to Detective Jim Hansen, who verified that Wayne Merriam was wanted in Seattle for the murder of his wife.

He was held pending the arrival of the King County detectives. He told Hansen that he had hitchhiked to Spokane from Stampede Pass, catching a ride with a trucker. He no longer had a gun with him.

Detectives Tolton and Keppel went to Spokane to return the suspect to Seattle to face charges of murder. Merriam declined to talk about Kaitlyn's death. Instead, he demanded to speak to an attorney. In fact, he had already been contacted by the Public Defender's Office while he was in jail in Spokane and was represented by counsel.

Bob Keppel talked to a witness who indicated that Wayne Merriam had been rational just after the shooting. The wife of one of Merriam's friends said that Wayne had called her on the morning of June 22 within hours of the murder. He had seemed quite calm, much calmer than she'd known him to be on other occasions. "He told me that he wouldn't be around, and told me to send the money we owed him to his parents. I asked him where he was going, and he just said he wouldn't be around."

The M1 carbine used to kill Kaitlyn Merriam was never located, although investigators questioned every business on the route to Stampede Pass to see if someone had tried to sell such a gun on the morning of June 22.

Wayne Merriam never went to trial. Instead, he agreed to a plea bargain, and he pleaded guilty to second-degree murder in Kaitlyn Merriam's death. On a chilly weekend in the first part of January 1979, he asked to be taken to her grave. His request was granted. One can only surmise his thoughts as he stood under heavy guard at Kaitlyn's grave. In a few seconds of violence, he had ended her life and it seemed that his, too, was finished. He would, however, be eligible for parole in less than a dozen years.

A conviction on first degree murder would have meant thirteen years and four months, with a consecutive sentence of five years because Merriam had used a deadly weapon in the commission of his crime. But he was only 21. It was possible that he would be free before he was 35.

And he was.

Kaitlyn would never have a second chance. Perhaps there never was a place far enough away or safe enough for her to run to. From the day she was 15, Wayne had considered her to be his and he was not prepared to let her go — ever.

Wayne Merriam served almost fourteen years in prison, and then he was paroled. He soon remarried. Apparently, he *could* live without Kaitlyn after all. If only he could have realized that before he ended her life.

Kaitlyn Merriam was only the first of dozens of women I would have to write about over the years ahead. But, because she was the first, I remember her and wonder what her life might have been like. As I write this, I realize that she wouldn't be 50 yet.

Young women who read this would do

well to beware of any boyfriend who loves them *too* much. How can they determine this? There are warning signs:

- If he tells you that you and he don't need anyone else, and you should be happy to spend all your time with him.
- If he urges you to avoid makeup, clothes that flatter your figure, and high heels.
- If he begins to cut you off from your friends and your family.
- If he calls you a dozen times a day to ask what you are doing and whom you are with.
- If he discourages you from seeking higher education.
- If he tells you constantly that he cannot live without you.
- If he begins to chip away at your self-confidence, making you feel that you are not worthy of having the things that are important to you.
- If he *ever* strikes you in anger.

Run. And if you are afraid to run, look on the Internet (www.google.com) for "Domestic Violence Groups" or go to the library to find one near you. There *is* support out there to help you.

Bad Blind Date

Almost everyone has suffered through that potentially disastrous social custom known as a "blind date." The very worst are usually well-meaning setups by mutual friends who are convinced that they are bringing together two strangers who will feel instant attraction. The would-be cupids are almost always wrong; individual tastes vary so much that nobody else can detect what we are looking for in the way of romance. If we were asked to jot down a list of qualifications, most of us couldn't even say what we're hoping for *ourselves*.

Occasionally, a date with a stranger does work — just often enough to keep matchmakers optimistic. However, the horror stories far outnumber the happy-ever-afters. Some are boring, some are totally embarrassing, and a handful are scary. That's why our mothers taught us to always carry mad money so we can take a taxi or a bus home.

Closely aligned with completely blind dates are the invitations we accept impulsively from someone we really don't know at all. Maybe you've had a long-term Internet relationship with someone, but the Internet is really only words on a computer monitor; you can't actually know if you are talking to a man or a woman, a teenager or someone collecting social security, a dependable citizen or a sexual pervert.

Thirty years ago, there was no Internet, and someone without meddling friends wasn't likely to get set up with a blind date. One young Seattle woman took a chance on a man she barely knew, telling herself it wasn't *really* a blind date because she had, at least, seen the man, and he looked presentable enough and certainly seemed safe enough.

Her date ended in the kind of horror she didn't know existed.

Twenty-one-year-old Victoria Legg worked as an entry-level clerk at Boeing's Marginal Way plant. She accepted a date with a man she barely knew because he reminded her of a former boyfriend who had left for military duty in another country. To someone more worldly-wise than Victoria, that wasn't a good way to judge character, but Victoria's coworkers found her to be "very naive."

She had led a relatively sheltered life and she had never been exposed to violence, not in the home she grew up in, or anywhere else. She felt she was an adult who was quite capable of making her own decisions. So, on July 17, 1970, when Victoria's mother warned her against going out with strangers, she reminded her that she was of age and it was time she did as she pleased.

If she wasn't allowed to make her own choices, how was she ever going to learn? She told her mother gently — but firmly — that she intended to keep the date with a college man named Cal that night. There was nothing to worry about: He was a nice guy — she was sure of that — and he was cute too.

The call that was to propel the Seattle Police Department's Homicide Unit into a massive investigation came into the police radio at 3:20 a.m. on the Saturday morning of July 18, 1970. Patrol officers Sergeant E. George, P. H. Wright, L. F. Stark, and H. P. Sloan had responded to a citizen's complaint at the North End Precinct that a woman's body had been found in Cowan Park. At that time of the morning, the homicide detectives' office was empty; their night shift ended at 11:45 p.m., and radio operators called the investigators who were next up to be notified at home.

Detectives George Cuthill and Bernie Miller woke up rapidly when their phones rang. They arrived at the scenic park a few blocks north of the University District within a half hour. It was warm — 64 degrees, even at that hour of the morning — and the sun rose to a day that was clear and dry.

Much of Cowan Park was a wooded ravine, a deep-green sanctuary in the midst of the city, its paths winding rapidly from the heavy traffic of University Way to a silent place where the only sound was wind in the trees and birds singing. It was peaceful and serene, but it would be a terrible place for someone who was afraid.

Cuthill and Miller were met by Sergeant George, who explained that the body of a young female had been found on a dirt path north and east of the Cowan Park bridge. George said he had touched nothing at the scene beyond checking the victim's wrist for the beat of her pulse. There had been no sign of life at all.

He said her arm was already very cold to the touch. He led the homicide investigators down the trail to the ravine area where the body lay. The air became dank and chill as they descended into the cool, leafy spot where a small stream rippled.

With the aid of flashlights, Miller and Cuthill could see the outline of a woman's body. She appeared to be lying on her back with arms and legs outstretched. Using strobe lights, they took their first pictures of the body and the scene where she lay. But they decided they would wait until dawn — which comes early in Seattle in summertime — before attempting a full-scale processing of the death site.

The area was secured with yellow crime scene tape, and patrol officers stood guard around the perimeters while the detectives talked to the reporting witnesses — a young couple who said they had been walking along a trail in the park a few hours after midnight when they suddenly came upon the dead girl. Beyond that, they couldn't offer any information. They didn't recognize her and they hadn't seen or heard anyone else in the park.

A very nervous young man fidgeted in Sergeant George's car. George had spotted the man walking away from the vicinity where the body was found. He had admitted readily that he had been walking in the area, but when George questioned him, he babbled, "I never saw a body at all. I don't know anything about it."

The detectives looked at his ID, jotted down his name and address, and let him go.

Now Miller and Cuthill waited beside the body until the first rays of light broke through the ceiling of trees above them. Shortly before five a.m., they were joined by Homicide Sergeant Elmer Wittman and Detective Ted Fonis. The investigators searched the area meticulously but found nothing that seemed connected to the murder. They moved closer to the hapless girl's body. She had probably been very pretty in life, but now her face bore evidence of a savage beating. Her left eye was blackened and swollen shut, she had bled copiously from her nose, mouth, and left ear. It also appeared that several teeth had been knocked from her mouth. Whatever else had happened to her, she had surely sustained severe brain injuries.

What appeared to be a nylon stocking was wound so tightly around her slender neck that it almost disappeared into the flesh beneath it. She wore a one-piece dress of brown and beige that was pulled up around her thighs, and her white shoes lay near the body. They found torn blue panties and pantyhose beneath her body. The victim still wore a gold wristwatch, a gold ring with a green stone, and a chain around her neck bearing a cross.

Obviously, robbery wasn't the killer's motive.

The detectives noted that the dead girl's skin and clothing were covered with dirt, brush particles, leaves, and bits of bark. The soles of her feet were extremely dirty — as if she had been walking in the area barefooted. It appeared that she had put up a tremendous fight for her life.

Although it would take the medical examiner's report to confirm their assumptions, they had little doubt that the victim had been raped either before or after her death.

Even for veteran homicide detectives it was difficult to view such a scene with detachment, but it was vital that they begin the dozens of steps necessary to preserve evidence. They had learned a long time before that they couldn't allow their emotions to interfere. Grimly, they went about the task according to time-tested procedures.

George Cuthill and Ted Fonis collected the victim's scattered clothing, along with particles of vegetation and dirt samples found near the body, and bagged it all in individual plastic bags, the seals marked with the date, time, and their initials.

A beige straw purse lay in the dry leaves near the girl's head. It was open, and Elmer Wittman peered into it. It appeared to contain the usual female paraphernalia — makeup, brush, comb, and facial tissue. There was also a payroll stub from The Boeing Company made out to Victoria M. Legg.

That was probably her name: *Victoria.* They had no idea yet how she had come to this secluded place by the stream or who had come with her — or she had perhaps encountered. Still, it was likely she hadn't walked so deep into the woods alone — not in the dark. And she hadn't been dead long enough to have lain here since the day before.

Bernie Miller photographed the entire area again, showing it as it now appeared in the daylight. Later, homicide detectives Wayne Dorman and Dick Reed, who were accomplished aerial photographers — if white-knuckle flyers — would be flown over the scene in a helicopter piloted by Detective Sergeant Jerry Yates. Often, comprehensive panoramas of a wooded area showed details that couldn't be seen from the ground.

Ted Fonis carefully encased the victim's hands in plastic bags and taped the bags securely at the wrists before her body was removed to the King County Medical Examiner's Office, thus preserving any evidence that might be caught beneath her fingernails.

At 7:30 a.m., the body was removed for autopsy by the chief medical examiner, Dr. Gale Wilson. While detectives Cuthill, Miller, and Fonis returned to headquarters to confer with the director of the crime lab, criminalist George Ishii, Sergeant Wittman directed five investigators to the scene —

Sergeants Ed Golder, Henry Ebbeson, and Detectives Roy Moran, Billy Baughman, and Mike Germann — to conduct an inch-by-inch search of the wooded park area. It didn't matter that it was a Saturday. The usual weekend crew in the Homicide Unit was made up of one sergeant and four detectives, but this murder was so savage that nobody complained about being called in for overtime.

They were dealing with what was potentially a huge crime scene. Detecting evidence — some of it minute — would not be easy in the rugged park landscape. However, Mike Germann and Ray Moran, working beneath the bridge overpass some 225 feet from the body, noted suspicious dark red stains on bushes growing there. They rushed the branches to the crime lab for tests. The stains proved to be human blood.

Just as they had feared, the crime scene perimeters encompassed a very large area, far larger than the usual scene. But the tedious search for physical evidence was the backbone of any strong homicide case, and every detective going through that woods on his hands and knees knew it. The most minute clue is often the one that clinches a case. Circumstantial evidence is all well and good and makes TV detectives and lawyers shine, but it is the kind of doggedly painstaking search carried out by Seattle detectives on that sunny morning in July that constructs a case that will hold up in court.

At eight a.m. on that bright summer morning, Detective Don Strunk had the hardest task a homicide detective ever faces — informing the family of the victim. He could tell when they opened the door that they hadn't slept all night; they'd clearly been waiting up for their daughter to come home.

As gently as possible, he talked with Victoria Legg's parents and sister. Fighting to retain some degree of composure, the Legg family said that Victoria had left at about eight the previous evening for a date with a man they knew only as Cal Lansing.* At least, they assumed that she had gone out with Lansing; they could not be sure, because no one was home at the time he was supposed to pick her up and none of them had ever seen him.

They said that Victoria had never dated him before. All they knew was that she had met him about a month previously at a TacoTime Mexican restaurant in South Seattle.

Her mother wept as she said she had

warned Victoria over and over again about dating someone she had met so casually. If only she had been home to meet her daughter's date of the night before, she wondered if *she* might have been able to save Victoria.

"She just said that she would be fine, that he seemed like a nice guy. I told her she couldn't know that so soon, but she thought I was silly to be worried."

It was a last-minute date, her family recalled, because Victoria had been planning to go shopping with two girlfriends the night before. But she had suddenly changed her mind and accepted Lansing's invitation to go to The Warehouse. Strunk knew that was *the* popular tavern at the moment for those in their twenties. It was on Eastlake, about two miles south of Cowan Park.

"You remember anything else Victoria might have said about Lansing?" he asked.

"She said he told her that he had just been released from a hospital where he was treated for a football injury. I think he was on the University of Washington team, and they just started summer practice."

As Strunk left, he could see the family was in deep shock, still trying to deal with the terrible news he'd given them. Sadly, the victim's mother had been right in her advice, but the end result was much worse than even she had worried about. Don Strunk assured them that the detectives were doing everything they could to find Lansing. He left his card and asked Victoria's family to call if they remembered anything more that she might have said about him.

Don Strunk talked next to a neighbor of the Legg family who said he *had* seen Victoria leaving with a date the night before. The neighbor said he'd even made small talk with the man. "He was a young fellow — husky — maybe five feet ten and up around two hundred," the witness said. "He was wearing a yellow sweater, and he had dark brown hair. Cut short and neat. He was a real clean-cut guy. We talked a little and he seemed like a happy-go-lucky type."

"Did you notice the car he was driving?" Strunk asked.

"Yes. It was a '62 or '63 Olds. Ivory color — four door sedan. I know my cars. It had Washington plates."

Strunk thanked the witness for his help and thanked providence for the man's precise memory. He'd come up with everything but the car's license number.

Checking the Traffic Violations Bureau for a record on a Cal Lansing, Strunk fared even better. There was an arrest noted for a Calvin Archer Lansing Jr., white male, 21, six feet tall, 210 pounds, with brown hair and a stocky build. He had been arrested two months earlier for drunk driving. Even more interesting, this Cal Lansing was listed as owning a 1963 Oldsmobile four-door white sedan, license number ABB-957.

Strunk obtained mug shots of Lansing, combined them with five similar-looking photos of men in a "lay-down," and returned to show them to the observant neighbor of the victim. The man studied them for a while, but he wavered between two of the photos and said he didn't think he could definitely pick one photo. However, his son and a friend had also seen Victoria Legg's date and both of them picked Cal Lansing's photo without hesitation.

While Don Strunk was trying to identify Victoria Legg's Friday-night date, Ted Fonis and H. D. Aitken were detailed to Dr. Gale Wilson's office to witness the autopsy of the dead girl. They told Dr. Wilson about the surroundings where she had been found and showed him the photographs detectives had taken at the park scene.

The victim's body was extremely dirty and countless pieces of twigs, grit, dust, and weeds from the park area adhered to it. There were a number of small abrasions on her legs and feet, both knees were skinned, her left elbow was skinned, and there were numerous small bruises and abrasions on her shoulders. There was a large bruise on the right side of her neck extending from the collarbone to the underpart of her chin.

The postmortem exam also revealed that the victim had suffered terrible injuries from a beating, either with fists or a thick branch. Both of her eyes were blackened — although the left eye had been injured much more severely.

One tooth had been knocked completely out, one loosened, and one broken off. Perhaps more shocking, vegetable matter had been forced down her throat — the Oregon grape and fern fronds that grew in the park location, some of them seven inches in length. If the stocking around her neck hadn't succeeded in strangling her, the native vegetation would probably have suffocated her.

Her dress was still zipped up the back,

but remnants of her panties were found around her waist. Her bra straps had been torn apart and the bra, too, dangled around her waist. Vaginal examination indicated that intercourse had taken place shortly before, during, or just after death.

Victoria had eaten a heavy meal within two hours of her death — a meal that consisted of Chinese food.

Dr. Wilson concluded that Victoria Legg had succumbed from asphyxia by strangulation and the "vegetable matter that an unknown person forced down her throat with an unknown instrument."

Her death had been unusually violent, the work of someone enraged, perhaps, by her refusal to have sex with him.

Victoria's family had provided the names and phone numbers of her closest girl-friends. The investigators started by talking with the girl that she had planned to go shopping with on Friday night.

"We had a tentative date," the girl said. "Victoria told me that she'd go shopping with me if Cal Lansing didn't call her back. I guess he called before she got home from work and her little sister answered, and he said he'd call Victoria later. Then she called me about a quarter to seven on

Friday and said she *did* have a date with Cal. They were going to The Warehouse."

"Had she been out with him before?" Wayne Dorman asked.

"No — I'm sure she hadn't. I don't really know anything about him," Victoria's friend said, "except his name and that Victoria met him at the TacoTime drive-in about a month ago. She told me she was attracted to him because he reminded her of an old boyfriend. She never did go out with him before Friday that I knew of, but I know she talked to him on the phone several times."

The fact that Lansing did indeed resemble Victoria's old boyfriend was most evident to investigators when they looked at an enlargement of a snapshot they'd found in the victim's wallet. The photo was of Victoria Legg and her former boyfriend; the boyfriend, now in the service, bore a decided resemblance to Cal Lansing.

Detectives questioned all employees of The Warehouse and found one bartender who remembered that Cal Lansing had been in the vast, uniquely decorated nightspot from around 9:30 to 10:30 on Friday night. However, he couldn't remember if Lansing had a date with him.

Looking at the many-tiered levels of the

immense tavern and the packed crowd of "under-30s" dancing to the constant throb of hard rock music from the combo suspended above the dance floor, the investigators could well imagine that it would be hard to remember who might or might not have been there on any given night.

Working on the information that Cal Lansing had been a football player, Ted Fonis called popular University of Washington football coach Jim Owens, who had taken his winning teams to the Rose Bowl. Fonis asked Owens if he had a student named Cal Lansing in his Husky football spring or summer turnout. Owens replied that he had not — nor had he ever had a Cal Lansing on his squad.

That told them one thing for sure: Cal Lansing was, at the very least, a liar.

A work friend of Victoria's had more information. He was an employee of The Boeing Company, a security guard at the huge plant's gates. When he read the article in *The Seattle Times* about Victoria's murder, he called Don Strunk and Ted Fonis to tell them that he had known the victim for some time and might have things that would help them find her killer. They drove at once to the Boeing plant and listened to his story.

The security guard was a middle-aged man who explained that he had known the pretty young clerk since she began working for Boeing. "She kind of confided in me like a daughter might to a father," he said. "Victoria was an old-fashioned, naive girl, the kind you don't see much anymore. She blushed a lot. Well, the last couple of weeks before Vicki died, this fellow had been coming to the parking lot and waiting by her car — it's a 1968 Buick — when she came out to lunch. I'd see them talking by her car. It was all kind of joking, you understand, but Victoria told me that he bothered her."

"How?" Strunk asked.

"I guess because she didn't know him very well, and he was real insistent about dating her."

"What did he look like?"

"He was about her age, I'd say — maybe 22, 23. I'd say six feet tall, over two hundred pounds. Kind of heavyset, with brown hair."

Ted Fonis showed him the lay-down of mug shots, and the guard identified Cal Lansing immediately as the man who had hung around the dead girl's automobile.

"I didn't like the look of him," he commented sadly. "He was almost stalking her, just creeping around her car, waiting for her like that. I would have told him to leave her alone, but she never asked me to do that — and it wasn't my business."

Armed with the address listed for Calvin Archer Lansing at the time of his traffic violation arrest in May, detectives drove to an area just west of the University District. They found the name Lansing on one of the mailboxes of the run-down five-plex and cautiously approached the apartment just up the stairs where the number on the door matched the mailbox.

Their knocks, however, went unanswered. When they peered through the window, they could see that the apartment had probably been vacant for some time. Cardboard boxes, dust, empty cupboards, and just a few junky pieces of furniture left behind told the story. They contacted a neighboring tenant and learned that Lansing *had* lived there, but he had moved out about a month before.

Even with this information, the detectives double-checked with the landlord and arranged to have patrol units check the address several more times.

They located an elderly relative of Lansing's, but the man they wanted wasn't there, nor was Lansing's car parked nearby. He had several family members living in the south end of Seattle, and the investigators drove "sneaker cars" around their homes, first checking alleyways and surrounding streets to see if the '63 Oldsmobile was parked there.

When they did contact Cal Lansing's relatives, they all said they hadn't seen him for months. One uncle finally admitted that Cal had called only the day before, but he didn't know where he was at the moment.

Elmer Wittman and Mike Germann went back once again to the five-plex. They had a hunch that he wasn't really gone from there for good. This time, they talked with the tenant who lived immediately beneath Lansing's former apartment. She said Cal Lansing had lived there for eight or nine months and had moved out only two weeks before. She'd known him well because he used her phone often.

"In fact," she offered, to the detectives' surprise, "he was here yesterday — in the morning — to pick up his mail."

"How was he? Did he seem nervous — or different than he usually acted?" Germann asked.

"No," she said. "He was like he always

was: in a good mood."

"Have any bruises or scratches on him?"

She shook her head. "None. I wasn't looking for any, though, but there was nothing obvious."

Lansing's neighbor told them that she believed Lansing had been receiving unemployment checks from the state and thought he was probably looking for his check.

"What's he like? You know him well?"

"Not really. But he had a violent temper when something set it off," she said. "He drank a lot of wine, and he was always talking about speed and narcotics. I don't know if he was really using, or if he was trying to sound cool."

Victoria Legg had only been dead for two days, but the investigators from the Seattle Police Homicide Unit had been working around the clock, one team taking over from another. They were fighting time and the chance that Lansing might take another victim. They disregarded the fact that it was a summer Sunday. An all-points bulletin in the eleven western states was issued for Calvin Archer Lansing.

By Monday morning, July 20, they had yet to find Lansing, even though he'd been seen briefly at most of his old haunts. They suspected he was still in the area.

Sergeant Elmer Wittman received a phone call from a female relative of Cal Lansing. She said she was extremely concerned because Lansing always came to her home for Sunday-night dinner, but he hadn't shown up the night before. "I just saw him on Friday night," she said.

"What time was that?" Wittman asked.

"He left my house about 7:30 p.m.," she said. "He was all dressed up, I remember. He had on a gold-colored sweater, a white sport shirt, and plaid slacks."

"Did he say where he was going?"

"No — but he called me Saturday morning about eleven a.m. and asked about his mail. He sounded normal and cheerful, like always. He was waiting for letters from several colleges where he's sent applications. Now I'm worried because Cal said he was coming over to see me in a couple of hours, and I haven't heard a word from him since."

So far, the investigators were getting two diametrically opposed descriptions of Cal Lansing. Some witnesses had said he was a weird stalker, a man with out-of-control temper tantrums, and a drug and alcohol user. His relatives — and Victoria's own neighbor — said that he was a pleasant,

471

well-groomed man who was looking forward to college in the fall.

Lansing's father told detectives that Cal had applied for a loan — a federally insured student loan — from a north end bank so he would have tuition money.

"I think he'll be checking with the bank this week to see what progress they've made on that loan. He applied for $1,000."

When he was asked if his son might have flipped out of control and killed Victoria Legg, Lansing's father looked doubtful.

"I don't think he had anything to do with the murder of that girl," he said firmly. "If he is avoiding you police, it's because he's worried about some traffic violations he has on his record."

"Yeah," Ted Fonis said. "We know about those. No big deal with that. We just want to talk to him and he can probably clear himself."

Fonis and Don Strunk contacted the bank officials and spoke with the officer who had processed Cal Lansing's application. She said she had mailed correspondence to him on the previous Friday, July 17, and had received his reply by return mail.

"In fact," she said, "it was in this morning's mail. I expect I'll hear from him again soon. His loan was okayed and he'll need to get in touch with me in order to get his check."

The number of places Lansing was likely to show up — and soon — was multiplying. Fonis and Strunk asked the bank staff to call them at once if he called them or came in to pick up his check. They made a similar agreement with the Washington State unemployment office where they had learned Lansing was due to report at 9:45 on Wednesday morning. If he wanted any more checks, he was required to check in and give them a list of places where he had sought work.

Every patrol officer in Seattle and all the sheriff's deputies in King County had Lansing's photo on their dashboards and the description of his white Oldsmobile. Surely, one of them would spot him at any moment.

But the hours passed without even a sighting. Strunk and Fonis worked on another lead that could place Lansing with Victoria Legg on Friday evening. No one had actually seen them together — not even her neighbor. He had seen Lansing, as had the bartender at The Warehouse. Was there even a slight chance that Vicki had stood Lansing up? Had she gone out with someone else?

They knew from autopsy findings that the contents of Victoria Legg's stomach indicated that she had eaten Chinese food within two hours of her death. Teams of detectives talked to the proprietors and waiters of every Chinese restaurant from the University District northward. It was a tremendous undertaking: Chinese food is very popular in Seattle, and there seemed to be Chinese restaurants in every block. The detectives visited dozens of them.

It was the team of Nat Crawford and Don Dragland who found an important witness. They located a counter girl in a Chinese drive-in on Lake City Way who immediately picked Cal Lansing's photo from the ten-mug-shot laydown they showed her.

She pointed to his picture and said, "Yes, I'm sure. *This* man was here on Friday evening just before closing. He came in about a quarter to ten and he was in a hurry. I can't remember just what he ordered, but it wasn't a large order — only about enough for two people."

But just as the two detectives got their hopes up, the witness said she hadn't seen whether Lansing had a girl with him or not.

"From my counter," she explained, "I

can't see the whole parking lot. There could have been someone with him, but when he headed for his car, he walked out of my line of sight."

Still, it was another important circumstantial piece of evidence. Vicki died two or three hours after she had Chinese food, and Lansing had bought an order for two around ten p.m.

As Monday ended, the investigative crew, which by this time included almost every member of the department's seventeen-man Homicide Unit, had reconstructed the events of Friday evening — but only to the point where the couple had presumably visited the Chinese drive-in.

Just as important, or perhaps more compelling, was what they had found out about Cal Lansing himself. He wasn't the friendly, All-American athlete he sometimes pretended to be. In reality he was nothing like the man Victoria thought she was dating.

The homicide investigators learned that Lansing was a brilliant — if erratic — scholar. He had been in and out of college, but never came close to getting his degree. He had also been in and out of mental hospitals. He *had* been in a hospital recently — just as he told Victoria — but it wasn't for a football injury: he had voluntarily committed himself to Western State Hospital in Steilacoom, Washington, twice in the past.

Cal Lansing was in the Seattle area, detectives knew, because he had called the home of relatives twice more. He had been informed during those calls that the detectives wanted to talk with him, but he told his family, "I didn't do it — and I'm not going to sit in jail for a year until they find the guy that did it."

When they asked where he was, he hung up.

The investigators continued to drive by each address where he might show up. They also visited every tavern Lansing had been known to frequent in the past — all with negative results. Their gut feeling was that he wasn't far away, but so far he was only a shadow to them, someone whom they felt was thumbing his nose at them just beyond their peripheral vision.

On Wednesday, July 22, Sergeant Ivan Beeson, Fonis, Baughman, and Strunk staked out the Washington Employment Security office in the early morning in the hope that the elusive Lansing would appear for his appointment at 9:45. Hours passed, but he didn't show up. They dropped their stakeout temporarily, sure that he was too smart to try to get his unemployment check. An hour later, the manager of the office called the police radio operator and whispered that Cal Lansing had just appeared in the office.

Detectives were in the building within only minutes, but the suspect had become suspicious and left.

"What's he wearing today?" Don Strunk asked, disgusted to learn they had missed Lansing once again. He was beginning to feel as though Lansing was *watching* them and knew exactly where his trackers were at all times, instead of the other way around.

The employment counselor said he'd never seen Lansing before, but recalled that "he was wearing a gray shirt, gray pants, and horn-rimmed glasses. He's got several days' growth of beard. The gal that usually checks him in wasn't sure it was him, so we told him that he would need a more extensive interview, and asked him to wait for a few minutes. He sat down in the chair I pointed out, but then I saw him get up and leave in a hurry. He's very antsy."

Outside the employment office, a cordon of squad cars with their bubble lights flashing surrounded the area, but a half hour's search failed to turn up Cal Lansing. Foot patrolmen and patrol officers were instructed to arrest him on sight.

The detectives were sure that Lansing had somehow slipped through their fingers. He was like a fox, sniffing the air, catching their scent, reading their minds. They kicked themselves for not realizing that sooner.

And then, suddenly, their police radios crackled: "Suspect Calvin Lansing is presently in the Washington Mutual Savings Bank on West Market Street."

Somehow, he had made his way many miles from where he had last been seen. He was attempting to pick up his $1,000 check. If he got that, he would have enough money to leave Seattle far behind.

"Tell the bank to stall him," Don Strunk told the radio operator. "Do whatever they have to do. We're ten minutes away."

Several teams of detectives headed for the bank. En route, the radio operator's voice reassured them by saying that Cal Lansing had been apprehended at the bank by patrol officers.

He had already been advised of his constitutional rights under *Miranda* by the arresting officers. He refused to tell them much more than his name. If he had a vehicle nearby, he wasn't saying. Sergeant Ivan Beeson and Don Strunk drove him to homicide headquarters in the Public Safety Building.

Detectives Roy Moran and Owen McKenna began an immediate search of the area around the bank in an effort to locate Lansing's Oldsmobile sedan. McKenna had a set of keys that bore General Motors markings that the arresting officers had found in Lansing's pocket. He and Moran suspected that the missing sedan was probably parked within walking or jogging distance, and it might well contain physical evidence connected with Victoria Legg's murder.

As they drove slowly around the area of the Washington Mutual Bank, McKenna spotted a middle-aged man sitting alone in a small foreign car parked near the bank. He glanced at his watch frequently, as if he was waiting for someone. In response to McKenna's questions, the man said that his name was Matthew Wrigley★ and that he *did* know Cal Lansing.

"I drove him to the bank as a favor to a friend," he said. Wrigley seemed bewildered at the turn of events that had ended with Lansing's arrest. "He's been staying at my place for the last four days."

"Do you know where his car is?" McKenna asked.

"Sure," Wrigley replied. "It's parked right out in front of our house."

Wrigley told McKenna that Cal Lansing had come to his north end home well after midnight on Friday night and asked one of his stepsons if he could spend the night.

"I woke up Saturday morning and there he was on the couch, asleep. His face was dirty and his right hand was bruised and bloody," Wrigley recalled. "So was his arm just above the wrist. I asked him what had happened and he said that he'd been in a fight over by Alki Beach — told me he got jumped by four guys, but he said he ended up 'beating the hell' out of them."

Wrigley said he'd known Cal Lansing for about a year. "After Friday night — er, Saturday morning — Cal just stayed on with my family. He seemed kind of lonely and we were planning a trip up into Okanogan County, so we asked him to come along for the weekend and he accepted. We didn't come back until about noon on Monday."

That would explain why Matt Wrigley hadn't heard about the Victoria Legg homicide; Okanogan County was far northeast of Seattle, on the Canadian border.

Lots of vacationers went up there to get away from the city and didn't read Seattle papers. Radio signals from the coast disappeared after cars reached the summit of the Cascade mountain passes.

As for the Oldsmobile, Wrigley said Cal Lansing had asked if he could leave his car parked at their home for the summer because he had "lost his driver's license and didn't want to be tempted to drive."

They had no problem with that. A day later, he had offered them a bargain price on the Olds if they wanted to buy it from him. "We told him we didn't need another car," Wrigley said.

With Wrigley's statement, too, came the explanation of the mysterious "escape" of Lansing from the Employment Security Office. Lansing himself hadn't even been there; he had told Wrigley that he had another appointment for a job interview, and asked the older man to sign in for him on the unemployment line. But when personnel there saw the name he gave, and advised Wrigley that he would need an interview, he had become nervous and fled. So officers looking for Lansing had had no chance of catching him. It had been Wrigley — who bore no resemblance to Lansing — who had slipped through the police cordon, himself unaware of the circumstances.

At headquarters, Cal Lansing was advised again of his rights. He stated that he did not wish to discuss the case, but he did want to talk with an attorney. He was given a pair of jail coveralls to wear and the investigators noted that both his knees were badly bruised and scabbed, his right hand had a deep cut, and his right arm was inflamed and hot to the touch. It looked as though it was infected. He declined to accept treatment for the infected wound on his hand and arm and continued to do so in spite of the advice of a jail physician.

Detectives talked to Matthew Wrigley's wife while McKenna examined the suspect's sedan, which was still parked in front of the Wrigley home. Mrs. Wrigley substantiated her husband's account of Lansing's coming to their home during the early-morning hours of July 18. She had noted that he was nervous and upset about his "fistfight on the beach at Alki." She had observed "skid burns" on his knees and what looked like fingernail scratches on his side.

He had asked her to wash some of his clothes — including a yellow sweater with bloodstains on it. She had washed some of his clothes but she put the sweater aside because it would need special treatment to get the blood out. In view of his story of a fight at Alki, she thought little of the fact that the sweater had blood on it. She assumed it was his own blood.

She turned all of Cal Lansing's clothes and possessions that he'd left in the Wrigley home over to detectives.

As he went over the Oldsmobile sedan, McKenna noted what appeared to be bloodstains on the steering column and on the registration holder. As he peered closely at the seat covers, McKenna saw what looked to be flecks of dark red. However, final determination would have to be made by criminalist George Ishii, as the covers were of a "speckled" red and silver design that made it impossible to tell with the naked eye what was part of the pattern and what might be dried blood.

As the Oldsmobile was hoisted by a tow truck to be impounded in a police holding garage, McKenna noted a dried holly leaf clinging to the underbody of the right front section. He removed the leaf and placed it in an evidence bag. Later, in court, this single leaf would become the subject of hours of cross-examination by Lansing's attorneys.

The Oldsmobile's trunk held several

pairs of men's shoes, various articles of male clothing, and a filthy blanket. The blanket was covered with dirt, twigs, and bits of leaves, and stained profusely with what appeared to be dried blood.

At the crime lab, criminalists Dr. George Ishii and Kay Sweeney, tested the blanket's stains. They were, as suspected, human blood, and the blood was of two types: Cal Lansing's *and* Victoria Legg's. Again, thirty years ago, forensic science could not yet identify a person by examining blood for combinations of enzymes, and although Ishii was aware of research on DNA matching, his tests were done sixteen years before that process would be used in solving a crime — and that, a single case in a Scottish village.

Just before noon on July 23, a citizen reported to detectives that he had been searching for a hubcap the previous evening along a parking strip on Ravenna Avenue when he found what looked to be a bloody T-shirt. This was the street that was a direct route from the slaying site to the Wrigley residence.

Detectives went at once to Ravenna Avenue and searched the parking strip. They recovered the red-smeared T-shirt, a pair of socks, an almost full pack of cigarettes, and a quantity of dried holly leaves — leaves just like the single leaf McKenna had removed from the underbody of Lansing's vehicle.

Holly leaves were hardly alien vegetation. The entire Northwest coastal area has ideal climate and soil to grow the red-berried bushes and trees that are seen only at Christmas in most states.

Driving a police vehicle with a Stewart Warner calibrated speedometer, one of the investigators began a mileage check from the spot where the bloody clothing and tire marks had been found to the Wrigley residence. The distance was three-tenths of a mile.

Within a week of Victoria Legg's murder, the Homicide Unit detectives had, through extensive legwork and meticulous gathering and cataloguing of physical evidence, built a tight case against Cal Lansing. Over a hundred pieces of physical evidence and a number of extensive witness statements were noted in the growing case file.

Cal Lansing was formally charged with first-degree murder. However, the actual trial of the stocky suspect would be delayed for a full year. In October of 1970, Lansing was declared mentally unfit to participate in his own defense and was transferred to the Western State Hospital for the third time.

It was July 1971 when Cal Lansing would face a jury of his peers in Superior Court Judge James Noe's courtroom. Some of the most bizarre and shocking testimony ever heard in a King County courtroom would be brought out as his attorneys Wesley Hohlbein and Lowell Halvorson fought to show their client as a profoundly disturbed individual. Under the M'Naghten Rule, the standard that most states use to delineate the fine line between sane and insane under the law, they had to show that Cal Lansing did not know the difference between right and wrong at the time of Victoria Legg's murder.

Patricia Harber, a veteran in the King County Prosecutor's Office who was the assistant chief criminal deputy, and deputy prosecutor Douglas Duncan would hold that Lansing was quite aware of his crime against Victoria.

The State maintained that Lansing had deliberately led his victim into the deep and isolated park so that he could attack her, and that he had most certainly made adequate provisions after the murder to facilitate his own escape.

Judge Noe presided over one of the largest courtrooms in the King County Courthouse, and most of the varnished oak benches were full each day. Many court sessions stretched long into the evening hours as Pat Harber presented the physical evidence to the jury.

Wes Hohlbein was known as an attorney from the school of Richard "Racehorse" Haynes and Gerry Spence, sometimes a bombastic actor and at others a relentless jackhammer who wore the Court's patience thin. He was definitely a showman, and regular court watchers tried never to miss a trial where Hohlbein appeared for the defense. Now, he cross-examined prosecution witnesses vigorously.

At one point in the trial, when the blanket alleged to have been present at the murder site was unfolded and held up in the courtroom, Hohlbein, who had been vehemently against the State's introducing the single holly leaf caught in the undercarriage of Lansing's Oldsmobile, demanded that the courtroom be swept so that "evidence" would not be lost on the chamber's floors.

Those of us covering the trial waited while the floor was swept. But the first sweeping did not satisfy Hohlbein, and he himself bent to sweep the floor with a whisk broom, taking at least fifteen minutes to be sure "no evidence is lost."

None of the histrionics appeared to touch Cal Lansing. Throughout the sessions, the defendant sat stolidly, betraying little emotion.

Dr. Richard B. Jarvis, testifying on the mental competency of the defendant for the prosecution, stated that he believed Lansing had a schizophrenic personality disorder but was not psychotic, and able "before, during, and after the crime to carry on a normal pattern of social activity . . . He was quite able to make a moral distinction about the concept of degradation on the victim, able to take steps to avoid detection and apprehension."

Asked by Wes Hohlbein if it was not possible for a person to suddenly become psychotic during the commission of a crime, Dr. Jarvis replied: "This idea of someone going out of one's mind with devastating swiftness just does not happen, in my experience."

For the first time, the checkered background of Cal Lansing became known to the general public as nightly newscasts reported each day's courtroom events.

Cal Lansing had been a popular, serious student, the vice president of his senior class in high school. In a battery of IQ tests, he had scored at vastly superior levels. One test indicated he was brighter than 85 percent of the population, another that he was more intelligent than 99 out of 100 people. He had attended two colleges.

And yet, Cal Lansing's family background made for a very negative case history. His parents testified that their marriage had been marked by hostility and fighting. His mother showed the jury scars she had received when her husband attacked her with a can opener and subsequently broke her leg. She also said that he had hit her on the head with a baseball bat and that she had chased him with a machete. As a child, Cal had witnessed these battles between his mother and father.

Calvin Lansing Sr. confirmed the stories and told the jurors of criminal activity he and his son had engaged in. The senior Lansing said that he had survived the Bataan Death March during World War II and still kept a scrapbook of his war experiences and the atrocities committed — a scrapbook in which his son had evinced much interest.

Both parents discussed an alleged incident that had occurred in a California jail where Cal claimed he had been raped by several men in a cell. This incident had seemed to have a lasting and damaging effect on Lansing.

On July 21, 1971, Cal Lansing took the stand in his own defense. In a flat voice, he recited details of his life and the crime he was charged with — details that shocked even veteran courtroom habitués. He admitted that he had had sexual relations with relatives, with his dog, and, on the very day that Victoria Legg was murdered, with a 4-year-old girl.

He said that he found the world around him "despicable." He related that he used marijuana and LSD but did not remember how many times he had dropped acid because "after ten or twenty trips you lose track of them."

In the same flat voice, devoid of affect, Lansing gave his version of the events of July 17, 1970. He recalled meeting Victoria Legg about a month earlier. That day or that week, she had accepted a date to go to a tavern with him.

"I was enjoying the evening very much — it seemed kind of pleasant. We danced and talked a lot. It wasn't deep conversation — just lighthearted."

The defendant said he had then suggested that they drive to Cowan Park and play on the swings, but when they arrived there the swings were occupied, so they decided to walk. After walking for a while, Lansing spread a blanket on the ground for them to sit on. Perhaps Victoria Legg had already begun to sense danger; perhaps not. At any rate, Lansing told the jury that she made a remark that suddenly made her seem threatening to him; he could not remember just what it was, but he felt that she was part of a conspiracy from California and that it was somehow connected with his own castration.

In response to that, he said he had tightened his arm around her neck and ordered her to perform a sexual act upon him. When she panicked and tried to run, he tackled her. "I don't know what happened except that I started beating her. I remember being fascinated with beating her — there was the joy of each punch and this feeling that it was my obligation to have sex with her."

The 220-pound defendant told of sitting on his victim and holding her by the ears while he beat her head against the ground.

"Somehow I knew that if I didn't have sex with her, I would either be killed or castrated or both."

As Pat Harber cross-examined Lansing, he answered quite calmly that he had raped Victoria Legg because "I wanted to degrade her."

"Isn't it true that you stuffed wild ferns and leaves down her throat because you heard voices in the park and wanted to silence her cries for help?"

"No," Lansing replied. "I did that because I was fascinated with cruelty and torture."

He told the jurors that after he strangled and raped his victim, he got partially dressed, picked up his stained socks and T-shirt — which he threw away later — and walked back to his car and drove away.

"I thought she was still alive when I left."

A psychiatrist for the defense, Dr. David Clarke, characterized the defendant as a paranoid schizophrenic. He said that Lansing had hallucinations after the homosexual "rape incident" in the California jail and warded off "demons" by a confusing process of "forcing them into the spaces between molecules."

As an example of the thought processes

in the defendant's mind, Dr. Clarke read one of many poems that Lansing had written:

Imagine the mindless
Oxen
Careening madly
Through a field of roses
Watch the beggar
Rape the girl child.
Her blood flow —
Like a new-made fountain
Nomadic man-made
Beasts
Swarm across the horizon
locust fashion
Devouring maiden roses.

The courtroom was hushed after that example of the defendant's poetic images. This, then, had been the man that Victoria Legg had chosen to date because he resembled someone she knew and trusted.

After a lengthy Saturday session, the jury retired to ponder their decision on the guilt or innocence of Calvin Archer Lansing and to decide whether he should receive the death penalty and be hanged for the murder of Victoria Legg if found guilty.

They had been sequestered for three weeks. Now they would evaluate the almost two hundred pieces of physical evidence introduced and thousands of words of testimony.

It took almost four days, with time off to sleep, but after thirty-one hours of deliberation, the jury sent word to Judge Noe that they had reached a verdict: guilty of murder in the first degree — but with no recommendation of the death penalty.

One month after this verdict was returned, Cal Lansing underwent another evaluation of his mental condition. He was found to be psychotic and not mentally capable of understanding the nature and seriousness of his sentence. Instead, Judge Noe ruled that the 22-year-old man should be held in maximum security at Western State Hospital.

One interesting — and odd — side effect of Cal Lansing's trial was that his father, Cal Sr., was so intrigued with murder trials that he became a fixture in the courthouse. For years, he appeared at every major trial and showed up almost daily in the courthouse and in the Public Safety Building across the street. He came to consider himself an expert on courtroom procedure, and apparently bore the homicide detectives and prosecutors no ill will for convicting his son of murder.

If — and when — Cal Lansing Jr. should ever be adjudged competent, he faced a sentence of up to life in prison. But Lansing vanished into the system. If he is alive today, he is 55 years old. He is not listed in death records, nor does he appear to be an inmate in any Washington State prison. Patients in mental hospitals are protected by privacy laws.

If Victoria Legg were alive today, she, too, would be 55. I cannot help but wonder what her life could have been like if Cal Lansing had failed to call her for the second time on July 17, 1970. She would have gone shopping at the mall with her girlfriend, rather than dancing with him. No one can ever know at what point during their date Victoria began to realize that Lansing was not at all the person she had expected him to be. While they were dancing? As they ate their Chinese takeout in his car? As they walked toward the swings in the park? A girl as shy as she was would never have walked down into the dark ravine with him.

Tragically, she was too naive to know how to turn back until it was too late.

The Highway Accident

Maybe it is true that there is nothing new under the sun, and that even the most shocking crime stories in today's headlines are really just reruns of what has happened before throughout ancient and modern history. Two of the most media-saturated murder cases in 2004 are, of course, the Laci and Connor Peterson homicides in Modesto, California, and the more recent Lori Hacking tragedy in Salt Lake City. As I write this, neither the Peterson nor the Hacking cases have been fully adjudicated in a court of law. However, Scott Peterson is in the midst of his trial as the defendant charged with the murder of his wife and the son who was within a month of being born. And Mark Hacking has been charged with the apparent shooting death of his pregnant wife and the subsequent disposal of her body. We know that Laci's and Connor's remains were found in San Francisco Bay. Lori Hacking's remains were found on October 1, 2004, buried in a landfill.

★ ★ ★

Despite our horror at the shocking number of females who fall victim to infamous serial killers, the truth is that the largest percentage of women who are murdered are killed by men they once loved and trusted: lovers, husbands, ex-husbands, and ex-lovers. Most women believe they can judge a man and perceive any aberrance that may exist in his secret heart. In the majority of cases, that is true. And those women who have made the right decisions about their love lives are sometimes too quick to judge women who guessed wrong.

That isn't fair. Some of the most intelligent women are fooled by men with perfect facades. And deluded for a very long time. I am not talking about the slick married man who convinces an innocent woman that his wife doesn't understand him, or the con man who marries wife after wife (some of them concurrently rather than consecutively) so he can get his hands on their money or property, or the sexual cheater who cannot be satisfied with being intimate with just one woman but must have multiple liaisons.

I am speaking now of the men — and, to be fair, of the women — who live lives that are totally fabricated. These deceivers leave their homes in the morning headed for jobs or for classes that don't exist. They promise a wonderful future, even though they must *know* that eventually the truth will come out. How carefully they have to choreograph their hours and their days, how many lies they have to tell, how many financial ledgers that require juggling and double entries. The true sociopath doesn't mind lying to his own family and friends. Indeed, he often lies even when there is no point in the falsehood; it would be simpler to tell the truth. For years, those who love the liar believe — because *they* do have consciences, and don't expect someone they love to lie to them. The very thought of the deceptive games people whose whole lives are phony must play all the time sounds exhausting.

Mark Hacking, 28, allegedly convinced his wife of five years, Lori, 27, that he was attending the University of Utah for two years after he had dropped out of school. He even sent out announcements of his "graduation" in 2004. The couple made plans to move to North Carolina, where Mark said he had been accepted at the University of North Carolina's Medical School.

It was as prosecuting attorneys of earlier decades liked to say, "all a tissue of lies."

On July 18, 2004, when Lori Hacking found out that her husband's name was unknown at the North Carolina university's registrar's office, she was stunned. How could that be? They were packing up their apartment, preparing for their move across the country. Mark had a new stethoscope with his name engraved on it. He was going to be a doctor — like his father. One moment, Lori had it all; she and Mark had been about to embark on a great step forward in their future, she believed that she was five weeks pregnant and she was thrilled, and the couple were even scheduled to attend a goodbye party that night thrown by their many friends. They went to the party, despite Lori's doubts, and she smiled as if she hadn't a care in the world.

The Hackings were caught on the security cameras of an all-night convenience store later that night, and Lori — who had been cheerful at the party — no longer looked happy. Hours later, Mark Hacking came in alone. The next morning, he frantically called police to say his wife had not returned from her morning jog. He said he had run her regular route twice, desperately looking for her. Local law enforcement investigators found that he was actually buying a new mattress during the time he said he was racing the jogging path, looking for Lori.

But a nearby garbage can was puddled with blood, and the Hackings' old mattress had been disposed of.

In Modesto, California, Laci Peterson was also pregnant — very pregnant — and, according to her husband, Scott, she had gone for a walk with their aging golden retriever on Christmas Eve morning, 2002, and had failed to return. Scott, of course, hadn't known that, he said, as he'd been fishing in San Francisco Bay that Christmas Eve.

Everyone who can read or who watches television knows the Peterson case, and the Hacking case is sure to garner as many headlines. They are both heartbreaking stories.

I read somewhere that the Mark and Lori Hacking story may well be a "textbook case," one for the record books in the field of criminology. I doubt that. When I think of the emails and letters I have received from beguiled and duped women over the years, I remember so many that were shockingly similar. One woman with three sons lived for years believing that her husband had died in a terrible accident — only to find him living quite happily and successfully 2,500 miles away. Another married a "professor" who simply disappeared one day. He turned up, too, teaching at another college. He'd done it several times before; when one life got boring, he simply fashioned himself a new identity.

And then there was the case of an Oregon couple who everyone thought were the perfect match. I covered that story in Salem in 1976. That was almost thirty years ago, and it appeared to be an anguishing twist of fate for a young man and wife who were so much like the Hackings. She was a schoolteacher and he was about to graduate and begin an exciting career. She was finally able to fulfill her longtime dream of becoming a mother, and she was so proud of him. All her sacrifices to support them and pay his tuition at Oregon State University were more than worth it.

She was planning his graduation party when their life together ended in what appeared to be a terrible accident on a curving road near the Oregon coastline.

When I first heard about the disappearance of Lori Hacking in Salt Lake City, I experienced a haunting sense of déjà vu. As you read this case, I suspect you will agree.

One proviso: as you read this, realize that I have had to change some names, and block out some photos. The reason? The guilty person in the Buckleys' story in Oregon was out of prison in a little more than ten years. The ending of the story was not at all what I expected. Was justice done? That is up to you to decide.

The sounds coming through the bedroom wall in the duplex apartment in suburban Salem, Oregon, were too loud and too disturbing for anyone to sleep through. It was very early in the morning on February 25, 1976, when both Marilee⋆ and Doug Blaine⋆ had the same dream, or rather, the same nightmare. Wrenched from deep sleep in the dark winter night, they sat up in bed. Doug fumbled for a light.

They could hear a woman screaming over and over, "No! No! Don't!" Then there was only silence, which was followed by a softer sound that was almost like a moan. That was suddenly cut short.

Blaine looked at the clock beside their bed and saw it was three a.m. He and his wife discussed what they should do. Although they had never heard the couple in the adjoining duplex fight before, they agreed that they were probably overhearing a domestic squabble. They hated to interfere in something that was none of their business. What should they do — go knock on the door in the next unit and ask, "What seems to be the problem?" Maybe pound on the wall? They couldn't phone because they didn't even know the last name of the people next door, much less their telephone number.

There were no more screams, now. They tried to get back to sleep, but Doug Blaine was troubled and he tossed and turned, watching bare tree limbs bend grotesquely over the streetlight outside as the wind pushed them.

After a while, he thought he heard someone open the front door of the adjacent duplex. Blaine got out of bed and, without turning on any lights, crept to his living room. Feeling somewhat like a busybody, he eased out of his front door silently and stood in the frigid dark where he knew he was hidden by his car. Everything seemed perfectly normal. Both of the neighbors' cars were parked in the driveway: a Volkswagen Beetle and a Chevy Vega. Far off, a dog barked and the trees creaked in the wind, but there was no other sound.

Back inside, Blaine heard nothing but the ticking of clocks and the furnace blower. He crawled back in bed and he and his wife tried to go back to sleep.

It was quiet for about twenty minutes, but then they heard drawers being opened and shut next door, closet doors squeaking, and bedsprings settling. Beginning to feel like a fool, Blaine looked out his front window once more. This time, the man next door was carrying what looked like laundry or bedding to the Vega. He made several trips back and forth to the car. Then he got in and started it up. Without pausing to let the engine warm up, he backed out, accelerating as he disappeared down Cedar Court.

Wide-awake, the Blaines discussed what they should do. It looked as if their neighbors had had a spat and the husband had left to cool off. They didn't know the couple except to nod and say "Hi" when they happened to meet. The wife was always friendly, but her husband seemed aloof. If they didn't even know the couple's names, they certainly hadn't the faintest idea about the state of their marriage. The only times they had heard any loud noise from the other side of the wall was when the couple had parties, and that had not happened very often.

It was after 4:30 a.m. when the Blaines finally decided they should notify the police; they couldn't forget the screams they had heard. If the girl next door was all right they would feel a little foolish, but feeling foolish was worth peace of mind.

Their call came into the Marion County Sheriff's radio room at 4:47 a.m. Corporal Tim Taylor and Deputy Ralph Nicholson were dispatched to Cedar Court. They knocked on the door of the neat duplex, but there was no response. Since the Blaines didn't know their neighbors' last name, Taylor gave the radio operator the license plate number on the Volkswagen parked there and asked for a check on the registered owner. The owners came back as Lori Susan★ and Walter Louis Buckley.★ Taylor asked the operator to look up the Buckleys' phone number and telephone the residence. Soon, he heard the lonely sound of a phone ringing again and again in the empty apartment.

If there was anyone inside, they either would not — or could not — answer the phone.

The Blaines were positive that the woman who lived next door had not left with her husband in the Vega. They pointed out that her car, the Volkswagen, was still parked there. Tim Taylor contacted the man who owned the duplexes. Even though it was still very early in the morning, he said he would be right over with a key to open the door for the deputies.

The door to the Buckleys' duplex swung open and the deputies stepped in. They saw that the place was immaculate. Tentatively, the two sheriff's officers peered into each room, calling out the Buckleys' names. No one answered. There wasn't that much to look at; there was a living-dining area, a kitchen, and two bedrooms. The southeast bedroom looked as if it were being used for storage. A drawer had been left pulled out in one chest. Oddly, there was a pile of walnuts on the floor in front of it.

The master bedroom — the southwest bedroom — was the room that shared a common wall with the Blaines' bedroom. It was as neat as the rest of the house. The queen-sized bed had been stripped of sheets, and clean sheets rested atop the mattress as if someone had begun to change the bed linen.

There were no visible signs of violence. The missing bedding was something of a puzzle, but then Doug Blaine had said it looked as if Buckley had been carrying laundry to the car. Well, that's why twenty-four-hour Laundromats stayed in business. People did their laundry at all times of the day and night.

Even though he hadn't found anything suspicious inside the empty duplex, Tim Taylor radioed in that he felt there should be a recheck of the premises in daylight. "The occupants will probably be back by then," he said.

Taylor left his business card on the dining room table with a note asking the Buckleys to call the Sheriff's Office on their return. Then they could write the complaint off in a simple FIR (Field Investigation Report).

But there were no calls from the Buckley duplex. Six hours later, Deputy Bernie Papenfus returned to the Cedar Court address and knocked on the door. There still was no response. But now in daylight, Papenfus noticed a faint red spot on the front step. It looked very much like dried blood. Once again, the landlord, who had also felt strangely troubled since he had opened the door for the deputies at five that morning, produced a key.

Their voices hushed, Papenfus and the landlord entered the duplex. It was bright and airy; the sun was shining through the windows. The home had been decorated with charm and good taste, with paintings, plants, and a wine rack with bottles of homemade wine bearing the Buckleys' names. Wicker lamps and end tables complemented the furniture. There was nothing out of place in the living room — not even a magazine or newspaper.

They moved to the master bedroom. Papenfus's trained eye noted another reddish stain that was barely visible on the rust carpet in the bedroom. Still, the room looked normal enough.

But cops see things that other people don't. Papenfus's throat tightened a little as he saw that the blue-flowered mattress was not sitting square on the springs. He raised it. The underside was a mass of bloody stains. Blood had soaked into the surface and it was still damp.

Hurrying now, Papenfus looked for more signs that something violent had taken place in this little duplex unit. He didn't have to look far. There were more dried scarlet streaks on the towel cupboard and on the entryway into the kitchen. The stains on the carpet were blurred, as if someone had tried to rub them out.

Deputy Bernie Papenfus had seen enough; something terrible had happened here during the night. Careful not to use the phone in the Buckleys' duplex, he radioed Sheriff Jim Heenan's office and asked that detectives respond to what could now only be considered a "possible homicide."

Lieutenant Kilburn McCoy and Sergeant Will Hingston left their offices in Salem and headed for the address on Cedar Court. Lieutenant James Byrnes, chief of detectives, and Detective Dave Kominek had left Salem very early to attend a narcotics conference in Portland. En route, McCoy radioed Byrnes to stand by because the circumstances at the Buckley home were most suspicious.

Byrnes would not be going to Portland, after all.

Kilburn McCoy learned that Lori Buckley, who was 26, was employed as a sixth-grade teacher at the Highland Elementary School in Salem. It was possible that she was in her classroom, teaching. That would explain why she was not in the apartment at eleven a.m. on a Wednesday morning. He called the school and learned that Lori Buckley was not there. However, she had arranged to have a substitute because she had a dental appointment scheduled for Wednesday morning. She was not due at school until the afternoon sessions.

The school office staff didn't know her dentist's name. They gave the detectives the phone numbers for Lori Buckley's relatives, suggesting that they might know her dentist.

While they waited to hear from Lori Buckley's family, the Marion County detectives moved around her home. They found more and more bloodstains marring the otherwise immaculate apartment.

Whatever had happened here, the scene had to be protected. Hingston and Papenfus strung heavy rope, cordoning off the entire property from the sidewalk back, and posted a sign that read, POLICE LINE: DO NOT ENTER. They half expected Lori and Walt Buckley to come driving up and ask them what in the world they were doing. But no one came by except curious drivers who gawked at the rope and the sign.

Finally armed with the name of Lori Buckley's dentist, McCoy called his office, only to find that Lori had not shown up for her appointment. It was to have been a preliminary session for a long-term teeth-straightening procedure. Lori's dentist was concerned when she didn't keep her appointment or even call. He said she was always thoughtful about calling to cancel if she could not make an appointment.

Lori Buckley's family arrived at her du-plex, worried and completely mystified. They talked with detectives outside, since no one but police personnel could go in until the place had been processed. Her family said that Lori and Walt had been happily married for four years. Lori had been teaching since her graduation from Oregon College of Education. Walt was at-tending Oregon State University in Corvallis. He was about to graduate with a degree in accounting. Lori's folks com-mented that Walt had recently applied to become an FBI agent. He had told them about the fifteen-page form he had to fill out, laughing about what specific details the Bureau wanted to know about every facet of his background.

Asked if it was possible that Lori and Walt had gotten into a brawl, her family was aghast. They could not imagine such a thing. That just wasn't possible. Lori and Walt just didn't have that kind of a mar-riage. They had never known them to have *any* kind of physical confrontation.

The Marion County detectives won-dered if it was possible that someone had entered the Buckleys' duplex during the night. Doug Blaine had admitted he didn't know the neighbors that well. He had seen a man going out to his neighbors' car and he thought it had been the man who lived next door, but he admitted he could have been mistaken. Could the Buckleys have been abducted by someone who had injured one — or both — of them?

Doug Blaine said he hadn't seen Lori Buckley at all. Just her husband with his arms full of laundry.

In whatever manner Lori had left her duplex, she wasn't there now. A thorough search of the apartment proved that. She wasn't in the closets or in the crawl spaces. She and her husband were both missing.

The Oregon State Police Crime Lab and ID Bureau in Portland responded by sending criminalists to the scene. Sergeant William Zeller and Troopers Sherie Kindler, Cliff Daimler, and George Matsuda set out at once to help. Chief of Detectives Jim Byrnes and Detective Dave Kominek were already on their way back from Portland.

It was apparent that someone had been gravely injured in this apartment. The bloodstains on the underside of the blue mattress measured between four and ten inches in diameter. That much blood could not have come from a minor cut.

Doug Blaine described again for the detectives what he had heard. "I've never heard a scream like that before. It was kind of a moaning scream like someone was being hurt, not like someone had just knocked the coffeepot off."

The sheriff's office sent out a teletype on the missing couple to all police agencies in the area. They were described as Walter L. "Walt" Buckley, 26 years old, five feet nine inches tall. He weighed 180 pounds and had light brown hair and a mustache. Lori Buckley was five feet five inches, weighed 130 pounds, and had long brown hair. Their missing car was a light green Chevrolet Vega bearing Oregon plates: DRY-255.

Detectives canvassed the neighborhood along Cedar Court looking for someone else who might have seen or heard anything unusual during the early-morning hours. But no one had.

A complete crime scene search of the duplex and its carefully tended yard disclosed more unusual or misplaced items. There was a Tab bottle cap on the kitchen counter, and bits of a Tab label and pieces of bottle glass under the sewing machine in the master bedroom. There were fragments of bloodstained glass behind the dresser on the north wall. There was evidence of blood residue in the bathtub and on the drain plug.

The clean, folded flower-patterned sheets that rested on the blue mattress were flecked with blood. A man's large-sized T-shirt and a knit shirt taken from a clothing basket in the bedroom were slightly stained with some red material. All of the bloodstains were tested and proved to be Type A.

An amazing response to the sheriff's teletype came from the Oregon State Police office in Lincoln City, a resort town on the Oregon coast. The state police reported that a Lori Buckley had been *killed* that morning in a traffic accident along the Van Duzer Corridor. The corridor is a winding highway between the Pacific Ocean coast towns and inland cities. The fatal accident in which Lori Buckley had been killed was almost fifty miles from the duplex where she lived.

The detectives shook their heads. How could that be? How could the Blaines have heard screams on the other side of their bedroom wall at three a.m. when Lori was in an accident so far away? If they had been men who believed in ghosts, which *very* few detectives are, they might have come up with some otherworldly scenarios.

It took the Marion County detectives a number of phone calls before they established that Walt Buckley was alive but had been injured in the accident that killed his wife. The Oregon State Police said he had been taken to a hospital in Lincoln City in Lincoln County.

The next report that seemed connected to the increasingly peculiar case was a call from Sergeant Lee Miller of the Polk County Sheriff's Office. Polk County lies between Marion County and Lincoln County and the Buckleys would have had to pass through it to get to Lincoln City. Miller said a hiker had found a pile of bloody bedding — sheets, blankets, a bedspread, and a mattress pad — among the forest undergrowth along Mill Creek Road in Polk County. Jim Byrnes checked the description of the bed linen against that of the list of the bedding found in the Buckleys' duplex. He found many similarities.

Byrnes and Dave Kominek left Salem and headed over to the coast. Crime lab technicians went to Polk County to pick up and bag the blood-soaked bedding found along a narrow dirt logging road.

When Jim Byrnes and Dave Kominek arrived at the scene of the fatal traffic accident, the Buckleys' Vega had already been towed away. They parked at Mile Post 14 on Highway 18 at 4:20 p.m., aware that there was precious little daylight left. But they could see where the Vega had gone off the shoulder of the road. It had crushed vegetation when it went over the bank and then dropped about twelve feet through a thick stand of fir trees. The two Marion County investigators commented to each other that there were no skid marks or torn-up areas on the shoulder of the highway; there were only parallel tracks in the soft dirt and grass.

Oregon state troopers Michael Luka and Wayne Price had been the first to respond to the report of the accident. A log truck driver had called for help over his CB radio. The trucker told the troopers that he had seen a man lying beside the road shortly after eight that morning. He had managed to call for an ambulance by relaying his emergency request through two other CBers.

"Then I got out of my rig and ran to help the guy in the road."

"Did he say anything?" Luka had asked.

The trucker had shaken his head. "He kept repeating, 'Lori. Lori.' Then I looked down through the trees and spotted the green car down in there."

Luka and Price told the Marion County detectives that they found Lori Buckley lying outside the Vega. Her feet had been partially under the right door, and her head was resting on a pillow. Someone had covered her with coats. But Lori Buckley had been dead for a long time when the troopers got to her.

They had photographed her body where it lay in the fir forest, and then released it to a mortuary. Her husband, Walt Buckley, had been rushed to Lincoln City for treatment.

There was no question that the Walt and Lori Buckley who had been in the accident along the Van Duzer Corridor were the same Walt and Lori Buckley who lived on Cedar Court. But Jim Byrnes and Dave Kominek were still trying to figure out just *how* they ended up miles away, almost at the Pacific Ocean.

Walt Buckley had given statements about the accident to Trooper Price — both at the scene and at the hospital. According to Price, he had explained that he and his wife had left Salem the afternoon before. They had planned to drive to the coast for dinner. They had eaten at the popular Pixie Kitchen in Lincoln City. He said they had decided to drive south a short way to have an after-dinner drink at the lounge in the plush Salishan Lodge. Buckley told Price he and his wife had left for Salem about midnight. They were on their way home when the accident occurred.

Buckley said they had lain in the ditch beside the highway all night waiting for help. He had done what he could to make his wife comfortable and to keep her warm.

The ambulance attendant who had transported Walt Buckley told the detectives that Buckley had been very tense — so tense that he had held his arms tight against his chest. Both of his fists were tightly clenched and full of dirt and grass. He had kept his eyes closed and mumbled incoherently as the EMT checked him for injuries. Although he had initially appeared to be seriously hurt, his injuries had proved to be only superficial.

It had looked like a normal, if tragic, accident. At her husband's request, Lori Buckley's body was scheduled to be embalmed as soon as possible. However, the mortician who removed her body from the accident scene had been busy that Wednesday afternoon and several hours passed before he began the embalming procedure. He had just made the first cut — an incision into the femoral artery of the thigh — when the phone rang and Dave Kominek told him to stop immediately. *Nothing* was to be done to the body until the accident investigation was complete.

Kominek went to the mortuary and viewed the corpse of Lori Buckley. He noted immediately that she had suffered many, many deep cuts around her face and shoulders. It would take a complete post-mortem examination to establish the cause of death, but her injuries seemed far too severe to have been sustained in a car wreck in which the vehicle was damaged as slightly as the Vega had been. There had been only minimal damage to the right front fender and grill. The windshield on the right, where Lori had reportedly been sitting, was shattered in a wide "spider-web," but it had not been broken clean through. It was safety glass with no sharp edges that might have cut her face and upper body. Odd.

Kominek received the clothing that Lori Buckley had worn when she was found. He looked at the blood-soaked blue-and-white-checkered blouse and the jeans. There were no cuts or tears in the clothing.

Marion County detectives questioned even what seemed obvious. They interviewed personnel at both the Pixie Kitchen and the Salishan Lodge about the evening of February 24 to see if anyone remembered serving the Buckleys. The Pixie Kitchen, which was usually jammed with lines of people waiting to get in, had been rather quiet on Tuesday night, but none of the waitresses remembered serving the couple. One waitress said she would have remembered Lori particularly because she had been saving to get braces for her daughter and she noticed anyone with a similar dental problem. The Pixie Kitchen cashier said there had been no out-of-town checks or credit cards used by customers on Tuesday night.

The cocktail waitresses and the bartender at Salishan Lodge were positive they had not served drinks to the Buckleys.

It would be days before the widespread investigation could be coordinated and evaluated. Lieutenant Jim Byrnes wanted to talk to Walt Buckley. Maybe Buckley would have some explanation as to why the edges of his story didn't come together cleanly.

Byrnes talked first with the emergency

room nurses at the Lincoln City Hospital. They had treated Walt Buckley at nine a.m. when the ambulance brought him in. One nurse said that his arms were stiff and shaking and that he had appeared to be in shock. He had cried out the same phrases over and over: "Lori — where is she? I couldn't stop. Lori yelled. I couldn't stop the bleeding," and "It's my fault."

"If he was acting, he sure was a good actor," the nurse commented. She said that Buckley had stared into space and cried intermittently as he was being treated.

One thing had been a little odd. Walt Buckley's feet had been very cold, as they would expect in someone who had lain out in the cold of a February night for hours. But his *body* was warm — so warm that his temperature was up one degree above normal. The staff had thought it was strange that he hadn't shown signs of hypothermia.

They had sedated Walt Buckley and he had grown a little calmer. He had talked of how he and Lori had gone out to have a nice dinner. He told them he was a college student majoring in accounting. He had explained that Lori was supposed to be in Salem that morning so she could have braces put on her teeth. But when the nurses asked, "Was Lori your wife?" he had started to cry again.

Jim Byrnes had to wait until almost six before he was allowed to talk with Walt Buckley. A local physician checked Buckley to be sure that he was well enough to talk to Byrnes. As the doctor left Walt's room, he nodded his consent and said, "He wants to talk to you and is very alert."

Jim Byrnes had a fairly good idea what had happened to Lori Buckley. He didn't believe that Lori had been alive when the accident occurred; he felt she had either been dead or very badly injured when the Vega had pulled away from the duplex on Cedar Court at 4:30 in the morning.

Now, as Dave Kominek stood by, Byrnes read Walt Buckley his rights under the Miranda ruling, and the widower signed the MIR card as Byrnes questioned him casually about subjects unconnected to the accident. He wanted to be sure that Buckley was alert enough to be questioned about his wife's death. Byrnes was surprised to find him as stable as the doctor had indicated.

Asked what he remembered about the night before, Walt Buckley first repeated a version of the evening's events that, in essence, corresponded with what he had told troopers earlier. He said Lori had been very tired when she came home from school the day before. He had suggested that they go out to dinner so that she wouldn't have to cook. Lori had agreed happily to that, so they had driven over to the coast, leaving about six. He estimated that they had eaten dinner about eight at the Pixie Kitchen in Lincoln City.

"What did you order?" Byrnes asked casually.

"I had the salad bar plate, and Lori had the combination plate."

Then, Buckley said, they had gone to Salishan Lodge where they had after-dinner drinks and walked on the beach. Oregon beaches are wonderfully smooth and wide when the tide is out, and tourists walk on them all the time. But Byrnes wondered how many people might have wanted to be out there after ten at night with a cold February wind blowing.

He said nothing about his thoughts.

It had been very late, Buckley said, when they started home. Much too late, really. He hadn't realized how exhausted he was. He sighed heavily as he said that he had fallen asleep at the wheel.

"The last thing I remembered was Lori

yelling 'Walt!' and then the car ran off the road."

Walt Buckley had tears in his eyes as he recalled how he had tried to help his wife. He had covered Lori up the best he could and tried to talk to her, but she hadn't responded at all. Finally, he had crawled up the bank to get to the road. He had hoped a car would come by and he could signal for help. But they had lain there for hours before the log truck stopped.

Jim Byrnes let silence fill the hospital room. Neither he nor Kominek said anything as Buckley stared down at his own hands. And then Byrnes told Walt Buckley that the sheriff's office had sent deputies to his home early that morning — and what they had found there. He asked Buckley if he and his wife had been lying next to the wreckage of their car after midnight, who was it who had been screaming and moaning in their duplex at three a.m.? Whose blood had stained their mattress and left telltale spatters around their house?

Jim Byrnes, whose flinty blue eyes had intimidated scores of suspects, watched Buckley's reaction. Despite the sedation, Buckley was nervous. Sweat dotted his forehead and he sighed deeply. Even so, while Walt Buckley began to modify his version of his wife's death in the accident — attempting to make his recall fit the facts he now realized the detectives knew — he refused to give a complete statement.

Instead, he talked *around* what had happened, coming close to something terrible and then veering off into extraneous detail. He admitted a great deal without really admitting anything. He said that he hadn't meant to hurt Lori. He talked about putting her in the back of the car, but then he mentioned that he thought he had heard her moan once as he drove through Salem.

The *back* of the car? *Salem?* Buckley had finally changed his story from that of the highway accident fifty miles from Salem, and Byrnes realized that he was talking about what had happened on Cedar Court.

"I drove to a doctor's office by the freeway but the lights were out," Buckley said weakly.

As Jim Byrnes and Dave Kominek stared at him, Walt Buckley repeated over and over again, "I was going home."

What did he mean by that? Had Buckley actually driven to the Oregon coast with his dead or dying wife and then changed his mind and headed toward his home? That was possible.

Walt Buckley was scared, worried about what would happen to him if he told the whole truth.

Byrnes asked him if he knew District Attorney Gary Gortmaker. (Gortmaker had arrived at the hospital a short while before. Gortmaker went to the scenes of homicides and worked side by side with detectives.)

"I don't know him but I've heard of him," Buckley said.

"Do you want to talk to him?"

Buckley nodded, and Byrnes and Kominek left the room.

Gortmaker pulled a chair up to Walt Buckley's bedside and answered his questions about the legal ramifications of the situation. After they had talked quietly for several minutes, Gortmaker stepped into the corridor. He told Jim Byrnes and Dave Kominek that Walt was ready now to tell them what had really happened to Lori Buckley.

The story that Walt Buckley told proved once again that no one can really know what goes on behind the closed doors of a neighbor's home. The most serene facade can hide turmoil beyond our most wild imaginings. What appears to be an ideal marriage can be, in reality, a bomb waiting to explode. As Walt Buckley spoke, the detectives quickly perceived that the neat and tastefully decorated duplex on Cedar Court had not been a real home at all, but only a stage where a massive deception was played out.

Walt Buckley admitted there were things in his marriage that even Lori had never known. He said he had managed to live two lives, not for weeks or months — but for years.

Their families, their friends, and Lori's school associates had been under the impression that they had had a perfect marriage. The Marion County detectives had already learned that in their preliminary interviews. Everyone they had talked to when they were searching for the missing Buckleys had described them as a loving couple.

Lori Buckley had always seemed happy at school and was a well-liked and competent teacher. She often talked about Walt's upcoming graduation from college. Although she loved her job, Lori had been eager for Walt to begin *his* career so she could resign from teaching and start having a family. Still, she had never seemed to resent the fact that she was the sole breadwinner in the marriage. She had not only paid the bills with her teacher's salary, but she was putting Walt through college.

And she had never mentioned any quarrels — not to her family, her friends, or other teachers.

As Walt Buckley began to talk about his *real* life, the detectives listening remembered that his and Lori's friends had described them as "a beautiful couple." They had both loved to play tennis, and several friends had recalled that Lori and Walt often did things on the spur of the moment, including drives to the coast. They had taken carefully planned vacations, too; during the summer of 1975, they had gone off on a junket to Europe.

Everyone they had interviewed had told the investigators that Lori had been as cheerful as always on her last day at school. She would have been tired — just as Walt said in his first statement — because she had stayed late working on a chili dinner for the school. Detectives knew that she had left for home around 4:20.

No one — *no one* — had described Walt Buckley as a man with a temper or as an abusive husband.

However, as he spoke now, it became rapidly apparent he had kept many secrets from Lori. Yes, she had been paying his tuition and supporting him. She had believed that he was about to get his bachelor's degree in accounting. She had been so proud of him, and thrilled that he might become a special agent with the FBI.

But it had all been an incredibly intricate sham. In reality, Buckley had been dropped from Oregon State University in 1974 — an academic suspension. He had then enrolled in Linn-Benton Community College, but anyone who checked his records would see that he hadn't completed any courses. He hadn't even paid his tuition. He had left home each morning with his briefcase as if he were going to school, but he didn't go to college classes. And he hadn't had schoolbooks in his briefcase; he had carried copies of *Playboy* and *Penthouse*. He spent his days as he liked, returning home at the right time had he been going to college in Corvallis, which Lori believed.

There was more to Buckley's machinations that Detective Kominek already knew. In looking through papers in the Buckleys' duplex, seeking some clue as to where the couple might have gone,

Kominek had discovered that Walt Buckley had been playing games with Lori's bookkeeping and their household accounts. It was apparent that each month, after Lori had written checks for the proper amount of the bills, she had given them to Walt to mail. But he hadn't mailed them; instead he had made out *new* checks for smaller amounts. This had left most of their bills only partially paid, with a growing accumulation of debt. Kominek had found many overdue accounts, and he had also seen where someone had altered the bills that came in so that this wouldn't be apparent.

It looked as if Walt Buckley had been "skimming" money from their joint bank account, but that was puzzling, too, because he hadn't removed the money from the bank; he'd only written duplicate checks for lesser amounts. There was no explanation for that double-ledger bookkeeping, although he might have been planning to withdraw a very large sum at some future time.

Walt Buckley *had* filled out a fifteen-page application to the FBI, just as he had told everyone, and it was dated February 19, six days before he killed Lori. But he had never submitted it.

Of course, Walt Buckley knew that the FBI wouldn't hire him. He had no college degree in accounting. He hadn't been going to college for two years.

Buckley continued his confession, describing the house of cards that had just grown higher and higher until it was bound to tumble. It may have been on the last night of her life that Lori Buckley finally discovered Walt had dropped out of school. There would be no degree for Walt, she would not be able to stop teaching, and there would be no babies. Worst of all, she discovered that the man she trusted implicitly had been lying to her for *years.*

Buckley said Lori had been angry at him that Tuesday night when she walked into the living room and found him "wasting his time watching television."

That's how it had started, at least in Walt Buckley's memory. The argument had been over television. He had fallen asleep on the couch watching the set, and he said she had turned it off and called him a "rotten whore." When he had fallen asleep, Lori had been sewing. He wasn't sure what had made her so angry.

How long she had known the truth was debatable. It must have been a sickening shock for her to discover that all her plans had evaporated. They were behind in their bills and she wondered where all the money had gone. She had bragged to everyone about how well Walt was doing in college; she had even been planning a party for his graduation.

Walt said that Lori had been furious with him — angry enough to threaten to leave their home at three in the morning and go to her mother's house. When he walked into their bedroom, she had been slipping on her shirt. "When she told me she was going to her mom's house, I picked up the quart bottle and hit her until it broke."

"What kind of bottle?" Byrnes asked.

"I hit her with a Tab or Safeway Diet Coke bottle."

He wasn't sure just what kind of bottle it was. He said he recalled only that it was a clear glass quart bottle. "I don't remember if the bottle broke the first time I hit her or not."

He did remember that Lori had been sitting on the bed, and the bottle had been on the dresser.

"She was mad and wanted me to stop watching TV and go back to school. I didn't want to disappoint her. I got mad and hit her. I put pillows over her to stop the bleeding. Blood was everywhere."

Buckley said he had carried Lori and the stained bedclothes out to the car and headed out of town. But he was sure he heard her moan when they were driving on Cherry Avenue. He said he stopped in a parking lot, but when he checked her, she was dead. He knew he couldn't go home, so he had headed toward the forest in Polk County. He had planned to leave both Lori's body and the bedding deep among the fir trees.

"I couldn't leave her there," he said regretfully. Instead, he said he had dumped all the bedding and some bags with the broken bottles near Buell, Oregon. But he couldn't bring himself to leave his wife's body there or in the river.

Buckley said he couldn't face what he'd done and that he had taken a bottle and tried to kill himself. But he didn't have the nerve to slash his throat or wrists. And so he had driven farther and staged an automobile accident, deliberately driving his car off the road and over the embankment.

The windshield had not broken in the accident, so Buckley said he had broken it himself. Then he had lifted his wife's body and positioned it near the car. After that, he had crawled up to the road. He admitted he had told the troopers that he had fallen asleep at the wheel.

"Had you been drinking — taking drugs?" Jim Byrnes asked.

Buckley shook his head. "I only had one drink all day. I've never taken speed or barbiturates."

He had no excuse for killing his wife, not really. He said he had no medical problems, and he had never suffered from blackouts — he just knew there had been an argument.

Jim Byrnes arrested Buckley at 8:25 p.m.; a guard was placed outside his hospital room for the night until he could be returned to the Marion County Jail.

Part of the puzzle was solved. Lori Buckley's killer was under arrest, but the investigation wasn't over. The question of why Walt Buckley had struck out at Lori so violently bothered the detectives.

Dave Kominek attended Lori's autopsy. State Medical Examiner Dr. William Brady and Dr. Joseph Much, the Marion County Medical Examiner, performed the postmortem exam. Lori Buckley had suffered a number of deep, gouging wounds to her scalp, forehead, neck, nose, shoulders, and left upper back. There were no wounds below her breasts except for defense wounds on her hands and arms where she had tried valiantly to fend off the cutting edges of the broken bottle.

Lori would have been left terribly scarred from these wounds and she would have lost a great deal of blood, but, according to Dr. Brady, she would not have died. None of the bottle wounds were fatal. Death had come from suffocation or asphyxiation, but not from manual strangulation. The hyoid bone at the very back of her throat was not cracked and there were no finger or ligature marks on her throat. It was more likely that Lori's killer had held a pillow over her face. Her lungs were fully expanded and discolored, which indicated trapped air. Perhaps Walt Buckley had been trying to stop her screams.

Walt Buckley came very, very close to getting away with murder. If no one had heard Lori's two screams, if the neighbors had not been at home, there might not have been such a careful investigation of the automobile accident. Lori Buckley would have been embalmed and buried, and her widower would have been the object of concern and pity. He would have had plenty of time to return to their apartment and destroy the blood-soaked mattress, throw away the bits of broken bottle, and wipe up the bloodstains. Since everyone, even their closest friends and relatives, thought their marriage was so loving, questions might never have been raised.

But questions *were* raised, and a thorough investigation followed. The Vega probably would not have been checked had the state police not been forewarned. When the car *was* processed, it held many clues that warred with the theory of an accident. Technicians found that the passenger side of the windshield *had* been broken from the inside, but the force had not come from a round, yielding object like a human head. Instead, some sharp, hard instrument had been used, centering the focal point of force in a small area.

The backseat was folded down and there was Type A blood in the far rear inside floor as well as in the wheel well. A gold rug in the back was stained with blood. Lori had not ridden in the front seat on her last ride; she had been in the back, already dead.

Her blue sneakers and a broken Tab bottle were on the floor in the front, along with a bloody hand towel.

When it was coordinated with what was

already known, the cache of bedding found in the forest in Polk County was very important. Alone, without being linked to all the other information detectives and criminalists had unearthed, it would have been almost impossible to identify and might never have been connected to a fatal "accident in another county." As it was, the flowered sheets were found to be identical to bedding back in the Buckley duplex. The bloody bits of a broken bottle were stained with Type A blood, Lori's type. A dishcloth wrapped around a chunk of broken bottle matched Lori's dishcloths. In all, twenty-two items had been taken from the woods and tagged into evidence.

Walt Buckley was returned to Salem by Sheriff Heenan and Undersheriff Prinslow and arraigned on murder charges.

Lori Buckley was buried on Monday, March 1. Lori had been an outdoor education enthusiast and she had frequently organized trips for sixth-graders to Camp Cascade. A memorial fund was set up with contributions to the "Camp Cascade Memorial Fund in Honor of Lori Buckley."

When detectives developed a roll of film they had found in the Buckley duplex, they found prints of a happy family gathering, obviously a celebration honoring Lori and Walt. There were a number of pictures of the couple. Walt was handsome with a luxuriant dark mustache; Lori was winsomely pretty. In one shot, Walt held his arm protectively around his smiling wife; in another, the two held a basket of flowers and champagne.

Lori didn't live to see those pictures.

Walt Buckley had been living a lie for a long time. Perhaps he was afraid Lori would leave him. Perhaps he truly loved her, in his own way. Maybe he only thought of losing the cushy life he had led. He may have panicked, or he may have been maniacally angry when she impugned his masculinity and scorned him for letting her carry all the responsibilities while he did nothing.

Walt Buckley pleaded guilty to murder charges during the first week in April 1976, and was sentenced to life imprisonment.

Sheriff Jim Heenan commented on the case: "One thing I know. I don't think any of us who worked on this investigation will ever look at an automobile accident again without having second thoughts."

In prison, Walt Buckley was depressed

and morose for weeks. In time, he became a model prisoner. After a little more than a decade, he was released on parole. He remarried, had a family, and found a job with the State of Oregon. Ironically, he now lives the life that Lori dreamed of.

You Kill Me — Or I'll Kill You

I have thought long and hard about including the following case, because it is, perhaps, too shocking for many readers. And that must sound strange, since a number of the cases you have already read in this book have been explicit, disturbing, and filled with details that most laypersons have never encountered before. I initially included this case in earlier *Crime Files*, but I've always taken it out at the last minute, concerned about insulting readers' sensibilities. Now I realize it is important, if only to warn women that you cannot invite men you really don't know into your homes — just to be nice, just to be polite, just to avoid hurting someone's feelings. Certainly the message was clear in "Old Flames Can Burn," but this case makes it so compelling that no one can ignore it. Women tend to be kind, and sometimes far too passive. Such traits can, in the final analysis, be the death of them.

Kiss Me, Kill Me is about homicide cases,

and delves deeply into the human psyche. Earlier, I discussed serial killer Harvey Glatman, a man addicted to autoerotic asphyxia. Even though I had been a cop, a counselor in a teenage girls' training school ("reform school" in the old days) and a crime reporter, *I* was in my thirties before I had more than a surface knowledge about obsessions like Glatman's. I covered this Oregon case a year or so later. And I must admit, it shocked me just as much. In a way, I'm relieved that the truly perverted acts of violence I sometimes encounter continue to astound me. If I should ever become blasé about the cases I come across, that would be the time to move on to another genre.

The perpetrator of the crimes in this next case was a man who was much admired, highly educated, and working in a field that helped people. But he was not what he seemed.

Not at all.

The fantasy life of this man exploded one frigid December night into one of the most grotesque and violent homicides I have ever chronicled. I know the Oregon investigators who captured him well, and I can say without reservation that they, too, were shocked.

This is not a Sherlock Holmes mystery because the killer was caught quite soon, identified by a victim who, by all medical probabilities, should have been dead. I'm sure her attacker *thought* she was dead. Still, teams of detectives from five Oregon law enforcement agencies would spend hundreds of hours after his arrest before they finished tracing the background of this murderer — a background that did, indeed, yield clues to the danger that smoldered within him.

Silverton, Oregon, is a pleasant, friendly town with a population of 7,400 people, located fifteen miles northeast of Salem, the capital city of Oregon. To reach Silverton, one drives along a winding road past farmlands and orchards, across the Little Pudding River and through Silverton's equally peaceful neighbor, Mount Angel — site of a jubilant Oktoberfest celebration at harvest time. On the surface, Silverton has not changed much in the last fifty years, and, indeed, it doesn't have a great deal of criminal activity when it's compared to metropolises like Portland and Seattle. Yet, there have been undercurrents of drug-related crimes that would have seemed impossible for the small towns of the Willamette Valley in earlier days. In 1975, the problems that Chief Cliff Bethscheider dealt with were a world away from those his father encountered in the 1940s and 1950s when the elder Bethscheider served as a lawman in Silverton.

Even so, the events of Tuesday and

Wednesday, December 9 and 10, would have seemed unusual to a veteran detective of any police department; fortunately, Chief Bethscheider's crew, though small, was highly experienced and well trained. *Prepared* for what they encountered? No. Nor would any big-city police department be prepared; it was just too far from what most of us like to think of as "normal."

It was shortly after 1:30 a.m. on December 10 when the phone rang in the Silverton Police Department. Ordinarily, the office would have been empty at that time in the morning, with calls being taken by a dispatcher in her own home, but Officer George Holland, a former Green Beret, had stopped in to eat a sandwich after his swing-shift tour of duty and was talking with Officer Frank Wilson before they both headed home. Holland picked up the phone and heard someone speaking so hysterically that it was difficult for him to understand the garbled words. It sounded as if there were a "possible rape" going on at that very moment.

Holland deduced that he was getting this information second- or thirdhand — or maybe even *fourth*hand. Evidently, the original complainant had no phone and had run to a neighbor, who relayed the call for help through several citizens-band ham radio operators.

He understood that the address given for the attack was in an apartment in the nine hundred block of Reserve Street. Holland and Wilson sprinted from the office and drove quickly to that location. They found a cedar-shake multi-residence building painted a bright blue. It was a quarter to two in the morning when the officers arrived, but they saw the bright red smears of what looked like blood on the front door of the first apartment. There were no sounds at all inside, and they pushed open the unlocked door, allowing them a clear view through the living room into a bedroom. A pair of human legs was visible in the bedroom. Holland walked through the living room, which was dark except for the flickering light of a television set.

The sight that confronted him was more appalling than anything he'd experienced, even during his years as a Green Beret. A naked young woman lay on her back on top of a pile of blankets next to the bed. She had been stabbed so many times that she was literally eviscerated, with her intestines exposed outside her abdomen. Her head had been almost severed by a gaping cut in the right side of her head. While

Holland stared down at her body, it seemed to him that someone had "finger-painted" in the still-wet blood, leaving swirls of scarlet all over what had been a beautiful body.

They wouldn't need to search for the death weapon; a razor-sharp knife with a tan bone handle, covered with blood, rested only an inch away from the body.

Acting reflexively, Holland bent to check for a wrist pulse and then touched his fingers to the left side of the woman's throat. He had not expected to find a pulse, and he found none, but the flesh was as warm as if the beautiful dark-haired victim still lived.

Suddenly, he realized there *was* a faint sound of breathing in the room, and for a moment Holland froze, wondering if the killer was still there in the shadows. Then his eyes fell on a tiny form on the bed. A 2-year-old girl lay there, her pajamas sprinkled with blood. Tentatively, Holland reached for the child, and was relieved to see that she was not injured; she was only asleep. Somehow, she had slept through the savage attack that had occurred only two feet away from her. He wrapped the little one in a blanket and took her, still sleeping, into the next room, where he called Chief Bethscheider and Lieutenant T. J. Woodall. Woodall was the small department's sole plainclothes investigator, and his fellow officers teased him, calling him "Kojak."

As Holland and Wilson made an initial attempt to piece together what had happened, a breathless young man ran up. He gasped, "I've got a wounded girl at my house. She's hurt bad!"

Wilson followed him to Ames Street, a block and a half away. The man led him into the kitchen and pointed to another young woman, who lay on the floor, covered with a blanket. She was pale as death itself, but she was alive. Wilson wondered how she could be; she, too, had been cut deeply just beneath her breasts — from one armpit to the other. And then someone using almost surgical precision had sliced her belly open vertically. She had also been eviscerated. But this woman had fought her attacker. She had defense wounds — deep cuts on her forearm, and one of her fingers appeared to be almost severed.

Wilson ran to his squad car and called for an ambulance: "Code Three," which meant lights and siren. Then he returned to the terribly injured girl and did what he

550

could to staunch the blood, hoping that somehow he could stave off irreversible shock.

The grievously injured girl would not rest, however, until she whispered to Wilson, "Kent Whiteside★ did this to me."

Chief Bethscheider and Lieutenant Woodall arrived at the apartment where the first victim lay dead. There they talked to a young man who lived in a downstairs unit. He identified the dead girl as Byrle "Fran" Steffen and said the injured girl was his girlfriend, Lee Connors,★ who had been staying with Fran because he had had an argument with her. It was just some silly disagreement, he said brokenly. "We would have made up by tomorrow." He gave his name as Will Grant.★

Asked if he knew anyone named Kent Whiteside, Grant nodded. "He's an older guy — somewhere in his middle thirties — and he lives over in Mount Angel. He likes to hang out with our crowd, even though he's a lot older than we are."

Grant said he thought Whiteside lived in a house with two male roommates.

By two a.m., the Silverton police had informed the Marion County Sheriff's Office in Salem of the murder-assault. There was no question that they needed assistance in the investigation from the much larger department. Silverton just didn't *have* homicides. Detective Woodall also notified the Mount Angel Police Department and asked them to place an immediate stakeout on Whiteside's home, but he warned them not to attempt an arrest. "We think he's very dangerous," he said.

While Lee Connors was rushed to Salem Memorial Hospital, Holland, Wilson, and Deputy David McMullen of the Marion County Sheriff's Office joined the Mount Angel officers. Quietly, they surrounded the gray two-story shake house where Kent Whiteside lived. Marion County Sheriff Jim Heenan, Chief of Detectives Jim Byrnes, Detective Dave Kominek, and District Attorney Gary Gortmaker were already headed for the crime scene in Silverton, while Marion County detective Mike Wilbur was sent to meet the ambulance bearing 22-year-old Lee Connors.

Wilbur's assignment was not a pleasant one. In view of Lee Connors's massive injuries, no one had much hope that she would survive. In order to obtain a "deathbed" statement — similar to an "excited utterance" or a "res gestae" statement in legal lingo — that would hold up in court in any trial of her attacker, Lee had to be told that she was "in imminent danger of dying." Legally, she had to be aware of her condition. No cop ever wanted to do that. The natural impulse was to say, "You're going to be okay. Everything's going to be fine."

Lee Connors's reaction was unexpected, but it demonstrated her tremendous will to live. She was angry with Mike Wilbur for even suggesting she wasn't going to make it. She assured him she wasn't going to die. He was glad to hear it, and so were the ER doctors who witnessed her reaction. That determination just might save her. She repeated her earlier accusation about Kent Whiteside, saying he had cut her and hurt Fran.

"Did you see the knife?" Wilbur asked.

"I never saw a knife at all," she gasped. "I didn't even feel it — it was too quick."

The Emergency Room nurses and physicians were as jolted by Lee Connors's condition as her neighbors and the investigators had been. She shouldn't be alive — but she was. Her pulse was racing at 110 beats a minute and her blood pressure had dropped to ninety over sixty, and it was falling rapidly — not a good sign. Her heart started and stopped erratically, and raced out of control with tachycardia, followed by no discernible beats at all. The doctors immediately did "cut-downs" to get intravenous needles into her veins, which had collapsed as the blood drained from them, and pushed as much blood and plasma as possible into her even before she went into surgery. To their surprise, she was not having difficulty breathing, but she was in deep shock. Fortunately, she was still in her "golden hour," when she could be brought back from the damage that shock does to the human body.

Mechanically, the admitting physician noted her injuries: a two-inch cut in her throat, a transverse cut through the lower breasts and the anterior chest muscle, a vertical cut from her sternum (breastbone) to her pubic area — so deep that it extended through the subcutaneous tissue and into the rectus muscle. There was also a diagonal slash next to her appendectomy scar. This was probably the most disturbing wound to view because it allowed at least two feet of her bowel to protrude. The defense wounds inflicted to her left forearm were into the muscle, and a tendon was exposed in her left hand. Lee was in "extremely critical" condition. Hours of surgery lay ahead, and even if she survived, there was still the danger of massive infection.

There had been no time as yet to wonder "Why?" or "How?" two pretty young women had been attacked so violently. At least Lee Connors was in skilled hands. Sadly, there was no need to hurry back to the scene of the attack, as Fran Steffen was beyond help. It was far more important to proceed carefully and meticulously in gathering evidence. The scene where Fran's body lay had been secured with crime scene tape and officers were stationed to guard it from anyone who might contaminate it.

It was oddly silent when police officers from Silverton and Mount Angel and the Marion County Sheriff's Office surrounded the house where Kent Whiteside lived. Most of Mount Angel's Christmas lights had been turned off, and a few evergreen wreaths swayed quietly in the wind. It was cold in the predawn December gloom as the officers and detectives were deployed front and back of Whiteside's house. They had every reason to believe that Whiteside was inside: his car was there, and no one could miss it. It was, as witnesses had described it, a yellow Volkswagen bug, decorated garishly by hand in

"John Deere tractor green" with red fenders. It was parked right in front of the house.

A Marion County investigator, his voice magnified twenty times by the loudspeaker attachment on his squad car, ordered everyone inside the house to come out. The waiting officers saw the door open within a moment or two. Two men emerged, their hands over their heads, their faces wearing completely bewildered expressions. They quickly identified themselves as Kent Whiteside's roommates.

"He's not here, though," one of them said.

"Isn't that his car?" Frank Wilson asked.

"Yeah," the roommate said, pointing. "But his motorcycle's gone."

The investigators searched the house and agreed that the suspect's roommates were telling the truth. Wherever Whiteside was, he was not inside. One of his roommates said that he had come home about six that evening and taken a brown leather satchel out to his car. Whiteside had been in an exceptionally good mood earlier that evening. "He was almost euphoric. He read a book for a while and then we went to Tiny's; it's a bar here in town.

"I asked him for a ride home," the

556

housemate recalled, "and he answered somewhat oddly — something like 'Not *again!*' like he was mad or something, but he did drive me home. I thought he was going home, too, but he said he was going back to Tiny's."

"What time was this?" Wilson asked.

"About 9:30."

Whiteside had told his roommates earlier in the evening that he'd like to find some "stray ladies."

Whether he had or not, they didn't know, but his other housemate said that he'd already gone to bed when Whiteside came running up the stairs shortly after one a.m. "He has to go through my room to get to his, and he was panting hard," the man recalled. "Five minutes later, he passed through again, wearing different clothes. He seemed like he wanted to talk, but I was half-asleep so he left."

As the officers impounded the tricolored Volkswagen, they heard the roar of a motorcycle approaching and looked up to see a man who answered Kent Whiteside's description riding toward them.

Frank Wilson approached him and asked, "Are you Kent Whiteside?"

"Yes, sir, I am," he replied mildly.

He was searched and handcuffed and

put into a squad car. When Wilson and McMullen attempted to question him about the horrifying attack on Fran and Lee, Whiteside looked at the floor, saying only "It was a nightmare."

None of them could argue with that. They decided that Detective Larry Lord of the sheriff's office would drive Whiteside to the Marion County Jail in Salem to be booked, while a full crew of investigators returned to Fran Steffen's apartment.

Looking at Fran's apartment as it must have been before the carnage began, they could see it was somewhat disordered but that the messiness appeared to be from a casual lifestyle and not from a struggle. It was the blood that was splattered everywhere that made the rooms look like an abattoir. Fran Steffen had lost an incredible amount of blood in the bedroom, and so, of course, had Lee Connors. The living room couch, bookcase, and records were all stained with droplets, now drying to a reddish-brown.

Chief Bethscheider and Detective Woodall from the Silverton Police Department, and the crew from Salem — Sheriff Heenan, Jim Byrnes, Dave Kominek, and D.A. Gary Gortmaker — found that the knife next to Fran Steffen's body was a hand-ground filleting knife with the brand mark *J Marttiini, Finland* on it. They also found a man's green plaid jacket in Fran's house with items bearing Whiteside's name in the pockets. A pair of men's wire-rimmed glasses lay on the floor nearby. The dead woman still clenched strands of long brown hair in her right hand.

In the predawn hours, Oregon State Police Crime Lab criminalist Corporal Chuck Vaughn and Sergeant William Zeller of the State ID Bureau joined the crew in Silverton, and began processing the murder scene. There was a likelihood that the suspect had been cut, too, so all the blood found would be tested for typing. Jim Byrnes, Vaughn, and Zeller searched Whiteside's oddly painted Volkswagen for more evidence. Inside, they found a scabbard that fit the Finnish filleting knife exactly and bore the same name, "Marttiini."

A voluminous photographic record grew from pictures taken by Byrnes, Vaughn, and Lieutenant Woodall. There was a corncob marijuana pipe in the apartment, as well as some butts — "roaches" — of marijuana cigarettes and a number of empty beer bottles. Just outside the front stoop of the unit, they found a copper bracelet, dented, with a carved dragon's-head design. The amount of marijuana was negligible. They weren't doing a drug bust, anyway: they were trying to solve a homicide.

As the investigators followed the path of Lee Connors's incredible flight from the Steffen apartment to the house of the first caller a block and a half away, they found a pair of women's jeans, soaked with blood, and turned inside out. Lee had worn only a blouse, bra, and underpants when she'd burst into her friend's home. Evidently, she had shed the jeans as she ran, possibly because they were tripping her. Her complete story would have to wait — *if* they would ever be able to talk to her.

Dr. W. E. Grodrian, the Oregon State deputy medical examiner who was called out to do a preliminary check of Fran Steffen's body, suspected that her aorta had been penetrated, in addition to her many other stab wounds. Oddly, there seemed to be no evidence of a sexual attack, save for the fact that she was naked when she was found.

It was now almost four in the morning, and there seemed to be little doubt that Kent Whiteside had killed Fran Steffen and attempted to kill Lee Connors. He'd been photographed, printed, and booked into jail in Salem after receiving treatment for a badly skinned lower leg — probably the result of his falling as he ran from the scene. Lee Connors had defense wounds, however, and she might have been able to fight him long enough for him to incur that injury.

In a sense, they would be working this case in reverse. They knew who the victims were, and they felt they knew who the killer was. What they did not know yet was *why*. Nor did the investigators know much about Kent Whiteside himself, beyond his preference for motorcycles and wildly painted cars. It was going to take a lot of teamwork to find out the motive for such monstrous butchery.

What they learned about Whiteside was the antithesis of what they had expected. It only served to make the slaughter in Fran Steffen's apartment even more incomprehensible, if possible, than it had seemed before.

Whiteside was a graduate of Stanford University, and he had served several years as a commissioned officer in the Air Force. His discharge had been honorable. Most of his background was impeccable.

Until two years earlier, Kent Whiteside

had been employed as a counselor at a nearby university. He had left that position to work as the director of a drug crisis clinic in a large Oregon city. Known for his compassion and his complete professionalism, he was highly regarded by the clinic's board of directors, which included many well-known Oregon citizens. The investigators had to wonder if they had arrested the right man! The history that they were coming up with was almost impossible to equate with the findings of the postmortem exam performed on Fran Steffen's body by forensic pathologist Dr. Larry Lewman.

The method of murder was hauntingly familiar to anyone who had read the scores of books written about, arguably, the most infamous murderer in criminal history: Jack the Ripper. Never identified despite the numerous theories about who he really was, "Jack," too, had eviscerated the hapless women who plied their trade in London's dark alleys in 1888. The devastation of a human body that lay on Lewman's stainless-steel examining table looked like the photographs of the Ripper's victims.

Five-foot-seven-inch, 130-pound Fran Steffen had been stabbed again and again and again by someone in the grip of maniacal fury. Her facial wounds were only superficial — her killer had concentrated mostly on her abdomen, exposing her small intestine. There were stab wounds in her small bowel, mesentery, and aorta. There was a deep, incised wound on the right side of the neck that had severed the carotid artery, the jugular vein, and the cricoid cartilage in the neck. There was a fracture of the fourth cervical vertebra — which would have left her paralyzed from the chest down, had she survived the attack — and deep slashes to her left forearm, finger, wrist, ankle, and thigh.

The immediate cause of death was, indeed, the punctured aorta — the large artery that originates from the left ventricle of the heart and whose branches carry blood to all parts of the body. When this artery is punctured, death follows almost immediately as the heart unknowingly pumps blood rapidly from the body. Fran would also have succumbed, but not as quickly, from the wounds in her neck and abdomen.

Neither Fran nor her friend, Lee, had suffered any wounds to the genital area. However, the very fury of the attacks seemed to indicate some sexual motivation, deviant though it might have been.

That motivation was explained, if a rational mind can accept such an explanation, in comments Whiteside made to Marion County detective Larry Lord on the ride to jail, and also in a scrawled note that criminalist Chuck Vaughn discovered in the clothes that had been removed from the suspect and bagged into evidence.

Whiteside told Lord that he had explained to a female friend shortly before the murder that he had an intense desire for a woman to kill him "like a Christian martyr." His fantasies revolved around a woman killing him with a knife. The belly had more sexual significance for him than the genitals. He blurted to Lord, "I even stuck a knife in my own stomach when I was 30." Whiteside said his strange delusions visited him only when he was alone. He said he had tried to be around people and stay intoxicated, believing that he would not act on his obsessions. "But it didn't work," he sighed.

When Lord asked Whiteside about the homicide, he replied, "You're right. I do remember the incident; some of it is vague — but I know what happened. But I want to talk to an attorney before I say anything else."

The note found in Whiteside's clothes

was a study in horror that indicated the drug counselor had planned the attack on Fran for at least a day before it occurred. The note was not a confession per se; it was more a final statement by a man who hoped to be murdered.

What he had written appeared to be designed to absolve his killer of guilt. It read:

Monday, December 8

Fran — Show this to the cops and you should be found innocent soon enough. This note is written to witness that I, Kent Whiteside, now set forth to threaten Fran with her life unless she does as told and shoves the butcher knife below the navel — aorta severing deep and then eviscerates and emasculates me. I tell her either she murders me this way or I gut and mutilate her and her friend. So, Fran was forced by me, to kill and mutilate me. She is innocent and will have acted under force and fear of butchering death. So I have found my purpose in life, leaving it via that lifelong fantasy come true — death by gutting done by a beautiful, naked slut. Who can say the drumm [sic] beat I hear is good or bad. Some part of me can hardly wait to see that 10" steel blade sliding murderously thru the flesh of my belly.

Kent L. Whiteside

Viewed in retrospect, it was, of course, apparent that Fran Steffen had refused to comply with her killer's weird masochistic fantasy. And so it was Fran, not Whiteside, who had died.

There were still many questions. The investigating agencies held a conference on the morning of December 13. Teams were set up to handle specific tasks to be sure that every vestige of evidence and background information on this incredible case was unearthed.

George Holland of the Silverton Police Department would work with Larry Lord of the Marion County Sheriff's Office to research additional background on Whiteside in an attempt to chart his movements in the forty-eight hours prior to the crime, and to interview his housemates and all those he had contacted after the killing.

Jim Byrnes and Dave Kominek of the sheriff's office would team up with Corporal James Gros-Jacques of the Oregon State Police to interview Lee Connors, who was fighting valiantly for her life in the Salem Memorial hospital. They would also talk in more depth to Lee's boyfriend, who had been in the same building — although in another apartment — when the attack took place.

Silverton Detective Lieutenant Woodall and Detective Vern Meighen of the Salem Police Department would talk with all the friends of Fran and Lee they could locate, photograph all witnesses, and coordinate the witness statements they collected with the crime lab to validate physical evidence with the personal recollections of the victims' associates.

It would be December 16 before Lee Connors was well enough to give a comprehensive statement to Byrnes and Gros-Jacques about what had happened to her. She recalled that she and Fran had attended a party the night before and had therefore gotten very little sleep. On the morning of December 9, Lee had worked her regular shift at the Two Grandmas restaurant in Silverton — where she and Fran had both been waitresses — from ten until two p.m. Fran and her small daughter, Melanie, had come in for lunch, and later the three of them had visited friends.

Fran had expected to have a date that evening, but it had been called off. Lee said she'd had a fight with her boyfriend,

Will Grant, and had planned to spend the night upstairs at Fran's apartment.

"I went to Will's apartment and brought my dog, Sam, back with me to Fran's," Lee remembered, "but Will took Sam home again later."

Lee said she and Fran, along with little Melanie, had watched television until Melanie got tired about 9:15.

"We were all tired that night," Lee said. "Fran left the living room to put the baby to bed, and I was kind of dozing on the couch when I heard somebody knock on the door about 9:35. When I opened it, Kent Whiteside was standing there. Neither Fran nor I know him very well, so I told him I was sleepy and just watching TV, and that Fran had gone to bed."

He hadn't seemed to take the hint. He stood there with a beer bottle in his hand.

"Was he drunk?" Byrnes asked.

Lee shook her head. "He didn't seem to be. But I couldn't shut the door in his face, and it didn't look like he was going away so I finally asked him if he wanted to come in. And he just walked in and sat in Fran's green chair and made small talk," Lee said. "I told him we were tired from a party the night before, and he told me that he was 'partying tonight.'"

At one point, Whiteside told Lee that he had to get something from his car, and he left, only to return in about five minutes.

"What did he bring in?" Gros-Jacques asked.

"I didn't see. I guess he must have had something in his pocket," Lee answered. "I didn't want to fall asleep with him sitting there and I kept hoping he'd take the hint and leave, but he just stayed on and on."

Trying very hard to keep in check the emotional memories that threatened to bring tears, Lee Connors closed her eyes, remembering that night a week earlier. "We heard Fran's voice from the bedroom telling Melanie to settle down," she said, "and Whiteside looked toward the bedroom. I don't know if he even knew I wasn't alone until then."

Lee estimated that it was probably around 10:30 when two of their younger male friends knocked at the door. She let them in and saw they were a little drunk. Still, she was relieved to see them. They asked Whiteside to go and buy beer for them, and he agreed, returning about eleven.

By this time, Fran had gotten up to join the group, but Lee dozed over the next two hours while Fran and the three men drank beer. When she woke occasionally, Lee said she noticed that Kent Whiteside seemed to be "out of it. He wasn't really included in the group," she said. "He wasn't part of the party, but he was still sitting there in the green chair, and he was still there when the other guys left about one a.m."

Lee recalled that she had drifted into deep sleep on the couch. She woke up sometime later — not knowing why, but sensing that a weight had just been lifted from her chest.

"I felt *funny,*" she said. "That's the only way I can describe it. I'd fallen asleep on my side, but I was lying on my back. I saw a shadow or a figure go toward the bedroom. I could see Fran between the bedroom and the living room. I think she was dressed. He was behind Fran and he had hold of her left wrist with his left hand. I heard Fran scream, 'Oh, God!'"

It was at that point that Lee realized that her jeans had been loosened and pulled down around her thighs and she reached to pull them up. Then she felt the blood. She stood up, almost tripping over her jeans. She moved toward the door and came close to falling down again. Somehow, she managed to get through the front door and recalled slamming it behind her. She remembered that she had begun to run toward her friends' house but realized to her shock that her intestines were hanging out.

"I needed both my hands to hold them in," she said. "So I stopped and dropped my jeans. I heard Fran's front door open and the sound of him gasping, and then his feet pounding as if he was running after me. I thought he was trying to catch me and drag me back, but then I heard his Volkswagen start up and tear off."

Somehow, she had made it the block and a half to safety, despite the fact that, at one point, her small intestine had caught on a protruding bush, and she had to stop and literally tug it free.

Even a week after Fran Steffen's murder, it still sounded like a nightmare, like nothing the detectives had ever heard before. Jim Byrnes showed Lee four photos of similar-looking men. She quickly identified a picture of Kent Whiteside as her attacker. She also recognized a picture of the jeans she'd worn that night. She was not familiar with the copper bracelet they had found. It would subsequently be traced to Kent Whiteside.

Lee Connors was only five feet two

inches tall and weighed just 103 pounds, but doctors said she had defied the odds against her and won. They cautiously predicted that she would be well enough to leave the hospital in a few weeks.

As for why Kent Whiteside had attacked her and Fran, Lee had absolutely no idea. Neither of them had ever dated him, and they considered a man of 35 a little too old to fit in with their crowd. They had barely known him as anything more than a guy who sat at the fringes of their social circle.

The investigators who talked with Cal and Sue Vonnet,* the young couple to whose home Lee had run, heard similar comments. Kent Whiteside had not been a meaningful part of Fran's life in any way at all — until the night he ended it. Cal Vonnet said that they had been in bed asleep when the doorbell rang and then Lee had come through the back door screaming, "Get me a doctor! I'm dying! I've been cut!"

"I helped her lie down on the floor," Cal said, "and then Lee said, 'Kent Whiteside went crazy and did something terrible to Fran.'"

Cal Vonnet said he had never heard Fran mention Whiteside at all, and he himself had never met the man. Cal's wife, Sue, was Fran's best friend. "We've been friends for years," she said, "and we roomed together in the past. I knew Whiteside when he was a counselor at the university where we went, but not very well. Fran met him in the spring a year or so ago, but she only knew him very casually. She didn't meet him again until this year — when they were going to the same restaurants and bars. And, even then, they only said hi to each other."

Sometimes, Sue said, Fran and Kent Whiteside had been at the same parties. "Everyone knew Fran had a boyfriend who visited on weekends, but she was kidding at this one party when she said that she needed a 'weekday boyfriend.' "

The Oregon detectives realized that Whiteside had evidently taken her seriously. During November, he'd tried to find out where Fran lived but none of her friends would give him specific directions. Then he'd dropped in on Will Grant and found out that Fran lived in the same building. A few days later, he'd come to Fran's apartment.

"After that, Fran tried to get a girlfriend to be there when he was there, because he was coming on too strong," Sue Vonnet said. "We thought he was a little strange, but we weren't afraid of him. We were never afraid of him."

Sue Vonnet said that Whiteside had been boorishly blunt at times. At one party he'd walked up to her and asked her without preamble, "Do you want to fuck?" She could see why Fran didn't want to be alone with him.

"He was an older guy trying to be cool. He hung around Tiny's Bar in Mount Angel and tried to join in our crowd, but we're all in our early twenties and he was an outsider. He seemed like a loner, and his weird conversations were pretty boring."

Will Grant, Lee Connors's boyfriend, said that he'd known Whiteside and had found him out of his element too. "He lied to me and said Fran had given him her address because she wanted him to drop by, but that he'd lost it. And then he asked me where she lived, and I thought it was okay to tell him," Will said sadly. "I wish I'd never told him."

"Did you hear any sounds from upstairs that night?"

"I slept right through it. I didn't notice any noise because they'd been pounding on the walls before, trying to get me to wake up. They were joking then."

It was apparent that Fran Steffen had had no relationship with the man who killed her. Still, she hadn't been truly afraid of him. She had only been a bit uncomfortable when Kent Whiteside kept dropping in to see her. She could have had no way of knowing that she had been chosen to play an important role in Kent Whiteside's ultimate fantasy.

Whiteside's psychopathology became clearer as Jim Byrnes and James Gros-Jacques talked to more people who had known him in the different areas of his very compartmentalized life. The Kent Whiteside who had skillfully directed the drug crisis clinic and counseled unhappy students for several years was a far different man from the misfit described by the younger set in Mount Angel and Silverton. A fellow clinic worker told Byrnes and Gros-Jacques that "everyone always loved Kent." Whiteside had been most competent in his job, frequently traveling in his capacity as director to give lectures and seminars on drug-related problems. He had had a bad experience in Vietnam while in the service, however, and friends related how he had occasionally broken down and sobbed over people he allegedly had killed while there.

A social-worker friend said that White-side had begun to deteriorate over the past year. When the woman he lived with moved out in February or March, his ability to cope seemed to vanish. He reportedly dipped heavily into drugs himself, trying everything but apparently not becoming hooked on anything. Oddly, it was old-fashioned alcohol that he became addicted to.

Whiteside's fascination with masochism was not a new aspect of his personality, however. He had told one confidante that he had stabbed himself twice — once when he was eleven and once a year or so before the night Fran Steffen was killed. A check on medical records for the suspect showed that he had suffered a shotgun wound at the age of 13, but there were no details on the circumstances. A self-inflicted knife wound when he was 30 had necessitated an exploratory laparotomy, but he recovered from the abdominal surgery without incident.

Lieutenants Woodall and Byrnes, Corporal Gros-Jacques, Detective Larry Lord, and Officer Holland searched the house where Whiteside, living on unemployment compensation during December, resided with his two housemates. The house had been empty and secured by police since the night of Whiteside's arrest, with his roommates lodged at a local hotel.

There was a startling painting in the living room of a man with a knife pressed against a woman's throat. The kitchen wall bore a painting of a horseman holding a stick on which a human head was impaled. Lord found only one small spot of blood on the bathroom sink, but Holland located a tan parka stained with blood. The parka bore Whiteside's name on the back.

As one of his housemates had described earlier, Whiteside's room could be reached only by passing through the other man's bedroom. Here, in his very private quarters, there was more violent "art." One wall was covered with photos and paintings, some of them depicting satanism and bizarre acts.

The investigators found a second knife in Whiteside's bedroom — a four-inch hunting knife with a black handle. And they located some puzzling items: in his closet, a male truss with numerous half-inch nylon ropes knotted to it; seven feet of nylon rope on the suspect's bed with knots in it; and notebooks that contained thousands and thousands of rambling words. Obviously, Whiteside's attic room had been the site of much reading, writing, and preparation for the final acting-out of his fantasy.

Next, the detectives talked to acquaintances of the suspect who had seen Whiteside immediately after he left his home after changing clothes on the night of the murder. He had arrived at the Gast Haus cocktail lounge and sat down at the bar, ordering two double bourbons and downing them without taking a breath. The barmaid noted that he was shaking as if he was having a "spastic attack," and that he kept staring at his hands. "His head wobbled too," she said.

Two of Whiteside's friends had gone over to him and suggested that they move to a table. He had told them that he'd "hurt someone" in Silverton. When they asked him if he wanted them to call the police, he said no. Nor did he want to talk about what had happened. "We'll talk about it tomorrow morning," Whiteside said, "at eight. We can meet and discuss it then."

At that point, Kent Whiteside had ridden off on his motorcycle and surrendered to the police who had surrounded his house.

Had he gone crazy on drugs? What had

triggered such a horrible attack? There had been no sign of drugs in Kent Whiteside's urine when he was examined just after his arrest, although he obviously had been drinking. Although alcohol was his drug of choice, it didn't seem possible that several bottles of beer had catapulted him into the carnage at Fran's apartment.

No, it seemed that Kent Whiteside had known what he was doing, had planned to force Fran Steffen to help him carry out his own death — his final realization of his masochistic fantasy. It was a premeditated act: the note he'd written to Fran was dated December 8. He had had twenty-four hours to think about what he planned to do.

He had been happy — "euphoric," according to his housemate's recollection of the early evening of December 9. He had come to Fran's house and waited for three and a half hours until the other guests had left and Lee was asleep on the couch before he acted. Lee Connors's unexpected presence had forced him to change his plans only a little. His note had mentioned cutting Fran's friend. He had apparently been stalking her, keeping an eye on where she went and who she was with. Under ordinary circumstances, Lee would not have been in Fran's apartment. But Whiteside had included her in his note. She had to be eliminated before he could carry out his obsession.

The filleting knife had been so sharp and the attack so swift that Lee hadn't even felt herself being sliced open. Forensic pathologist Larry Lewman told Jim Byrnes that if the blade had gone a millimeter deeper or a bit to the right or left, she might never have awakened at all. As it was, only her superhuman effort had allowed her to flee.

Had Fran gasped "Oh God!" because she had seen what had happened to her friend — or because she realized that she herself was about to be stabbed? No one will ever know, any more than they will know if Whiteside had actually presented his plan to Fran and given her the choice of stabbing him or dying herself.

Fran Steffen, the beautiful young mother who had grown up in the peaceful town of Silverton, only to die at 22 at the hands of a berserk masochist, was buried in a simple ceremony. Her little girl, the child who had blessedly slept through her mother's murder, went to live with her father, the memory of her mother growing dim over the years to come.

Lee Connors recovered from her

wounds. Today, she would be almost 50. It is highly unlikely that she has ever been able to erase the searing memory of that December night, or that she ever will.

Kent Whiteside first pleaded innocent by reason of mental defect. On February 18, 1976, he changed his plea to guilty of murder and attempted murder. On April 8, 1976, he was sentenced to life in prison for the murder charge, and the second charge was dismissed.

The Whiteside case was an outstanding example of the effectiveness of interagency cooperation: the Silverton Police Department, the Marion County Sheriff's Office, the Oregon State Police, the Salem Police Department, and the Mount Angel Police Department all worked together to gather physical evidence, statements, and background on the suspect and his victims in a case fraught with incredible aspects. All of them hoped devoutly that they would never see another like it.

At the time of Kent Whiteside's sentencing, a life sentence in Oregon meant that prisoners could apply for parole after about eleven years. But Whiteside had become a cause célèbre. He was a handsome man, and a local woman from the upper stratas of society fell in love with him, announcing that she wished to marry him. She also decried any notion that said Kent Whiteside was guilty of the crimes he had confessed to.

Whatever happened behind closed doors, Kent Whiteside didn't serve that much time in prison. Through sealed legal proceedings, he was given a pardon in a few years and released from the Oregon State Penitentiary. As recently as 2000, he was living in another state thousands of miles away from Silverton, Oregon. He would be about 65 now. If he has reoffended, the men and women who investigated his crimes of December 1975 have not been informed of it.

A strange finale to a strange case.

"Where Is Julie?"

As we have seen earlier in this book, many homicidal mysteries go unsolved for decades. And others may never be solved. But it is extremely rare to find cases where answers never come at all. In my view, the very worst tragedies are the sudden disappearances where there is no body, precious little evidence, and no proof of what may have happened. The majority of the stories I have investigated where someone simply vanished concerned young women. Has the missing woman decided on her own accord to walk away from her life? Is she, like some overly dramatic teenage girls, trying to make her parents or her boyfriend worry about her? That has happened. Was she abducted against her will? Is she being held captive somewhere, prevented from contacting those left behind? Is she being tortured or has she been sold — as our mothers used to warn us — into prostitution in some distant country?

Is she dead or alive?

In the last few years alone, there have

been several disappearances of attractive women who seemed to have been swallowed up by the earth. I think the whole country rejoices when there are news bulletins about the very occasional happy endings. Teenager Elizabeth Smart, who almost everyone thought was dead, came home to her family in Salt Lake City in 2003 when Utah police officers spotted her walking with the bizarre self-proclaimed prophet who had kidnapped her.

But Brooke Wilberger, 19, Utah college student, who disappeared on May 24, 2004, while visiting her sister in Corvallis, Oregon, is still missing. Like most of the missing women, Brooke was going about the mundane chores of life — washing the glass chimneys of the lights in her sister's apartment complex. Still missing, too, is anchorwoman, Jodi Huisentruit, 29, of KIMT-TV in Mason City, Iowa. Jodi was undoubtedly seized by someone who watched her as she walked from her apartment toward her car between three and four a.m. on June 27, 1995.

On November 22, 2003, Dru Sjodin, 22, was talking to her boyfriend on her cell phone as she walked out of a Grand Forks, North Dakota, mall after work. He could hear some kind of struggle on the line and then nothing. A convicted rapist, Alfonso Rodriguez Jr., paroled only six months earlier after serving twenty-three years in prison, was arrested six days later and charged with Dru's kidnapping — but he would not say where she was. After many months of searching, and with the help of Denny Adams, owner of Territory Search Dogs, and his search bloodhound Calamity Jane, Dru's body was found on April 17, 2004. It had been buried in the snow in Crookston, Minnesota.

The first television announcements that Dru had been discovered had sounded so hopeful that I can recall saying aloud: "Thank God." The sheriff in charge of the investigation into her disappearance was misleading when he announced, "Dru Sjodin is home."

But only her body was home. Dru herself had been dead for months, probably since shortly after she was abducted. Her family and the others who loved her at least knew where she was and that she was not in pain or fear. But she wasn't really "home." Only her mortal remains had come home.

On May 15, 2004, Calamity Jane found the body of 21-year-old Erika Dahlquist, missing since the previous October 30. By herself, the resourceful bloodhound found Erika and lay next to the remains of the pretty blonde until Adams tracked *Calamity* down.

Even U.S. Congressional intern Chandra Levy's skeletal remains turned up in a Washington, D.C., park months after she vanished. Most people who followed Chandra's disappearance believed she was gone forever, cleverly disposed of by the man who killed her. Most rumors said that she had been hidden under a cement parking lot. Her killer, of course, is still free.

Rumors are seldom much help in homicide investigations. Sometimes, the missing women are just gone. Forever.

Just as the mystery of who killed Sandy Bowman continued for thirty-five years, and stayed in the top layers of my memory all that time, there is another sad puzzle that keeps coming back to me. A beautiful young wife whose name is Julie Weflen vanished seventeen years ago in Spokane County, Washington, and each year on the anniversary of her disappearance — September 16 — I think of her, and wonder what happened to her.

If Julie had vanished today, I'm sure that her disappearance would have garnered the kind of headlines that Elizabeth Smart, Chandra Levy, Dru Sjodin, Brooke Wilberger, Laci Peterson, and Lori Hacking have. As it was, newspapers from Spokane to Los Angeles covered Julie Weflen's vanishing with at least one feature story. None of the coverage helped in finding her.

At least, Sandy Bowman's body was found within a few hours of her death, although admittedly that is small — if any — comfort. But Julie is still gone. Now and then over the years, I have written about her, hoping to trigger some memory in the mind of a witness who may not even know he or she *was* a witness to foul play.

And I admit that I hope the person who took Julie away from her husband and her family, and from her many friends, will read this, too, and be made aware that his days as a free person are coming to an end.

It would serve him better to turn himself in now than wait for the Spokane County sheriff's detectives to come for him.

Julie Miner Weflen was a modern young woman whose wide smile and petite figure belied the strength at her core. Dark-haired and dark-eyed, Julie was quite beautiful. She had perfect posture, something she had had to fight for when as a teenager she was diagnosed with scoliosis (curvature of the spine), had surgery to place a steel rod in her back, and then spent six months in a cast from her chin to her hips.

To see her, nobody would have guessed what her job was. She looked like a kindergarten teacher, but she was actually a power station operator for the Bonneville Power Administration. She had been with the BPA as a safety officer since 1977 when she was only 18. When she applied for the promotion, executives in the power company blinked: this was a man's job. Indeed, she was the only woman out of six applicants. If she was hired, she would be responsible for the lives of linemen out on the poles. She would have to know instantly which lines to reroute when a lineman was repairing a power outage. Second only to that was the importance of knowing which switches to throw so that widespread blackouts wouldn't occur.

Julie had studied for three years, mastering twenty lessons every six months, sending her answers to tests to Bonneville by mail and then taking oral examinations to assess her knowledge. She did all this and put in at least forty-hour weeks on the job at the same time.

Undaunted, Julie convinced Bonneville higher-ups that she could do it. Out of the six applicants, she was one of the two promoted. She had to memorize complex electrical formulas and the training was tough, but she had proven she could do it, even though she initially suffered hazing and jokes in the male-oriented world she worked in. She figured it was just part of establishing herself, and she let it slide off her back. The very men who teased her soon grew to respect her.

Julie met Mike Weflen in Portland at a jazz concert in 1980. He was a handsome man with thick blond-brown hair and slate-blue eyes who was five years older than she was. Mike, 26 then, and a troubleshooter for a condominium developer, had dated his share of pretty girls. But he knew at once that Julie was special. "You can just sense a kind of comfort when you meet some people," he recalled.

At the end of the evening, he asked her out to dinner, and from that moment on, they were together.

Julie's parents liked Mike, and his folks were delighted to meet Julie. "The best description of Julie," Phyliss Weflen, Mike's mother said, "is that she *radiates* love."

Mike and Julie dated for three years and then they were married on June 25, 1983. They were both outdoors people, although he was a skier and she loved riding horseback. They dreamed of having a family and he promised her she would have her own horses one day. Looking back, he smiled as he said, "You know, we really didn't have any particular common interests; we just got along."

The Weflens moved to the Seattle area a year and a half later. Mike worked as a commercial painter. When Julie was offered another promotion with the Bonneville Power Administration in Spokane County, east of the Cascade Mountains near the Idaho border, Mike told her to go for it. He figured he could start a painting business in Spokane as well as in Seattle, and they both liked the idea of a quieter, safer life in the far less metropolitan area of Spokane County. Julie had gone to school in Oregon, and Mike was from South Dakota, and they both preferred the slower ambience of a small town to living in a big city.

Sometimes Julie's salary was higher than Mike's, but it didn't bother either of them. They were a team, committed to each other. At first, Julie worked on various shifts inside a BPA building that was fenced and locked, and Mike never worried about her. But she hated shift work because it seemed as though they had no time off together. That was one of the reasons Mike took painting jobs: he could correlate his work time with hers.

They were both happy when Julie was promoted again, to "pool operator." Part of that job required her to go around to the substations in the county and check on them, but that was almost always during the daytime. "If she worked nights," Mike recalled, "I'd follow her in my truck, but I really never worried about her on the job during the day, and neither did she. I did worry about her sometimes at night."

Julie went off to work in jeans, heavy boots, and a hard hat, and Mike found that he had been right about relocating his business: he soon had more jobs than he could handle by himself. They were able to buy a nice little house with a barn on fourteen acres, twenty miles north of Spokane, just beyond the town of Deer Park. Soon, Julie had two horses, Sonn and Tony. Sonn was a palomino quarter horse, and her son Tony was a chestnut brown. They even had "two cats in the yard" as the popular song went: Si was a Siamese, and Shakes was black and white.

Julie was one of the gentlest souls Mike had ever met. She wouldn't kill bugs, and she carefully took spiders outside and let them go. She raised four orphaned kittens on a doll's bottle.

"One time," Mike recalled, "she thought a skunk had one of the kittens and she came running to me, shouting, 'Get your gun!' — but it turned out the skunk was only chewing on a chicken bone. Of course, she wouldn't have let me shoot the skunk anyway."

Even though Julie wasn't yet pregnant, she and Mike agreed that one parent should stay home with the children, and they had discussions about which of them would quit his (or her) job and be the main child-care-giver. They had traded the role of wage earner back and forth ever since they'd been together and it had always worked out. If Julie believed in equal rights for both sexes, then Mike was just as fair-minded in his thinking.

Mike painted their house gray and white, and Julie decorated the interior in a comfortable "country" style. She hung gingham curtains and covered pillows with the same fabric, with a color scheme of pink, blue, white, and mint green. She collected knickknacks that featured ducks and flowers, and a hand-carved "Home Sweet Home" plaque that summed up what their house meant to them. There was a delft-blue carpet in the sunken living room with a braided rug on top of it, and a fireplace for the icy winter nights.

"We were so happy," Mike remembered. "Things were just starting to come together."

Their lives were as perfect as lives can be. They were very much in love, and they looked forward to having children.

The summer heat of eastern Washington was dissipating and the evenings were growing downright chilly as September 1987 was half over. The leaves on the beech trees were beginning to turn bright yellow, and the Weflens were thinking they would soon have to get in hay for Sonn and Tony before snow fell. Just as lilacs bloomed everywhere in Spokane County in the spring, fierce winter storms could be counted on to leave towering drifts. Julie would probably have to deal with more power outages as lines snapped from the weight of ice storms, and Mike's painting business would be less busy, with only indoor jobs.

On Tuesday, September 15, Mike and a fellow painter headed for a job in Ritzville, a small town eighty miles southwest of their spread in Deer Park. They expected to be gone at least overnight, but Mike hoped to get home by Wednesday night.

He called Julie Tuesday evening to tell her they were making headway on painting the new house they were working on in Ritzville. "Things were normal," Mike said. "She told me she had been to our accountant and everything looked fine. She did the books for my business. I told her I would try to be home late the next night, but I'd call her at five to let her know for sure."

Julie said that the man who was their farrier might be there at five, so Mike reminded her to take their cordless phone out to the barn with her.

Mike did call Julie at five Wednesday afternoon, but the phone rang on and on. The two men hadn't quite finished the house in Ritzville, so they planned to work as late as they needed to and head home Thursday. There were no cell phones in 1987, so he had to go to a phone booth each time he called home.

"I tried calling Julie again at 7:30 and there was still no answer," he said. "Tried again at eight. Same thing. I kept getting my own voice on the recorder.

"I wasn't worried because I knew that Julie was probably over at our horse trainer's house. Sally only lives eight miles from us, and when I'm gone, they visit a lot."

Mike ordered a pizza for himself and his friend, picked it up, and they ate hurriedly before they went back to painting.

It was close to midnight when they quit painting that Wednesday night. They figured they could finish the last of the trim in a few hours in the morning. The two men went back to their motel prepared to fall into bed, exhausted.

As he recalled what happened next, Mike Weflen's voice mirrored the fear he'd felt when they got to the motel. "There was a note hanging on the motel door," he recalled. "It said, *Call BPA. Your wife's been kidnapped.*"

Mike stared at the brusque note in his hand, uncomprehending for a minute, and then ran for the nearest pay phone. He called the power company. All they could tell him was that Julie's empty BPA van had been located at the Spring Hill substation near Riverside State Park.

There was no sign of Julie anywhere around there, Mike was told.

As Mike stood in the phone booth, a Ritzville police car pulled up. The officer who stepped out said he'd been looking for Mike to be sure he got the news about his wife's disappearance.

"He could see how upset I was," Mike recalled, "and he warned me not to try to go to Spokane. He said they'd pick me up if I was speeding. I just looked at him."

He leapt into his truck and drove as fast as he could toward Spokane. No cop pulled him over, but he spent a terrible hour on the road. He was in shock, unable to believe that Julie was really missing; he kept telling himself that she would be found by the time he got there. He was still in his work clothes, his hair and skin spattered with paint, when he strode into the

Spokane County Sheriff's Office in Spokane at one a.m.

It had to be some kind of crazy mistake. How could Julie have been kidnapped? She had been doing her regular job in a safe area. It didn't make any sense. Maybe she'd been hurt — maybe she was in a hospital somewhere.

The deputies on duty told Mike Weflen everything they had learned so far. Julie had been out in the field and due back in the BPA headquarters at 4:30 p.m.

He nodded his head impatiently. "Yeah, that's right. She gets home at five."

But she hadn't answered the phone when he called at five. He berated himself for not being concerned about that, remembering all the times he'd called her.

The sheriff's officers said that people who lived in the Spring Hill area had become concerned when the BPA rig was parked for so long at the substation with the door open and the tailgate window open.

"They finally called us about 9:30 tonight," the deputy said.

At least there was no waiting around to see if Julie had left of her own accord. Her disappearance was already being treated as if foul play was involved.

Mike called his closest friend, Don Miller, and the two men drove to the substation. They couldn't get right up to it because the road was blocked off and sheriff's deputies and Washington State Patrol troopers were questioning everyone who drove up. The scene was almost as bright as day because floodlights had been set up. Handlers and German shepherd search dogs were moving around the road and the substation trying to pick up a scent, although they seemed to keep returning to the van itself.

Mike learned that Julie's purse and car keys were still inside her van; her yellow hard hat had been found on the ground outside.

By holding their flashlights at an oblique angle, Spokane County sheriff's deputies had noticed that a section of gravel near the BPA Dodge van looked as if there had been a struggle. The ground and rocks were in disarray from the driver's door to the front of the van. Moreover, there were some deep tire marks in the gravel that suggested another vehicle had peeled out of there.

The van was very dusty from the dry roads in the area, but there were scuffing, sliding marks in the dust, imprinted by what looked like jeans. That also suggested that Julie had probably put up a tremendous fight with whomever she had encountered.

The sheriff's detectives had arrived at three a.m. on Thursday morning. The most obvious answer as to what had happened was also the most ominous. Someone must have driven by and seen Julie working alone inside the Cyclone fence enclosure. Or someone had followed her. There had been a struggle, and Julie had fought like a tiger. But she was only five feet four inches tall and weighed 110 pounds. Strong and athletic though she was, she wouldn't have been able to best even an average man. Although there were several houses within sight, no one they had yet encountered had heard screaming.

BPA coworkers at the scene were able to reconstruct Julie's movements until the time she vanished on Wednesday. She had notified the main office that she had arrived at Spring Hill at two p.m. It was her usual practice to spend an hour inspecting a substation. She routinely left the driver's door of the van open so she could hear the radio dispatches from her headquarters.

Julie had finished her inspection by three p.m., but then she had noticed that one of the nitrogen tanks was leaking and said she was going back to use her "leak tech" bottle.

The sheriff's investigators urged Mike Weflen to let them handle the search for Julie, but there was no way he could just go home and wait. From the beginning, he had to be part of the effort to get her back.

He could not allow himself to think that Julie might really be gone. Just as any human would be, Mike was in shock, of course, and in denial about what the worst news could be. "I expected to find Julie that first day," he said. "I thought, 'Well, somebody took her and they probably raped her. But she's out there, and she'll be okay, and we can handle it together.'"

But the first searchers found no sign of Julie, and even an all-out effort for the next forty-eight hours by the sheriff's department came up empty.

Mike Weflen barely slept. For two months, he and his friends spent their evenings parked near the substation, out of sight, and watched the vehicles that traversed the road. Sometimes they sat in the ditch and watched the substation itself. They quickly became aware of certain vehicles that drove by the Spring Hill substation often. "We even disabled one deliberately," Mike recalled, "so the detectives would be able to find it and search it."

One detective who didn't consider Mike Weflen a thorn in the side of law enforcement was Mark Henderson. Mark and Mike already knew each other from playing golf, and Henderson privately believed that Mike "would make a good detective."

The men were a year apart in age, and Henderson — whose father, Calvin Henderson, had once been the commander of the Crimes Against Persons Unit in the Spokane County Sheriff's Office — was second-generation law enforcement. Calvin had had a heart attack from the stress of the job, and Mark was often asked, "Why would you want to be a cop when you have *seen* what it's like?"

"But I loved it," Henderson said later. "They didn't grasp that part of it." He'd started as a cadet when he was only 19, and made detective in 1983. He understood Weflen's pain and loss and the need to keep looking for his wife.

"Mark was really good at putting people at ease," Mike said. "I can't say enough about him. This isn't just another case for him. It's comforting to know he's doing everything he can."

Helicopters hovered low over the trees on the 225 square miles of the search area. Even after the sheriff's department had to pull back a full-time effort, there were at least twenty-five people who showed up at seven a.m. every weekday at the substation to search; on weekends, there were over a hundred.

It was the worst possible kind of terrain in which to look for someone — rocky, rugged, with thickly treed hills, deep crevasses, rivers and lakes. There were a thousand — ten thousand — places to hide a body. Caves were explored and rivers were dragged, but they found no sign of Julie Weflen.

By the end of the second day, there was a $20,000 reward, and the Bonneville Power Administration donated the same amount, plus the use of their vehicles and helicopters. Some of Julie's fellow workers took two weeks' leave of absence so they could join in the search for her. Members of the Weflens' church congregation at Trinity Baptist flocked to pitch in.

Mike knew that he was the first suspect the sheriff's detectives would look at. He didn't mind; it was just something to be eliminated so the real investigation could continue. He had been in Ritzville painting a house since Tuesday night; there was no way he could have been at the Spring Hill substation on Wednesday afternoon. The painting crew working with him had seen him all afternoon, as had the motel staff and the clerks at the hardware store where he had bought more paint.

Asked to take a polygraph examination, he did so at once. He passed it cleanly. There was no indication that he had any guilty knowledge of Julie's disappearance.

The Spokane County detectives tried to find some motive for anyone to want to hurt Julie Weflen. They found no one at her job who had a beef with her, and no one among the Weflens' friends. She hadn't spoken of being afraid of a stalker, or of an encounter with any man that might have upset her. The most obvious answer was that she *had* had a stalker, someone watching her who either followed her to the substation on that September day or who saw her working alone there.

But who? They checked on the whereabouts of men with records for violent or sexual crimes in the area and came up with several — and cleared them. They compared Julie's disappearance with that of Debra Jean Swanson, 30, who had vanished as she jogged along a lakeside trail in

Coeur d'Alene, Idaho, on March 29, 1986. The pretty schoolteacher had never been found. Coeur d'Alene was in another state, yes, but it was only nineteen miles east of Spokane.

The cases were, indeed, too similar not to discount a connection.

Mike and his friends went door-to-door in ever-widening circles around the Spring Hill substation in what old-time detectives call "heel-and-toeing," canvassing for possible witnesses to Julie's abduction: "What did you see that day?" "Anything that was unusual?" "Is there anything on your property that we should search — garages, outbuildings, trailers?"

At first, Mike Weflen's friends tried to protect him from the media, but then he realized, as days became a week, that Julie could have been taken farther and farther away from Spokane and that he had to get the word out. Patiently, he met with reporters and appeared on local television news as well as national shows like *West 57th Street* and *Hour Magazine*.

With the help of hundreds of people who wanted to help find Julie, Mike and the search team sent out thousands of flyers bearing her picture. Ten thousand buttons with Julie's photograph and yellow ribbons were distributed to stores and hospitals and to police stations around the country. With the gracious donation of space from billboard companies, eight billboards went up from the Canadian border to California.

Mike kept organizing bigger and bigger search parties as the hunt for Julie continued. "I realized that the police were looking for an arrest and a conviction, and *then* finding my wife. I wanted my wife back, period. They were worried about my screwing up evidence. Sometimes, I felt I was working against both the police *and* the person who took my wife."

For the first two months she was gone, Mike couldn't stand being in their house without Julie. It was as if she had only stepped outside to go to the barn. But he couldn't go home. She was everywhere he looked. The house was as neat as it had always been. All of her things were there, but Julie wasn't.

Finally, in mid-November, two months after Julie disappeared, he knew he had to go home. Friends had been feeding Sonn and Tony and the cats, but the home he and Julie had made and their pets needed him. It was wrenching for him to walk through the door, to see her clothes still hanging in the closet. He opened the refrigerator and saw the zucchini cookie dough she'd made in early September still waiting in the freezer to be sliced and baked.

Mike kept his phone number posted everywhere, and answered every call left on his answering machine. One woman woke him at one a.m. to say that she had heard a woman's voice calling for "Mommy."

"We got right out there," Mike said, "and we searched the area she had given me until four a.m. We didn't find anything."

There were many so-called sightings.

Mike called six truck stops in Montana after someone thought they had seen Julie riding with a trucker. He called every major city's hospitals and all the northern border crossings after a psychic assured him that Julie was in Canada.

Comparing Mike Weflen's efforts to find his wife to Scott Peterson's halfhearted attempts to find *his* wife, Laci, the difference is instantly apparent. Weflen usually managed to sleep only three or four hours a night. He worked just enough to pay the bills he had to pay.

I drove to Mike Weflen's Deer Park home in October 5, 1988, to talk with him.

Julie was still missing, and the gray and white house that I stepped into was exactly as she had left it a little more than a year before. I was writing an article about the search for Julie for a national woman's magazine; for Mike, it was another way to get Julie's picture out around the United States.

As he told me about Julie, it was clear that he had managed to build only a thin shell against the pain and stress of not knowing. It didn't really matter where *he* was: the memories went with him. Mike had tried flying to his boyhood town in Aberdeen, South Dakota, hoping to ease his anxiety, but nothing changed. He had come to accept that life went on day by day.

We spoke of the possibility that Julie had amnesia, that she might have been hurt somehow on the job and didn't remember her name or what her life had been up until September 16 the year before. I think both of us knew this was usually something that happened on soap operas, rather than in real life.

After we had talked for hours, I asked a question that I considered intrusive, but felt I had to ask: "Have you ever thought she might have left you on purpose?"

He paused for only a second. "No. Never. Of all the scenarios I ever pictured, that would be the easiest for me to accept. But no — not if you knew Julie. She wouldn't leave her horses," he said, breaking into a rare grin, "and she loves me a little more than she loves her horses."

It had been a good but not a ridiculously sweetie-sweetie relationship, he explained to me. They had argued like any other couple. About the only thing they had ever argued about, though, was the fact that he sometimes envied the time Julie spent with Sonn and Tony.

"I'll go anywhere to find her," Mike told me. "I'll listen to anyone to get a grain of truth. How do I go on if I stop? How do I go on without her?"

He vowed that he would not give up looking for her, even though friends had urged him to start living again and to think about dating. He had no interest in that. "I can't leave the memories. I don't know how to get back into the world — or if I want to get back into it. I always focus on Julie. My life *is* Julie."

Talking with Mike Weflen was one of the most difficult interviews I've ever done. As I write this, it is a week away from the seventeenth anniversary of Julie Weflen's disappearance. She would be 45 now; Mike is 50.

Eventually, he did move tentatively back into the world, something I believe Julie would have wanted him to do. Many years later, he married again, and today he has children. He and his current wife plan to write a book about Julie. Until then, there will always be one last thing he can do for his first love.

Over the years, one after another suspect in Julie's abduction has been cleared. There remain some likely possibilities, however. Mark Henderson is still a detective with the Spokane County Sheriff's Office, and he has never forgotten Julie, either. I talked to him this week, and he told me her disappearance remains a mystery. "There is no body, no sightings," he said with a sigh. "Sometimes I think I'll be retired when her killer is arrested."

But he did say *when;* he did not say *if.* Henderson believes that an arrest may be very close. With the tremendous advances in forensic science, items of evidence that could not identify the prime suspect in 1987 can now be very dangerous to him. They have been resubmitted to a very sophisticated crime lab for testing.

It took thirty-five years to catch Sandra

Bowman's murderer — more than twice as long as Julie Weflen has been missing. Now that Sandy can rest, the time for Julie's justice is coming. Until then, I would ask readers the same questions that Mike Weflen has asked over and over: "What did you see that day?" "Anything that was unusual?" "Is there anything on your property that we should search — garages, outbuildings, trailers?"

Mark Henderson would still like to hear from anyone who may have information about that day in September 1987. Please call the Spokane County Sheriff's Office at (509) 477-4760.

When Julie Weflen's abductor is arrested, I will be so happy to include the updates on my website at www.annrules.com. If anyone wishes to contact me with information, they can do so through the website. I will keep your identity secret if you like.

About the Author

Ann Rule is a former Seattle policewoman and the author of twenty-one *New York Times* bestsellers, including eight previous Crime Files volumes: *Last Dance, Last Chance*; *Empty Promises*; *A Rage to Kill*; *The End of the Dream*; *In the Name of Love*; *A Fever in the Heart*; *You Belong to Me*; and *A Rose for Her Grave*. Cases from this acclaimed series were anthologized by Ann Rule in *Without Pity*. She is also the author of *Green River, Running Red*, a revelatory account of the infamous Gary Leon Ridgway serial murders; *Every Breath You Take*, the only true-crime book written at the request of the murder victim; . . . *And Never Let Her Go*, the nationally renowned case of deadly seducer Thomas Capano, which was made into a CBS miniseries; and *Bitter Harvest*, which unravels the shattering case of Debora Green, a doctor and loving mother driven to lethal acts of vengeance. Her other bestsellers include *If You Really Loved Me, Everything She Ever Wanted, Small Sacrifices, Dead by Sunset, The Want-Ad Killer, The I-5*

Killer, Lust Killer; and her classic *The Stranger Beside Me,* the unnerving chronicle of Rule's dawning horror as she realized her friend and coworker, Ted Bundy, was a serial killer. She has also written a #1 *New York Times* bestselling novel, *Possession.*

Ann Rule has testified before the U.S. Senate Judiciary Subcommittee and often presents seminars to law enforcement agencies, including the FBI Academy, as well as district attorneys and victim support groups. She served on the U.S. Justice Department task force that set up VICAP (the Violent Criminal Apprehension Program now in place at FBI headquarters) to track and trap serial killers. She lives near Seattle. For more information, visit her website at www.annrules.com.

The employees of Thorndike Press hope you have enjoyed this Large Print book. All our Thorndike and Wheeler Large Print titles are designed for easy reading, and all our books are made to last. Other Thorndike Press Large Print books are available at your library, through selected bookstores, or directly from us.

For information about titles, please call:

(800) 223-1244

or visit our Web site at:

www.gale.com/thorndike
www.gale.com/wheeler

To share your comments, please write:

Publisher
Thorndike Press
295 Kennedy Memorial Drive
Waterville, ME   04901